Ethnic Chauvinism

Orlando Patterson

Ethnic Chauvinism
The Reactionary Impulse

 STEIN AND DAY/*Publishers*/ New York

First published in 1977
Copyright © 1977 by Orlando Patterson
All rights reserved
Printed in the United States of America
Stein and Day/*Publishers*/Scarborough House,
Briarcliff Manor, N.Y. 10510

Library of Congress Cataloging in Publication Data

Patterson, Horace Orlando, 1940-
Ethnic chauvinism: The reactionary impulse

Includes index.
1. Ethnicity. 2. Social groups. 3. Conformity.
4. Deviant behavior. I. Title.
GN495.6.P37   301.45′1   76-54912
ISBN 0-8128-2180-7

For David and Evey Riesman

Contents

Preface

Ethnic allegiance and its apparent revival are among the most crucial issues of our times. And yet, in spite of a massive outpouring of works on the subjects in recent years, they remain little understood.

The majority have concentrated on specific ethnic groups; relatively few have tried to come to terms with ethnicity in general. We know much, perhaps too much, about the Jews, the Blacks, the Irish, the Poles, but we still know little about the nature and extent of the ethnic revival, and even less about the thing-in-itself we call ethnicity.

Thus there is a great need to move both outward and inward from the deluge of descriptive monographs that now dominate the literature on the subjects. Several sociologists have attempted to pursue the subjects outwardly. I find almost all these attempts unsatisfactory. There are certain kinds of social processes that have a way of betraying the disciplinary limits of sociology, and ethnicity is one of them. There is something unfinished, almost interrupted, about such works. They seem to have covered everything worth covering; yet after we have read them, we feel that there is more, or should be more, to learn about the subject.

There are two reasons for this. One is the reluctance to treat the subject historically. We can never understand the outward contours of a subject like ethnicity by restricting ourselves to a detailed case study; at the same time we lose our grip on its historical character by simply analyzing it in a static, comparative way. In the first part of this work I have tried to understand the outward form of the subject in both historical and comparative terms. The task was far more demanding than I had anticipated. Had I known what I was getting into when I began this work, I would never have proceeded. I am happy now for my lack of foresight. The outward pursuit of ethnicity took me into the most remote corners of history, especially Western history. Very soon I felt like a hunter pursuing an elusive prey. By the time I had tracked it down, I found myself at the very roots of Western culture.

But alas, having trapped what I thought was the beast, I found a great surprise waiting for me. The thing I had cornered was merely an epiphenomenon. Having exhausted the limits of sociohistorical analysis, I found that the chase, the real chase, had only just begun. The failure to recognize this, to confuse the epiphenomenon with the real thing, is the second reason for the dissatisfaction with almost all sociological works on ethnicity. The second part of this work attempts to avoid this error.

Ethnicity is, above all, a form of commitment; it is an ideology, or more properly, a faith; one that is often secular, but is also frequently a secular faith layered on a more profound religious faith. Thus, to attempt to understand ethnicity without an analysis of its doctrinal aspects, its ideologies, would be as foolish as attempting to understand Christianity or any other religion without considering its theology. Cult is to the believer the outward social manifestation of myth; myth expresses inner spiritual meaning and at the same time gives meaning to cult. Myth, and in its formal aspect, doctrine, is therefore intermediary between social form and inward reality. What is true of religion is true of its secular counterpart, ethnicity.

But doctrine itself, it turns out, can be pursued in two ways: from the outside, objectively, and from the inside. Speaking of the study of religious doctrine, Paul Tillich has written that "there is a place [for] detachment and scientific objectivity ... but it touches only the surface." The first two chapters of the second part of this work explore objectively the origin and nature of the doctrinal core of ethnicity in Western thought. At the same time, its intellectual antithesis, universalism, is brought to light.

At the end of this intellectual hunt, however, I found that my quarry had once again eluded me. The beast I charged with the spear of objectivity was not a windmill, but worse, the discarded skin of some mythical serpent. The rest of Tillich's warning, part of which was cited above, kept me going:

There are objects for which the so-called "objective" approach is the least objective of all, because it is based on a misunderstanding of the nature of its object. This is especially true of religion. Unconcerned detachment in matters of religion (if it is more than a methodological self-restriction) implies an a priori rejection of the religious demand to be ultimately concerned. It denies the object which it is supposed to approach "objectively."

This is an extreme statement, and may be primarily true of the attempt to understand religious doctrine. I suspect, however, that it is at least partly true of ethnicity as a secular faith. Having come this far, I was not prepared to turn back. Hence the last chapter of this work. When I finally cornered the beast, I found myself facing a mighty adversary indeed, what frequently goes by the name of "the modern crisis," the problem of exile, alienation, rootlessness, of being and identity.

I found the beast, I am sure I did. But did I slay it? On this I am less confident. Who could be, facing such an adversary? I lacked the weapons for an execution: weapons that are essentially philosophical, perhaps even metaphysical. I did the best I could, which was to retire unscathed and with some grace, I hope. There will be other books, to be sure; if not by me, by others better equipped and with the temperament of hedgehogs rather than foxes. If I have succeeded in identifying some part of the way to the beast, I will consider this venture worthwhile.

I owe a great debt of gratitude to many people in the

preparation and writing of this book: To Daniel Bell, William Wilson, and Victor Turner for reading and criticizing earlier drafts of the manuscript; to the Institute for Advanced Study, Princeton, and especially to Clifford Geertz, for providing me with the leisure, tolerance, and support that made it possible for me to write this book instead of the one I went there to write; to Marty Lipset, from whom I learned much while teaching with him a course on ethnicity and stratification at Harvard during which the work first took shape; and to the Tuesday Club at Harvard for an evening of the most savage criticisms.

Above all I must thank David Riesman, who not only read the manuscript with the greatest care and offered numerous detailed criticisms and comments, but who taught me much of what I know about America. I have learned from his works, which began to influence me from my earliest undergraduate days; from his letters and conversations; and from teaching with him in his celebrated course, *Character and Social Structure in America.* Participating in the teaching of this course hardly a year after landing in America was very much like being thrown into the deep end of a civilization when one had hardly learned to creep in it. But with such an excellent guide I learned to swim fast. That was six years ago. The germ of this work was planted in our conversations then. I hope the fruit repays in some small way all the kindness and attention.

Nerys Patterson was not only an interested and responsive listener, but offered many incisive criticisms along the way. I also drew on her wide knowledge of early and modern Celtic cultures.

INTRODUCTION

CHAPTER 1

The Tradition of the Sorcerer

The inward struggle of two great forces underlies the progress of human culture. One pulls us toward the bosom of the group; the other pushes us toward the creation of ourselves as separate and distinct individual beings. Immanuel Kant saw in the "antagonism" of these two forces what he called the "asocial sociability of men." "Man," he wrote, "has an inclination to *associate* himself, because in such a state he feels himself more like a man capable of developing his natural faculties. Man has also a marked propensity to *isolate* himself, because he finds in himself the asocial quality to want to arrange everything according to his own ideas. He therefore expects resistance everywhere, just as he knows of himself that he is inclined to resist others.[1]

The really interesting difference between these two forces is that the centrifugal pull of the group is apparently innate, while the struggle for individuality is a force human beings create. As Kant saw, it is not natural. Precisely for this reason it is the more human and the more desirable. In the progress of human culture, it is not the innately natural but the most unnatural in us that has accounted for our achievements. Otherwise there would be no difference between the culture of the New Guinea headhunter and of the industrial civilization which is our own.

There is no evil in being natural or in the forces that have their roots in our animal composition. But neither is there any virtue in them. This simple truth, alas, has escaped all those who think in the romantic tradition of modern Western thought, from Herder and Rousseau to the present legion of lesser minds who would have us run like frightened chickens from the complex, changing, and fascinating demands of our urban industrial culture back to the pristine fold of the tribe, the ethnic group, the traditional community, or whatever else they choose to call it.

Without the group we cease to exist not only as human beings but as a species. Through the group we achieve the basic necessities of body and soul. Through its interdependence we insure our safety, magnify our comforts, and mollify the dreadful loneliness to which our humanity, unchecked, pulls us. But our nature is part of the condition of our humanity; it is not itself our humanity, nor can any conformity with it ever become the criterion of our happiness.

In exploiting the group, we do not qualitatively differentiate ourselves from the animals. Most living creatures exploit this principle. Some, like the social insects, in many specific respects are more adept at it than we. "Go to the ants," Professor Edward Wilson and his fellow social biologists would no doubt caution us. We differ from the lower animal in this regard only in the degree to which we have optimized the principle: in our ability to differentiate and specialize and in our skill at using the principle of group life to create artifacts—mental and physical—which then become the basis for further creations. Through exploiting the principle of group life we create and sustain culture, which in turn accumulates and reinforces the group in an endless cycle of self-regeneration.

Anthropologists never tire of telling us that in our capacity to create culture we are unique. They are right if by uniqueness they mean to emphasize the *magnitude* of our culture-creating capacity. They are wrong if they mean that group life and its cultural emanations are peculiar to humans. The social insects may not possess culture in the technical sense, since what they do is wholly prescribed by their genetic code. There can be no difference between what is prescribed by nature and what is actualized. They, surely, are the most natural of creatures, and no doubt to romantic thinkers the very happiest.

Higher up on the evolutionary scale, we find the beginnings of variance between the genetically prescribed and the socially actualized, in the primates, some vague signs of a liberation of group life from the tyranny of the gene. If not culture, at least something of a protoculture exists, if we accept the well-documented findings of Irven DeVore and other primatologists.

Even so, the liberation is paltry and comparatively trivial. The genetic code still reigns supreme among the primates. It was left to human beings to complete the great evolutionary task, to so increase the degree of culture-creation that results, finally, in the group's determination more by the thing it has created—culture—than by the genetic factors that created it.

With humanity, the group becomes the central product of not one but two blueprints, two codes: an inner code, the biological, which continues in a secondary way to influence group life in the basic needs and drives it, generates, and what, by analogy only, we may call an outer code, the cultural blueprint born of the group, yet able to feed back on it, strengthen it, expand it, and at times even destroy it.

While the capacity to create culture liberates humanity from biological determinism, culture itself can come to play the same role as the genetic code. What is the point of liberation if it is achieved at the expense of another form of submission—the tyranny of tradition? The fact that one's spiritual manacles are man-made is of no more comfort to the true lover of freedom than is the knowledge to the slave that he has made his own chains or has made possible the society that oppresses him.

I am not repeating the old anthropological tale that all cultures are tyrannical. And I certainly reject the deterministic theories of romantic thinkers from Herder to Kroeber, and of Platonists from Hegel to Parsons, that culture is always some kind of "super-organic" systemic essence that of necessity reduces human choice to nothing. Were that the case, the creation of culture would hardly be a cause for celebration in the evolution of human beings, for it implies that humanity is even worse off than the beasts in having not one but two sources of constraint.

Yet culture *can* become tyrannical. Unchecked, there is a tendency toward closure, and for many human beings succumbing to the dictates of tradition is all too easy. It is the struggle with this dehumanizing tendency of culture, and with those who would accept it, that makes possible perhaps the most noble and quintessentially human of all qualities: the drive for individuality.

Only human beings desire to be distinct, not just as members of a group, but, with wonderful perversity, in opposition to their group; to be different, not in the way in which the head of a primate pack is different from the rest of his group, but different in being like no other head or follower of the pack, and, even more humanly, different in a way that runs counter to the interests of the group's traditions. No other species shares this trait. As a distinguished social biologist once remarked, "In the non-human species ethnicity reigns supreme." We do not know precisely how or when his special quality of human beings emerged. We do know, however, that it is not instinctive, as is that other force against which it struggles, and that it is found in all human societies, from simplest hunting-gathering bands to complex modern societies.

Many would undoubtedly disagree with our claim that the struggle for individuality is a universal occurrence. It is commonly thought that individuality is a peculiarly modern phenomenon, or, at any rate, emerges only in complex, literate societies. Most traditional, and certainly all preliterate societies, goes the common view, exhibit little or no trace of individuality. The individual in such societies, it is claimed, lives under "the tyranny of the group," is submerged in it, and seeks only to enhance it.

This crude, oversimplified view of man in preliterate societies died hard in anthropology. Nor was it sustained purely by ignorance of the culture of traditional peoples, for as late as the 1950s Robert Redfield, the leading figure in the Chicago school of anthropology held fast to it. It has persisted, rather, because of the impact of the romantic tradition in anthropology, the perpetuation and thinly veiled modernization of the Rousseauian image of the noble savage of primitive societies as somehow more integrated, more harmonious, more at peace with nature, more natural, and, by implication—though never explicitly stated—somehow more good. This tradition reached its climax in the anthropological romances of the Chicago anthropologist Robert Redfield, whose ideal "little community" left no room whatever for human variation or individuality. Nor is this tradition dead. The continued obsession with community among modern anthropologists has both normative and scientific roots. Whether dead or not, however, the traditional anthropological view of the little community is something of a caricature of what really existed.

There is an important distinction between conforming individuality and deviant individuality. It is easy to confuse the conforming individualist with the mere conformist, since both work within the group for the achievement of essentially the same goals, the enhancement of the group's ends. The survival of the group is the paramount principle for both. In some societies, especially hunting-gathering bands, it is obvious why this must be so. Outside the primary band, life ceases to exist; there are no other groups to turn to.

However, it is possible to work toward group ends in different ways. The conformist seeks to further the ends of the group by becoming as near as possible like every other member. For him or for her, safety lies in sameness, in the total rejection of all deviation. Homology is the guiding tenet: a beautiful or handsome person is one who most resembles oneself; a truthful thought is one which most closely conforms with one's own. Ugliness and ignorance become the same thing: difference. This is your classic ordinary conformist. He is in every sense the "tradition-directed" character type defined by David Riesman in *The Lonely Crowd.*

The conforming individualist, even among hunter-gatherers, also works for the survival of the group; he has to do so for his own survival. But he does so by exploiting not the principle of homology but the principle of interdependence. He begins to see the virtue of specialization and differentiation for the group, so he creates a new role and makes himself master of it, risking the wrath of the majority of conformists. It is a calculated risk. He gambles on the fact that the conformists will see the value of his difference for the survival of the group as a whole and, as such, their own individual survival. As often as not, if his individualism is a genuine social contribution, he will be tolerated, even perhaps appreciated, especially if he is shrewd enough to allay their fears by generosity. This is precisely what the headman does in neolithic tribal societies. He gives. He constantly demonstrates his sincerity and commitment to the group by freely and unselfishly returning whatever surpluses he has generated by his own greater initiative and intelligence. Sometimes he gives, materially, even more than he can afford. He also gives freely of his superior wisdom. His status and his difference are reinforced and, at the same time, made bearable by the mass of conformists.

Such a conforming individualist is careful never to pull rank and never to exercise influence directly. He is not the Kantian individualist who "resists others" and "expects resistance everywhere"; he exercises influence through demonstration. It is of the conforming individualist that Lucien Lévy-Bruhl speaks when, in his famous work on *The Soul of Primitive Man,* he writes:

... his personality is for him an individual clearly distinct from all the rest, opposed to them, and apprehended by him in a way that is unique and very different from that in which he perceives individuals and objects around him. But this direct apprehension, vivid and consistent as it may be, forms only a small part of the idea he has of his own personality. The predominating elements of it are collective in origin, and the individual hardly grasps himself save as a member of his social group.[2]

The other type of individualist is the true deviant. Like the conforming individualist the deviant strives to be different, to be unique and creative, but he is far more daring and iconoclastic.

For him, creativity becomes an end in itself and a means for the promotion not of the collectivity, nor of some abstract entity called the group or tradition, but of his own ends and the ends of other individuals. Because he enjoys the act of creation for its own sake, because he places the interest of his own individuality and of those with whom he comes in contact above that of the group, he becomes a danger to the group. Because he will question even the basic values of the group's tradition, indeed even challenge the gods, he must be purged. And he is purged, in the primitive society, either by execution or by exile.

Whenever we come upon the deviant individualist in traditional society, we find him in exile. In his isolation he creates. And to these exilic creations humanity owes almost all its great developments. It is no accident that so many of the greatest minds in the history of humanity have been exiles, whether within or without the societies of their birth. No prophet, one of the greatest of all exiles once said, is accepted in his own country. Christianity was born in the iconoclastic deviance of Jesus, and in the agony and exile of the desert. Nor is prophecy possible in one's own country. The Sophists knew this and based their lives on this principle. So did the Cynics, and the Stoics. So have almost all the greatest scientists and literary figures of the modern world.

Joyce, who knew more about exile and its relationship to individuality and creativity than any other modern genius, once gave as the three guiding principles of his existence the combined pursuits of exile, cunning, and silence. These are the three most salient qualities of the primitive sorcerer, who is the prototypical individualist and creator. The sorcerer has no name. He cannot show his face. He is exiled in the bush, a mysterious creature playing with mysterious forces. To the Azande, as to most other peoples, sorcery "is performed at dead of night, for if the act is witnessed the sorcerer will probably be slain. No one, except the fellow sorcerer who has sold him the medicines, knows that he possesses them." [3]

P. Huvelin, a member of the French school of sociology at the turn of the century, was the first person to identify the sorcerer as the originator of individuality. One of the first signs of the emergence of individual rights, he argued, was the willingness of the members of a society to condone the use of ritual processes for the achievement of individual goals and the protection of individual property.[4] And speaking in defence of the sorcerer, R. R. Marret, drawing on Huvelin's work, makes the following penetrating observation, which clearly identifies the generic link between the sorcerer and the modern individualist, especially the professional intellectual.

... a reputation for magic in the sense of a more or less bad and anti-social kind of wonderworking is thrust upon him by the very fact that he is a professional and hence has the public against him, according to the principle that whatever is private in rude society is suspect. As Huvelin points out, so long as society remains undifferentiated, all custom rests on the common belief and wears a religious character, so that every manifestation of individuality is destitute of sanction, when it does not actually amount to a crime. Hence, when social organization begins to come into existence through the division of labor, individual activity is obliged to disguise itself under a cloak of religious forms, which gives the professional an ambiguous character, not only in the eyes of others, but even in his own eyes, since others suspect, while he himself is obscurely conscious, that powers and practices which originally came into being for the public service are being exploited for private ends. Whether it be the professional doctor or the professional smith, his right to be a specialist has been purchased at the cost of seeming, and being, something of a humbug.[5]

Seeming and being ambiguous, isolated, "something of a humbug" whose actions are "destitute of sanction," have always been, and still remain, the costs of genuine individuality and creativity. And yet, it is to these humbugs that humanity owes all its greatest advances both during and after neolithic times.

Lévi-Strauss has drawn our attention to the role of the sorcerer and other closely related deviant thinkers in primitive society in his discussion of what he calls "the neolithic paradox."

It was in neolithic times that man's mastery of the great arts of civilization—of pottery, weaving, agriculture, and the domestication of animals—became fully established ... each of these techniques assumes centuries of active and methodical observation, of bold hypothesis tested by means of endlessly repeated experiments.[6]

Lévi-Strauss argues that the paradox is solved when we recognize that between the primitive thinker and the modern scientists there exists not a great evolutionary gulf so much as two modes of scientific thought: "One roughly adapted to that of perception and the imagination; the other at a remove from it."

In the same way, too, the mode of being of the sorcerer lies parallel to that of the nonconforming individualist in civilized society. As the "fundamental problem" of what Lévi-Strauss calls "the shamanistic complex," "revolves around the relationship between the individual and the group," [7] so does the basic problem of the nonconforming individualist.

The degree to which the tradition of the sorcerer is tolerated may be a measure of the progress of human civilization. Simmel's classic essay on "The Stranger" [8] may be read as a celebration of the tradition of the sorcerer in modern, secularized form. The stranger, he tells us, is the "synthesis" of the totally uprooted wanderer and the totally rooted individual. He is "the man who comes today and stays tomorrow—the potential wanderer, so to speak, who, although he has gone no further, has not quite got over the freedom of coming and going." The stranger epitomizes "the union of closeness and remoteness involved in every human relationship ... the distance within this relation indicates that one who is close by is remote, but his strangeness indicates that one who is remote is near." It is the stranger who makes trade possible and as such is one of the major bases of civilization. But the stranger does more. He makes objectivity possible. Because he is not rooted in the particularities of the traditionalist he can view their passions and conflicts with detachment and can win their confidence and their intimacy. This objectivity, Simmel tells us, makes him a freer man, but it also makes him seem more dangerous. But, above all, it is the stranger who makes a universal conception of mankind meaningful. "That is, with the stranger one has only certain *more general* qualities in common, whereas the relation with organically connected persons is based on the similarity of just those specific traits which differentiates them from the merely universal."

The central truth and irony of the tradition of the sorcerer is that he or she is deviant, individualist, exile, creator, and revolutionary, but above all else human, wholly human. The sorcerer lives alone not because he despises humanity but because he recognizes only humanity. It is perhaps wrong to consider the sorcerer and his tradition as one of exile. For it is not those who deny their traditions, who wander in spirit and body, who seek freedom from all constraints, and who relate to other human beings only as individuals, who, in short, follow in the tradition of the sorcerer that are in exile. It is the rest of humanity who are exiles. It is the closed tribal group that exiles itself; it is the traditionalist who cuts himself off from his time; it is the ethnic chauvinist who isolates himself from the rest of humanity. We live in a looking-glass world. Everything has been turned around because most people prefer to pursue a path away from humanity. By making the antihumanistic the norm, we have come to see the humanistic as deviant.

Getting human beings to reverse their perverse perspective has been a long struggle. The struggle still continues. In spite of the fact that the tradition of the sorcerer has been accepted, the acceptance has been grudging. And in no civilization has the tradition ever become dominant. In the history of human societies it is the conforming individualist who has always ruled, and it has been his image of reality that has remained dominant, even in times and at places where the tradition of the sorcerer may have made the civilization possible.

In his distinction between rebellion and revolution, Camus has given us one clue to the reluctance to accept the tradition of the sorcerer, even where it has been pivotal for a civilization. The sorcerer is an existential rebel. He stands against history on behalf of humanity. His rebellion is the ultimate source of all genuinely humane values. By saying "no" to tradition, he says "yes" to the common values we share as human beings; "yes" to the fact that history exists and is constantly changing—*must* constantly be changed—to serve the ends of human beings. As Camus wrote in *The Rebel,* "It is those who know how to rebel against history, at the right moment, who really promote its interests." The revolutionary, on the other hand, assumes the posture of the rebel in a one-shot manner. It is an assumption of convenience. At heart, the revolutionary remains a conservative and reverts to form once he has won control of the state. As in the American, French, and Russian revolutions, no sooner had the act of insurrection served its purpose than it was betrayed. Harold A. Durfee notes in his excellent paper on "Albert Camus and the Ethics of Rebellion":

The revolutionary will no longer tolerate the rebel but demands conformity. At this point the original genius of the rebellious spirit is negated. But then, if the rebel is true to himself, he sets the limits to history by his defiant act and thereby affirms values common to all. Such authentic rebellion is the claim to unity but not conformity.[9]

Nowhere was all this more evident than in classical Greece. We think of the birth of human freedom, individuality, and democracy there; we think of the love of truth for its own sake; and of the zest for creation and for human progress. Yet, when we examine the works of the dominant and most famous Greek thinkers a stunning anomaly appears: they are all reactionary, antidemocratic elitists; in short, they are all conforming individualists, who, to take the case of Plato, would go so far as to condemn reason itself in favor of the perpetuation of tradition.

For a nonclassicist and ardent humanist, the first reaction to this strange contradiction is bemusement. As one digs deeper, the fascinating truth emerges. Greece was a land full of exiles, resident aliens, freedmen, and slaves, Greeks from other states and non-Greeks. And it is these men and women who forced the native Greek citizen to accept, however reluctantly, the tradition of the sorcerer with all its implications. It was they who made Greece great. But nowhere were they allowed to dominate. The Cynics, to take just one group, were, as E. R. Dodds tells us, the self-conscious hippies of the ancient world, and Xenophon, the classic chauvinist, could never understand why Aristippus preferred to be "everywhere an alien rather than imprison himself in a country." [10]

In Greece of the sixth century B. C., the tradition of the sorcerer first made itself indispensable. In becoming so, a crisis was created for the conforming individualist, one that is still with us, if we find it possible to take the latest work of Robert Nisbet seriously.[11] As in so many other areas of Western culture, the reaction of the Greek conforming individualists presents us with a set of prototypes that have remained true of all such reactions to the present time. There were four such prototypical reactions. Two of these have been identified by Dodds as the myths of "the Lost Paradise" and "the Eternal Recurrence." The third is what I shall call "the Madness of Heraclitus," and the fourth "the Pythagorean Syndrome."

In preclassical Greece, as in all other societies, the sorcerer was the original individualist and intellectual. F. M. Cornford, the scholar who has done most to illuminate this period of Greek thought, tells us: "In contrast with the priests of more advanced countries who hold office, hereditary or derived from a central authority, the shaman has no organization. His claim is based on divine inspiration, proved by his superior spiritual, intellectual and artistic gifts.[12] It was the shaman who combined in one person the three types of experiences which Plato and other, later, traditional thinkers of the classical period were to parcel out as distinct modes: the experiences of seer, poet and philosopher. "Beyond the horizon of the ancient Greeks," writes Cornford, "there exists abundant evidence for the combination of prophet-poet-sage, and the implied belief that all exceptional wisdom is the prerogative of inspired or mantic persons who are in touch with the other world of gods and spirits." [13]

The separation and secularization of these same three modes of deviant experiences by the exilic thinkers of the Mediterranean initiated the explosion of thought and social structure in the Greek world from the sixth century onward. After that not only

Greece but the Western world were never to be the same again. Everywhere tradition was challenged and changed. No group of people benefited more, both materially and intellectually, from these changes than the conforming individualists themselves. Yet they remained terrified.

The first of their prototypical reactions was the yearning for "the lost paradise." From as early as the Hesiodic period we find a longing for the good old days. By the time of Plato the myth of "the lost paradise" is fully developed. All virtue lies in the past. All change is evil. The golden age, of course, is the tribal past where tradition (it was and is still assumed) reigns supreme and conformity is the unbreakable rule.

Closely related to the myth of "the lost paradise" is the myth of "the eternal recurrence." [14] While the myth of "the lost paradise" is based on nostalgia and is often accompanied by pessimism, the myth of "the eternal recurrence" is based on wishful thinking. It confronts the trauma of change by denying it. Plato's incredible achievement was to persuade not only his fellow conforming Greeks but most Western philosophers for over two thousand years after his death that nothing really changes. This seemingly irresistible priestcraft rested on the notion of universal forms, the idea that the reality we receive from our senses is not the real truth but only the forms of these realities which exist in our minds. Nothing really changes, for the absolute remains one in its eternal form.

Not all Greek conforming individualists could live with such mystical solace. In Heraclitus there was an almost tragic response. On the one hand, Heraclitus completely accepts change as inevitable, even necessary. Change is the essence of reality. "Fire lives the death of air, and air lives the death of fire; water lives the death of earth, earth that of water ..." "Everything flows and nothing abides; everything goes away and nothing stays fixed ..." "You can't step twice in the same river ..." "It should be understood that war is the common condition, that strife is justice, and that all things come to pass through the compulsion of strife ..." [15] These are a few of the frantic sayings of a man obviously obsessed with change. One can partly understand, then, the temptation of a scholar such as Victorino Jefera to see Heraclitus as the father of all radical theories of social change: "... in Heraclitus the rational or intelligible is a process, something in motion. The world is changeful but it is also rational." [16]

This interpretation rests on a highly selective reading of the fragments. For Heraclitus, from his mountain fastness, issued the following also: "Men should speak with rational awareness and thereby hold on strongly to that which is shared in common—as a city holds on to its laws, and even more strongly ..." "Law involves obeying the counsel of one ..." "The masses glut themselves like cattle ..." "To extinguish hybris is more needful than to extinguish a fire ..." "The many are bad, the good are few."

These are clearly the reactionary rantings of someone terrified by change. It is foolish to attempt to reconcile the two sets of views in a single system of thought, one of the unpardonable sins of so many historians of ideas. The simple truth is that Heraclitus was self-contradictory and possibly quite mad. But his was a special kind of madness: it was the madness of the person who wants it both ways; both the past and the present as it made what would become the past. He wanted time and he wanted eternity. He wanted to rule the many now, which meant that he had to accept the means of control in his time, but he wanted to rule the many as the many were once ruled. He wanted change, for he benefited from change, but he wanted stability, for he was terrified of change.

The fourth prototypical response of the conservative Greek mind, the most complex and the most ingenious, was the ex post facto attempt to appropriate the tradition of the sorcerer by the idealization of his tradition in a former period safely removed from the present. While vehemently rejecting the tradition as it lived in his own times, the traditionalist attempted to get the best of all worlds by accepting it and using it to justify his denial of it in his own time. This, of course, was consistent with the other three responses. For if the past was always good, clearly even the sorcerer of the golden age must have been good. It is in the golden age that men were men and thinkers really thinkers. Orpheus could be accepted in all his "divine madness," according to Cornford, "as founder of mysterious, prophet, poet and son of the Muse Calliope," and could even become the model for, and source of legitimacy of, the conservative philosopher of the historic period, rationalizing their tendency to "deliver their oracles as men having an authority transcending common experience." [17] But not Protagoras, or Hippias, or Antiphon, or Gorgias, or Alcidamas, or Zeno. Not any man or woman in whom the tradition lived contemporaneously.

In this way, the traditionalist stands the radicalism of the sorcerer on its head. Yesterday's revolutionary becomes today's conservative saint. Revolutions are glorious, as long as they took place long ago. No prophet is or can be accepted in his own country, nor, we must now add, in his own time.

We have called this appropriation and distortion of the tradition of the sorcerer by the conservative mind "the Pythagorean syndrome," because it was most glaringly revealed in the manner in which the reactionary Greek thinkers of the classical period came to terms with the explosion of scientific thought around them. Unable to accept the fact that almost all the major advances in Greek mathematical and scientific thinking were made by radical thinkers who were either contemporaneous or too close in time for comfort, the conservatives attributed almost all their great innovations to Pythagoras, who became a legendary figure from the golden past. In this way tradition was preserved and glorified. Along with it was the view that there was nothing new to be known. Euclid's claim to have discovered the principles of geometry could be dismissed as the pretensions of an imposter. The legendary figure of the golden age had already seen them. Thus the very process of scientific discovery was itself subjected to the theory of forms. It was not just the objects of knowledge which were universal forms, already and forever existing, but the very way we come to know them. Thought itself was not really real and in no way new. Thought, intellectual creation, like all other forms, was already there, had already been seen.

In his masterful study of the sociology of classical Greek scientific thought, Walter Burkert exhaustively explored this problem and in the process exposed both the distortion of their scientific heritage by the conservative thinkers and the true motives that lay behind this distortion. His final account of the matter deserves to be quoted in its entirety. The fascination with Pythagoras, he tells us, comes from:

... the feeling that there is a kind of knowing which penetrates to the very core of the universe, which offers truth as something at once beatific and comforting and presents the human being as cradled in a universal harmony. In the figure of Pythagoras an element of pre-scientific cosmic unity lives on into an age in which the Greeks were beginning, with their newly acquired method of rational thought, to make themselves masters of their world, to call tradition into question, and to abandon long cherished beliefs. The price of the new knowledge and freedom was a loss of inner security. The paths of rational thought lead further and further in different directions, and into the Boundless. There the figure of the ancient Sage, who seemed still to possess the secret of unity, seemed more and more refulgent. Thus after all, there lived on, in the image of Pythagoras, the great Wizard, whom even an advanced age, though it be unwilling to admit the fact, cannot entirely dismiss.[18]

All four responses of the Greek traditionalists live on today among conservative thinkers. Like the Greeks of the classical period, we live today in an age of tremendous changes in our material condition and in our social and intellectual lives. Ours also is an era in which the masses demand, and partly receive, both freedom and equality. The conservatives of our own time also view these changes with alarm and the most acute ambivalence. Like the Greek prototypes they enjoy fully the benefits of change and modernity, indeed, are compelled to promote it, yet find themselves unable to live with it. Howard Hughes's elevated withdrawal, cryptic utterances, and ultimate insanity bear an uncanny resemblance to the madness of Heraclitus. So, too, does the military-industrial complex of our era, which, in one stroke, ravishes the countryside, pollutes, and endangers the atmosphere—all in the name of progress—while simultaneously venerating tradition and demanding the denial of social change, especially if it is meant to benefit the poor. They share the same madness. The same persons whose affluence rests on the industrial civilization that undermines authority mourn in dismal works the "twilight of authority." The same legislators who vote for the production of war planes even the military admits that it does not want, cut, with astounding meanness, funds from an already inadequate food stamp program, knowing that it will lead to the deprivation of millions of needy families. For as Heraclitus said: "The masses glut themselves like cattle ..." "The many are bad and the good are few ..." "And it should be understood that war is the common condition, that strife is justice ..." Many of the same Americans who celebrated most fervently the bicentennial of their revolution in the very next breath denounced and undermined the wars of liberation in Africa and Asia, and supported repressive regimes in southern Africa and South America. And everywhere around us we hear the yearnings of the conservative mind for a golden age, nostalgia for the good old days, for the old South, the small town, and the frontier—their endemic prejudices, racial and class inequities, and unspeakable violence notwithstanding. And it is no accident, finally, that we find today a return in social thought to both romanticism and Platonic idealism, to the glorification of the primordial group and the delusion that human societies are in their real forms cybernetic systems in a state of eternal equilibrium.

It would be wrong to think that these prototypical reactions are held only by the conservatives who constitute the power elite. There is another group of conservatives which is as great a threat to the tradition of the sorcerer in that their ideas are clothed in traditional liberal rhetoric. This group may be called the romantic right. Their reactions to change and modernity are essentially no different from those of the established conservatives, but they imagine themselves to be in opposition to these and they sometimes delude themselves and others into thinking that they are spokesmen for the left and/or the counterculture. In fact, they are the most eloquent voices on behalf of the conservative tradition.

In his moving defense of modernity, Samuel C. Florman has recently identified the principal figures on the romantic right and has incisively exposed the true nature of their thought. These are Jacques Ellul, Lewis Mumford in his later works, René Dubos, Charles A. Reich, and Theodore Roszak. Florman observes of these writers that they "are united in their hatred and fear of technology, and surprisingly unanimous in their treatment of several key themes." These themes turn out to be couched within the same four prototypical reactions we have identified. To take one example, they are all obsessed with the myth of the Golden Age. As Florman writes:

It is difficult not to be seduced by the antitechnologists' idyllic elegies for past cultures. We are all moved to reveries by talk of an arcadian golden age. But when we awaken from this reverie, we realize that the antitechnologists have diverted us with half-truths and distortions.... The callous brutality, the unrelievable pain, the ever-present threat of untimely death for oneself (and worse, for one's children) are the realities with which our ancestors lived and of which the antitechnologists seem totally oblivious.[19]

Nor are these reactions peculiar to the traditionalists of the capitalist world. The communist states of Eastern Europe display the same alarm and ambivalence among the entrenched and gloomy old men who rule and who manifest "the Pythagorean syndrome" hardly a couple of generations after their own revolution. Lipset and Dobson pointed out recently:

Modern societies—both Communist and non-Communist—face a growing dilemma posed by the fact that key institutions and their elites are increasingly dependent upon intellectuals—yet the leaders in these same social units (i.e., the intellectuals) are among the major critics of the way in which the society operates, sometimes calling into question the legitimacy of the social order and its political structure.[20]

A "growing dilemma" would seem to be an excessive under-statement in describing the intense and irresolvable agony of the traditionalists of our times. There is one critical difference between the condition of the conservative mind today and in classical Greece, which remained, to the end, a preindustrial society. In spite of the crucial role of the city, the great majority of people still earned their livelihood in a rural, peasant economy. The dilemma of the conservatives referred merely to one sector, the urban, albeit the seat of their civilization. In the end, it was still possible to return to the blind authority and untroubled slumber of the rural order, which indeed was exactly what the Western world did after the decline of Rome. We can say with absolute certainty that another dark age is no longer possible, however much reactionaries may long for it. Industrial civilization is here to stay. Its only alternative—and it is not inconceivable—is extinction of the whole human race in a nuclear holocaust. Barring that, the conservative mind must face and live with the facts that the civilization he still controls is largely the work of those who live and think in the tradition of the sorcerer and that this tradition is no longer merely supplementary but quintessential. In modern society, the tradition of the sorcerer has, at last, come into its own, but it is yet to find a permanent voice.

It is this more than anything else which now so horrifies our conservatives, especially the conforming individualists who dominate our polities. It is important to recognize that their prototypical reactions are all of the same order. The conservative mind is in full revolt, and for perhaps the first time in human history finds itself on the defensive, as the cunning of the sorcerer speaks from every key social foundation, with all its silent eloquence, and as the truth about who is really in exile is slowly revealed.

It is the purpose of this work to explore in depth one such manifestation of the current conservative revolt, the manifestation we have come to know as ethnicity. It is perhaps the most pervasive, intense, and insidious of all the conservative revolts, the one that threatens most the conquest of the tradition of the sorcerer.

So many have taken up the conservative mood, so great has been the retreat of the liberal mind from its traditional role as the poet of the sorcerer, that it is hard to find a single voice today who boldly and self-consciously defends the tradition. James Joyce was the last man of genius who had the courage to defend the great tradition which stands opposed to all traditions, to the very idea of tradition. It was Joyce who, after half a lifetime, came to the "explosive" truth that "romantic evasion is contrary to modern life" and that "behind realism can lie the key to the world." [21] *Ulysses* is the literary apotheosis of the sorcerer. Bloom, an Irish Jew, is, as Harry Levin noted, "a walking antithesis." Joyce's hero had to be, as Levin says, "a metropolitan type, neither native nor foreigner, a denizen of the megalopolis, a wanderer of the diaspora, equally at home and ill at ease in any city in the world." [22] In preparing for this triumphant celebration, Joyce placed the younger version of his hero, Stephen Daedalus, in a confrontation with his chauvinistic Irish peers. After hearing the conforming individualists, all high on Irish ethnicity, speak in terms of the golden age, and the other prototypical reactions we identified earlier, Daedalus, echoing the ancient "sorcerer" and exile whose name he bore, responded: "When the soul of a man is born in this country there are nets flung at it to hold it back from flight. You talk to me of nationality, language, religion. I shall try to fly by these nets. . . . Do you know what Ireland is? . . . Ireland is the old sow that eats her farrow." [23] And so he did. What Stephen Daedalus said of traditional Irish culture is, to all who think in the manner of the sorcerer, true of all traditions. It is to young Stephen Daedalus, poised on the edge of flight from the "great sow," ready to use the nets of nationality as the wings to escape from it, like the trickster-hero of the West Indian folk, Anancy the Spider-man, who flies on the same web he uses for the homes that are his points of departure, to Stephen Daedalus then, and to the humanistic ideals he cherished, and to the exile, cunning, and silence that were his weapons, and to the universalism that was his destination, and to the antitraditional tradition of the sorcerer which we share that this work is dedicated.

I

CULTUS: THE ORIGINS AND FORMS OF ETHNIC LIFE

A social order, a "culture," a "form of life," is a *problem*—never a solution.... Greek philosophy, the universalistic and exclusive and transcendent claims of Christianity, "Natural Law," the Reformation, the Enlightenment, 1789, and the Marxist or other attempts to provide a successful and more profound replay of it—all this is an ineradicable part of the Western tradition: if you think *all* of it away, almost nothing, and certainly nothing viable, is left. Yet all these elements contain the assumption that a culture, tradition, "form of life," is not a law unto itself, that external norms do exist in terms of which it is to be judged. Hence any contrary simple-minded philosophical model, which could only be put forward seriously by someone blind to our social and historical realities, leads to a paradox: this "form of life" itself contains the important principle that it should not treat itself as its ultimate norm.

Ernest Gellner, *Thought and Change*

CHAPTER 2

The Origins and Nature of Ethnicity

If we are to understand the nature and origins of ethnicity, we must turn to the conforming mode.

There are two fundamental bases of group life: the tribal and the territorial. A group may be held together purely by kinship. Agnatic and affinal bonds in such systems are the essential integrative elements in the basic fabric of social life. The social network is primarily the kinship network. The community is held together through a sometimes complex system of crosscutting ties and allegiances. In such systems, the centrifugal pull of blood ties is counteracted by the exogamous bond of affinal ties. Women (and men) are exchanged by potentially competing groups and in many such societies, as Lévi-Strauss was shown, the circulation of brides corresponds to a countercirculating flow of bride wealth, thus linking different groups in terms of persons and property.[1]

While the village is certainly not unimportant in such societies and indeed is the physical context of tribal activity, the really important social contacts and activities are determined not by one's spatial location but by one's social location in the "web of kinship." Even the ways in which the land is owned and exploited are determined not on a local basis but by the effective kin group, members of which cut across several localities. R. H. Lowie has cautioned us not to make the mistake which Henry Maine and

Lewis Morgan did of assuming that the principles of kinship and locality are of necessity mutually exclusive. The two usually went together in primitive societies, although kinship was the more important. The emergence of the state involves a shift, albeit a radical one, in emphasis from one principle to the next.

The basic problem of the state is thus not that of explaining the somersault by which ancient peoples achieved the step from a government by personal relations to one by territorial contiguity only. The question is rather to show what processes strengthened the local tie which must be recognized as not less ancient than the rival principle.[2]

A society organized primarily on the basis of kinship differs radically from one based primarily on territory or locality, a community in which residential propinquity is the critical factor in the determination of one's most important social activities. The shift from a kin-based, essentially tribal society to a territorially based system is one of the major evolutionary changes in the development of human groups. We can observe this development among contemporary preliterate or tribal societies. The trouble with such observations, however, is that the initial shift from tribal group to territorial state is often an externally induced revolution—one imposed by the Western colonial powers in their arbitrary demarcation of colonial state lines.

Fortunately, the history of Europe and certain Oriental societies reveals this shift from the kin-based principle of social organization to the territorially based unit. Archaic Greece is probably the best example of such a natural development. Here, in spite of the paucity of information, we can detect the movement from the kin-based world of Odysseus, which prevailed as late as eighth-century Attica, to the territorially based community of early classical Greece. Attica is of special interest, however. The change was never complete: an attempt was made to combine both principles of social organization, leading to the creation of a special kind of state.

A more complete transformation, one about which we have

almost no information, was the transformation of primitive, tribal Rome to a territorially based city-state. By the time we have adequate information on Rome, the shift to territoriality was already nearly complete. The only remnant of the former tribal system was the hereditary patrician aristocracy.

The transformation of a community from a kin-based system to one based on territory is associated with two other critical developments. One is the emergence of a genuine ruling class. Such a class is not possible in the tribal system, or the primeval hunting-gathering band, mainly because surpluses do not exist on a scale allowing for their emergence. To be sure, a few individuals, through either good luck, initiative, or superior intelligence do produce more than their basic subsistence needs as defined by the community. However, such individuals typically redistribute their surpluses in an egalitarian way. In return they gain superior status. These are the conforming individualists. In the long ages of the neolithic type of social organization, they never hoard their wealth and certainly never pass it on to their descendants. Hence, each generation must produce its own set of high-status individuals in a highly egalitarian manner. Among such highly egalitarian groups as the Yaruro Indians of Venzuela, for example, we find chiefs who have status, but no power or control over resources.[3] Sooner or later the tendency to hoard slowly comes to assert itself. The conforming individualist and his kinsmen challenge by a slow, cautious process of accretion the most basic rule of the neolithic tribal system, its egalitarianism, and they begin to do this by first distributing only a part of what they accumulate. This is made possible by the fact that the successful conforming individualist or "chief" in almost all egalitarian primitive societies acts, as Malinowski tells us, "as a tribal banker, collecting food, storing it, and protecting it, and then using it for the benefit of the whole community."[4] It is a short step from communal interest to personal self-interest. The transition, at first, may not even be recognized by the incipient monopolist, for he may completely identify both sets of interests.

Eventually the hoarding group consolidates its position by

another means—judicious marriages with other hoarders. There emerges, in the form of the hoarding lineage, the first and throughout history the most important group of conforming individualists, the parasitic collection of individuals we have come to call the ruling class.[5] Greece of the Homeric period was going through just such a transition. If we speculate about the social life of Greece from the Iliad,[6] what seems to be implied is a typical Indo-European migratory tribal group with only the most rudimentary form of political organization, certainly not one we could dignify with the term *state*. We can speculate that it was a primitive, egalitarian society consensually regulated by a group of older men who temporarily assigned strong powers of leadership to a warlord or chief. The world of Odysseus is more settled. The authority of the ruler, however, is extremely limited and the society is still mainly a group of independent farmers. Odysseus' father, Laertes, the former king, is just another farmer with almost no special powers. There is a court, but it seems to be mainly a big house where surpluses are stored. The possibilities of hoarding, however, already exist, and its exploitation by a few—the feasting suitors—is already beginning to alarm some of the more sober folk.

By the Hesiodic period, beginning with the late eighth century, the ruling aristocracy has emerged. Mason Hammond is right in seeing them as "basically agricultural magnates." He writes further:

In the small archaic communities of Greece, they were presumably the more successful farmers and perhaps the chief warriors, who had horses and chariots. It is probable that they built up their military and political strength by surrounding themselves with followers and by reducing the lesser farmers to increasing dependence. It may be that they fortified their predominance by inventing or extending the concept of kinship, if not within the tribe at least within a smaller group called the phratry.[7]

By the middle of the eighth century aristocratic rule was well entrenched, and Hesiod's grim picture of their ruthless exploitation was, if anything, too benign.

It is quite clear why the new ruling class finds it in its best interest to shift the focus of social life from kinship to territoriality. The kinship principle is essentially egalitarian. It is not possible for a dominant group to control such a system since one's primary loyalty within it is to other kinsmen rather than any other group of people. By emphasizing the region as the major basis of social life, an incipient ruling class subtly dilutes the principle of kinship as the major basis of loyalty and transfers it to the region. If it is to remain a hereditary aristocracy, the ruling class cannot take this transformation too far. Its own legitimacy rests on its claim of descent through blood lines from former generations of dominating kinsmen.

To solve this problem the hereditary ruling class does two things, one material, the other spiritual. In the material realm, it performs valuable centralizing state functions which offer clear military and economic increments to the group as a whole. Its existence makes the existence of everyone safer in relation to external foes (the tribal system is no match for centralized, well-organized state armies), and in the economic sphere its managerial role, more particularly that of its bureaucracy, often generates a higher level of income for all. Greater absolute material comfort is gained at the expense of greater inequality.

A net increase in material and military security is often not enough to maintain the legitimacy of the newly emerged ruling class. It is all too easy for the relatively deprived lineages to break away from the new hierarchial state, leaving the ruling lineage with only itself to rule. This, incidentally, was the major social tragedy of the Celtic peoples, especially those of the British Isles. The incapacity of the dominant Celtic lineages to contain the fissionary tendency of subordinate lineages accounts for the failure of powerful centralized states to emerge among them, and this in turn explains their vulnerability to a long succession of Latin, Germanic, and English conquerors.[8] To prevent this, the new ruling aristocracy must legitimize its status pretensions by manipulating the supernatural symbols of the tribe.

To do this it elevates the tribal gods to the role of central importance in the supernatural realm. All pretribal systems have a hierarchy of supernatural entities, ranging from the supreme being who is god of all the tribe down to the gods which relate only to specific segments, lineages, or sublineages of the tribe. Below these are the ancestral spirits worshipped exclusively by their descendants. The lowest and most immediate of such ancestral spirits are the household gods.

The interesting thing about this supernatural hierarchy is the fact that the significance of the gods and spirits in the daily life of their worshippers is the direct opposite of their position on the supernatural totem pole. The least important god in actual religious worship is the most supreme god, the god of the tribe.[9] Among almost all tribal peoples, such supreme gods are remote from the affairs of men and women. They rarely come into play during the day-to-day religious rites of the community. Only on the rare occasion in which the group acts as a tribe—for example, in intertribal warfare—is the blessing of such a god sought. Descending the hierarchy of the pantheon, the gods become more and more important in the activities of various segments of the community; these lower-level gods relate exclusively to specific kinship groups or associations which meet more frequently than does the tribe as a whole.

Below the lineage or clan ancestors are the households gods, the gods most frequently worshipped. It is to them that the greater part of the community's ritual acts are devoted. They are most present not only because they relate more specifically to particular groups, each with its own peculiar ancestral spirit, but because they have most recently departed the real live world of men and women. They literally breathe down the necks of the living. The reputed superstitious dread of the tribesman refers to his constant awareness of these household and lineage gods, not to the gods of other households or lineages, and certainly not to the tribal god, who is so distant as to be almost nonexistent.

The newly emerged ruling lineage, if it is to confirm its status successfully, first makes the tribal gods the most important gods. The supernatural hierarchy must be made consistent with the new secular hierarchy. Thus more and more of the ritual of the community must be devoted to these higher-level gods and the most significant of all religious rituals must be those devoted to the supreme being or beings of the pantheon. In this way the fissionary pull of particular ancestral worship and kin ties is muted, and the push of emerging loyalty to the tribe as a whole, rather than to the more immediate kin group, is reinforced.[10] In the Greek world we detect this development on a ritual level where there was the growing significance of the state cults, and on an intellectual level, where there was a rapidly emerging conception of a unified, divine essense transcending all particular kin-related deities. This intellectual development was to culminate in the Platonic conception of god, a conception which, however, was more a logical extension of Indo-European hynotheism in its continuing commitment to the particular worship of the communal and state dieties. Under the Semitic influence of Zeno of Citium, it was also to culminate in the intellectual monotheism of early Stoa.[11] And both culminations were to have a profound, if questionable, impact on Christian thought during the patristic period.

Once this shift in religious loyalty is achieved, it is an easy matter for the new ruling group to monopolize the rituals related to the higher-echelon gods. In this way a state cult emerges, with the ruling class reinforcing its status through its domination of the cult.

The second task of the incipient ruling class is to place its own ancestors among the dominant spirits in the ancestral world. That is, it must create a religious ideology in which the inequality on earth is reflected in (or, as Durkheim would say, is "represented" in) a parallel inequality in the ancestral realm. The ideologists of the ruling group set about reinterpreting the oral tradition of the past in such a way that the ancestors or founding fathers of the ruling lineage become the eponymous ancestors of the tribe itself. It was the aristocracy's ancestors who founded the tribe and as such from the beginning were its rulers. What is has always been. The right to rule is thus derived from the founding act of the aristocracy's ancestors and is further reinforced by the special role of the living aristocracy in the worship of the newly important tribal gods.[12]

The process just described represents one of the two major ways in which the state as a formal social organization originated.* However, other types of state systems were to emerge from it and since the form persisted among some peoples while other neighboring peoples had other, more evolved, forms, it is necessary to give it a special name. We shall follow Morton Fried and call it simply the pristine state, but because the pristine state emerged in two ways, we shall call this type the kin-hegemonic pristine state.

The kin-hegemonic pristine state, while it constitutes one of the first forms of the state, can remain the political framework for very advanced levels of human culture. In antiquity, the Hebraic state in Palestine and the states of classical Greece represent some of its highest achievements. In more recent times, the African kingdoms of Ashanti and Dahomey are perhaps its best examples.

For the purpose of this work, the most important feature of the kin-hegemonic pristine state is the fact that it represents not just the first form of the state but also the beginnings of ethnicity. Ethnicity was born with the kin-hegemonic state, although it was not to remain with it, since other state forms soon disassociated themselves from the tribal elements of the pristine state. Surely, it could be argued, as many sociologists have done, we ought to go back further and seek for the origins of ethnicity in the tribal group itself. There is a very good reason why we have not, and in discussing it we will not only show how ethnicity necessarily originated only with the kin-hegemonic pristine state, but reveal one of the critical features of ethnic allegiance.

The native name of the tribe very often translates to mean the same thing among most primitive people, namely, the word "people." The significance of this cannot be exaggerated. To the tribesman, there is no need to demarcate his group from other

---

* The second manner in which the pristine state evolved led to the emergence of the theocratic pristine state, to be discussed below.

groups, since other groups are simply not within his sphere of reference. "We the Tikopia" means "we humanity," or more properly, "we the segment of humanity worth taking seriously." This is not to say that the tribesman is not aware of other peoples. He often is, but "others" are not socially or morally meaningful. Indeed, to the tribesman it is often to be doubted whether they are human beings at all. The words tribesmen have for strange peoples always emphasize their nonhumanness. They are monsters, Cyclops, strange, perverted creatures lying somewhere between humanity and the beasts, between the natural and the supernatural. They are people who speak in strange tongues, sounding like ba, ba, ba; in other words, they are barbarians. They are the stuff of which folktales and sometimes epics are made. Or, even better, if one is forced to relate to them, they are mere brutes fit only to be slaves, vocal animals, to be abused, sacrificed, and sometimes eaten. As Mircea Eliade points out, the boundary of the tribal territory is also the boundary that separates cosmos from chaos; "cosmicized," "inhabited and organized" space, "our world," from foreign space which "shares in the fluid and larval modality of chaos." [13]

Except in a bizarre and incorporeal way, other people simply do not enter into the social and moral universe of the tribesman. What all this means then is that the tribesman never finds it necessary to define himself as a distinct group vis-à-vis other groups. There is no real ethnic consciousness, because the need for it does not arise.

This does not mean that the tribal group does not inspire group solidarity. Certainly Robert Redfield was right in claiming that this is an essential feature of tribal life. However, it is absolutely important to distinguish between what I shall call *existential solidarity* and *ethnocentric solidarity*. The tribesman has the former but not the latter. In existential solidarity, the togetherness of members is an assumed reality. It is the being-in-the-world of each individual group member, so it can never become the consciousness of the individual. To be conscious of being different is to add immediately a critically new dimension to being that would fundamentally alter its nature, make it something that it is not. Consciousness, indeed, would destroy its truth; this being the fact that "we"—"the Tikopia," the Achaeans, the Ibo—are not all there is that truly and absolutely constitutes the reality of human existence.

Ethnocentric solidarity, on the other hand, is *conscious* togetherness. It makes something new of tribal solidarity by making it at least partly dependent on the existence, on the *real* existence, of other groups. It introduces the quality of contradistinction; indeed it is possible for ethnocentric solidarity, through consciousness, to exist without the reality of existential solidarity. Consciousness can create its own social being, for we know that many groups have existed only because of the consciousness that they are not other groups, and having come into being through this negative creativity of consciousness, social being is then generated through will and artifacts and myths, through the culture-creating genius of human beings. Just such a creation is the ethnic group we call black Americans. If we do not understand this, we understand nothing about the group.

Ethnicity does not even require the existential solidarity of a tribal group. On purely logical grounds, we clearly cannot trace its origins to it. We do know, however, that existential solidarity is easily transformed into ethocentric solidarity and this is precisely what occurred with the emergence of the kin-hegemonic pristine state. In the genetic sense, then, tribal solidarity is related to the emergence of ethnicity. The tribal group may be viewed as a protoethnic group. It bears a part of the historical nucleus of ethnicity. In the tribal group, there is a positive nuclear social charge, "us," but there is yet no "them." With the kin-hegemonic state, "them" comes into being and in the fusion of "us" and "them," the nucleus of ethnicity is born. This happens to have been the way it came about. It may even have been historically necessary. But what is historically necessary is not necessarily logically required. During later times ethnicity was to emerge in quite the opposite way: consciousness preceding being, "them" preceding "us."

Why, it may be asked, does consciousness of others as real people, as "them," come about with the emergence of the kin-hegemonic pristine state? For one thing, it is often the case that it is precisely the real threat of other hostile groups that stimulates the emergence of the ruling lineage and the centralized state form. The superior military might and security of the centralized state is often one of the main reasons why the dominated segments of the tribe do not break away in response to the aristocratic claims of the new ruling class. Secondly, even without the threat of hostile peoples, it is not long before the ruling aristocracy finds the existence of such hostile forces in its own best interest. So if they do not exist, they will be made to exist by the external aggressiveness of the new ruling class. What better way to unify a tribal group on a tribal basis than to have a common tribal enemy? And what better way to demonstrate its utility to the tribe as a whole than to lead the tribe to victory against other tribes? Having a hostile "them" is always one of the most convenient ways of legitimizing the claims of an insecure emerging ruling class. So it was at the dawn of antiquity, so it is even today.

A third factor accounting for the inevitable tendency of the kin-hegemonic pristine state to make the transformation to ethnicity is trade. The tribal state can only emerge after a group begins to generate surpluses, and the economic base of the ruling class is the disproportionate hoarding of such surpluses. Sooner or later, the ruling class will recognize the value of exchanging its own surpluses for those generated by other groups. In this way it increases the level of its own luxury and differentiates itself further from the masses. More important, trading allows the ruling class to acquire superior power in the form of exotic and more potent weaponry. By monopolizing surpluses and the fruits of trade, if not trade itself, a Stone Age ruling class is able to equip itself with, say, the iron- or bronze-age tools of its neighbors, while the masses continue to depend on bows and arrows. How this reinforces its internal hegemony should be perfectly obvious.

With the emergence of the awareness of other peoples as enemies or as traders, the nucleation of "us" and "them" is

completed and ethnicity as a distinct human experience comes
about. The Greeks, even as late as the classical period, continued
to identify the foreigner among them with the enemy. This
included the group of resident aliens among them known as the
Metics. Thus all private transactions between Metics and the state
were handled in a separate department under the polemarch or
war archon.

There existed a second, but less typical, evolutionary path
between the tribe and the pristine state. This is the path followed
by many Oriental societies and several of the pre-Columbian
civilizations of the Americas. The state systems that emerged in
Mesopotamia, the Nile valley, Meso-America, and Peru evolved
as responses to entirely different sets of environmental and social
challenges from those which stimulated the development of the
kin-hegemonic pristine state. Ecological conditions were the
critical prime movers in the development of this kind of pristine
state. We are not here thinking of the organization of large-scale
irrigation works, for it has been fairly convincingly shown,
especially by Robert M. Adams, that in spite of the concurrence of
these systems with irrigation works, Karl Wittfogel was wrong in
seeing the construction of such works as the casual factor in the
emergence of this type of pristine state. The opposite, indeed,
seems to have been the case. That is, the intensification of
agriculture and, with it, increased production, led to the emergence of pristine state systems, which then made possible the
organization of large-scale irrigation works.[14] What is not con-
tested, however, is the view that unusual ecological factors posed
major intellectual challenges, which, in their resolution, led to the
emergence of this type of pristine state.

Kent V. Flannery has given us some idea of what these
challenges were.[15] They involved the deliberate development of
new varieties of plants and domesticated animals and the
establishment of new symbiotic relationships with peoples living
in neighboring, though differing, ecological zones, especially those
in the highlands. For a primitive people, such deliberate social
engineering and scientific manipulation of the flora and fauna are

even more impressive than the construction of large-scale irrigation works. Of Mesopotamia, Flannery writes that:

Successful cultivation seems to have intensified exchanges of natural resources and cultivars between groups, and there are hints that the diversity of environments made village specialization in certain commodities the best means of adapting to the area. We have suggestive evidence that by 4000 B.C. the redistributive economy had produced regional temple-and-market towns which regulated the produce of a symbiotic network of agriculturists, engaged in intensive irrigation, transhuman herders, and perhaps even traders . . .[16]

Now we know from Sahlin's work on Polynesia that whenever such dramatic increases in productivity take place institutionalized stratification, and, as such, the state, inevitably comes about as an essential adaptive technique. In his own words, "the degree of stratification . . . is an adaptive feature of related increasing productivity." [17]

The extreme nature of these challenges were clearly such that they demanded the skills not of the conforming individualist but of the revolutionary deviant. It is not unreasonable to conjecture, then, that the religious deviant—the prototypical scientist and intellectual, it will be recalled—played the key role in the development of this type of pristine state. The risks were enormous, for they obviously entailed the complete destruction of the older religions with their acceptance of, and theological reconciliation with, nature. But the rewards were in keeping with the magnitude of the risks. The deviant geniuses met the challenge successfully and their reward was the institutionalization of their status at the head of these systems during their early, formative stage. (Later in the post-pristine, dynastic stage of development, they were to be replaced by secular, conforming individualists who, however, were obliged to legitimize their position by claiming divine status). All these early Mesopotamian states were theocracies, which is why they have been labeled theocratic pristine states.

Mason Hammond tells us:

The Gods, through their priests, ensured wide control over both polities and economies. Even if kingship developed from an originally elective chieftainship and not from the secularization of a religious representative—or incarnation—of the deity, monarchy remained closely connected with the temples and with the gods even after it had acquired a military aspect and a desire for hegemony over other cities.[18]

These are the main differences between the two types of pristine states: First, the causal chain linking material conditions, hegemony, and centralization in the theocratic pristine state was the direct reverse of that for the kin-hegemonic pristine state. In the theocratic pristine state it was the extremity of the physical environment, requiring various intellectual and social breakthroughs that stimulated the need for a centralized authority system and led in turn to the emergence of a dominant class and state system. In the kin-hegemonic pristine state, it was the hoarding of property and the intermarriage of hoarding lineages which led to the emergence of a ruling class, which led in turn to the emergence of centralized authority to preserve this hegemony and finally, stimulated an increase in overall productivity by a more efficient exploitation of the environment.

Second, private property played a critical role in the emergence of the kin-hegemonic pristine state, whereas communal and, later, state ownership of all property—at least in theory if not always in practice—was the critical attribute of the theocratic state.

Third, the invention of the kin-hegemonic pristine state was the work of the conforming individualist, the conservative hoarder taking minimal risks who slowly consolidated his position through the traditional technique of intermarriage with other conforming individualists equally successful at hoarding. The theocratic state, on the other hand, was the work of the deviant individualist, the radical religious thinker taking major risks in order to meet a major challenge in the environment and in the process totally transforming his society.

Fourth, religion played a dominant role in the creation of the early Oriental state and remained the basis of legitimacy in that state, the priest class being at the head of the hierarchy in its early formative period. In the kin-hegemonic pristine state, on the other hand, religion was always a secondary factor, being used to reinforce the already emerged ruling class. Kinship and descent remained the primary legitimating agency. This thesis is strongly supported by the work of the leading student of early Indo-European society, Dumézil, who has argued that the tripartite hierarchy was the cardinal feature of the proto-European state and that within this hierarchy the role of the priest was always at best ambiguous in his relation with the secular rulers and, most often, decidedly inferior in status.[19] Certainly, by the time of recorded history the religious specialist, insofar as he existed, played an inferior role in the pristine Indo-European state.

It is, however, the fifth and final difference between the two types of pristine states that is of greatest relevance to us, and this is the differing role of ethnicity. It is a remarkable fact that the theocratic pristine state was in no sense an ethnic state. All the evidence we have suggests that these societies, from the very earliest period, tended to be extremely inclusive with respect to alien and conquered peoples.[20] Indeed, the entire history of ancient Mesopotamia can be seen as one of conquest and absorption. This is true even of conquered peoples who began their career among the conquerors as slaves. For one thing, there is that very remarkable document, the code of Hammurabi, one of the earliest extant law codes. A considerable portion of this code is devoted to the treatment of slaves, and what immediately strikes the modern reader is the relative humanity of the slave laws, especially when compared with the later Graeco-Roman slave laws.[21] Recent work by Gelb has gone so far as to suggest that the mass of prisoners of war taken by the Babylonians were not kept in a permanent slave status, as was formerly thought, but after a period of state slavery lasting for no more than three years, the great majority were enfranchised and fully incorporated into the mainstream of Babylonian society.[22] Several centuries later the same tradition arose among the Persians, whose tolerance to conquered peoples has become justly famous.

In contrast with this tradition of tolerance and mutual absorption, the exact opposite occurred among the inhabitants of the pristine states of the Mediterranean, where, as among the Greeks, intermarriage with freedmen or free Metics was forbidden and citizenship was denied to all except those who belonged by birth and kinship to the community of native Greeks. Ethnicity was born with one, and only one, of the two types of pristine states, the kin-hegemonic state.

The other major type of state system that evolved from the kin-hegemonic states of the ancient world was the juridico-territorial state. In the kin-hegemonic pristine state, the ruling class, in shifting the focus of group loyalties from a primary emphasis on kinship to a primary emphasis on territory, was treading on very risky ground. Because its hegemony was sanctioned on the old kinship principle of descent, a too complete commitment to the territorial principle could undermine its own hegemony. Finding the right blanance between the principles of territoriality and descent was the peculiar dilemma of the aristocracy. Some of them were very skilled at it, as were the early Germanic peoples. Others, like the Greeks, a normally clear-headed, if chauvinistic, people with a marked distaste for ambiguity, were thoroughly confounded by it. Cleisthenes' attempt to reorganize Athenian social structure along the principle of locality with the deme as the basic unit, while preserving the terminology and idea of clan affiliation, was so utterly unworkable that one is left to believe that no right-thinking Greek, least of all Cleisthenes, really took it seriously. When we finally learn about it, from none other than Aristotle, the system has acquired a mathematical formality which, given the known biases of our source, immediately confirms our suspicions. By Aristotle's time so much intermarriage across class lines had taken place that, to the average Greek, aristocracy had come to be defined in socioeconomic rather than in biological or "blood" descent terms. As the intellectual father of all racist theories of inequality, Aristotle was understandably appalled by such a state of affairs, so much so that he simply abandoned the reality of the Greek world around him in the development of his biological theory of class.

Other ruling classes, however, were neither as skilled as the Germans nor as shrewd as the Greeks in maintaining the balance between territoriality and rule by descent. The Romans, more than any other group of people, were to shatter the balance—throw out their kings, circumscribe and make impotent, though never formally eliminate, their governing aristocracy, and develop one of the most thoroughly juridico-territorial political orders not only in antiquity but in all times. All this in a remarkably short period of time.

The most critical feature of the territorially based state is the citizen's loyalty to a state not tribally but spatially and juridically demarcated. The land and the laws defined one's membership in the Roman state. To be a Greek citizen one had first to have been born a member of a regionally demarcated Greek tribe and share its culture. Anyone not Greek was barbarian and automatically excluded. The Greeks never gave up this basic ethnic principle, although they added to it the additional principle of regional exclusiveness among themselves. The Romans, on the other hand, were essentially inclusive and antiethnic in their bestowal of Roman citizenship. They were, in fact, the first Indo-European people to have transcended tribalism fully and to have created a truly cosmopolitan world order in which all men were potentially members. Imperial success, combined with a juridico-territorial conception of the state—one which sharply differentiated the *res publica* from the *res gestae*—forced the Romans, almost against their will, to become not "the first humanists of history" as Victor Ehrenberg too enthusiastically and Eurocentrically claimed, but the first imperial power to pursue, in a sustained manner, at least one of the major tenets of humanism. The Greeks, within the confines of their homeland, whatever their incomparable intellectual achievements, were at heart ethnic chauvinists and often downright racists, and never could understand this great antiethnic principle of Roman life, even when, as a conquered people, they enjoyed its consequences and were allowed, in Horace's fine phrase, to make their captors captives to their art and culture.

The territorial state, especially its imperial variant, while essentially nonethnic, is critical for an understanding of ethnicity, for within its confines most of the other major forms of ethnicity were to emerge.

In its territorial and imperial expansion, such a state naturally leads to the displacement of many peoples. Previous empires had subjected conquered peoples, but Rome was unique in the concurrence of several important features. It transferred vast numbers of people from their homeland to the metropolis and other parts of the empire as slave laborers. Large numbers of displaced persons also migrated to Rome, voluntarily or in statuses other than slavery. Following the crisis in the supply of labor created by the Solonic reforms, the Athenian ruling class also resorted to slave labor on a large scale, though in absolute numbers never as great as Rome. There was a large group of free, non-Greek traders in Greece itself—the Metics. In the ultimate fate of these displaced persons we detect a second and unique feature of Roman civilization.

Neither the freedmen nor the Metics were ever assimilated fully into Greek national life despite a policy of naturalization under the influence of the liberal reformist Solon. As the number of Metics grew, the chauvinistic Greeks, alarmed, abandoned naturalization by the end of the sixth century. In Rome, after a period, free foreigners were fully incorporated. So, astonishingly, were freedmen after a generation. To be sure, "nothing," as Duff tells us, "could wipe out the original stain of slavery" [23] during the lifetime of the libertini, but it is a remarkable fact that Roman law permitted the marriage of freedmen and free Roman citizens. It was even possible for a few ex-slaves to achieve the status of *restitutio natalium,* in which, by a legal fiction, the former enslavement of the freedman was declared to have been illegal and freedom by birth was completely restored. Freedmen, moreover, were active in all aspects of public and private life. By the second generation the mark of slave status was completely removed. Nothing attests more fully to the inclusiveness of Roman society than the extraordinary role of freedman and their descendants in the imperial bureaucracy, where for a time they dominated the imperial household and several of the most important offices of the empire. Between the time of their entry into the society and complete absorption we find evidence of a sense of ethnic identity among such displaced persons. This ethnic identity may have already existed, as was the case with the displaced Greeks and Jews in Rome. In other cases, however, the experience of being displaced generated a common sense of identity with fellow tribesmen or nationals in Rome.

There is every indication that Thracians and Lydians from Asia Minor, Persians, Parthians, and Arabians as well as Egyptians and Ethiopians and Syrians, who along with other displaced persons were brought to the Italian peninsula as slaves, developed a strong sense of ethnic consciousness and cohesiveness in the alien setting. These people may originally have had a sense of solidarity, but a solidarity not culturally or symbolically based. There was very little or no sustained contradistinctive consciousness along ethnic lines because most of these people came from the nonethnic states of Asia Minor and the Near East. Perhaps the best examples of the development of ethnic consciousness in the new imperial setting were the rebellions in the late Republican era. Most of the servile rebel leaders, especially the Syrians, consciously used newly formed ethnic identity as a basis for uniting the slaves in armed revolt against the Roman slave masters.[24] The important point is that it is only in the alien setting that ethnic, as opposed to state, consciousness emerged. Newly emerged ethnic consciousness in the community of worshippers centered on the many alien gods which the immigrants, forced and free, introduced: gods such as Isis, Mithras, and Cybele. The contrast here with Greece is also striking. The Greeks forbade resident aliens to worship in any of the kin-based cults, and participation in the worship of the state cults was rigidly restricted. They were generally hostile to foreign gods, though they took the position that it was impractical to abolish them. Even in the rare case in which, for special reasons, a foreign god was accepted, a rigid segregation of worship was imposed. Thus there were two *thiasoi* for the worship of the Thracian goddess Bendis, one for Thracians, one for Athenians. Apart from one or two of the old Roman deities, all aliens were free to participate in the worship of the Roman gods. Freedmen were prominent as priest attendants and in the emperor worship. The Romans avidly worshipped all the new gods brought in by the immigrants and there was no segregation of worship.[25] Religion, while a basis for temporary ethnicity, was in the long run one of the primary means of a two-way assimilation of foreigners to Roman ways and of Romans to the ways of the foreigners. Religion engendered ethnic consciousness, but by promoting assimilation it paved the way for the destruction of that very ethnic consciousness.

I shall call this kind of ethnic solidarity *adaptive ethnicity*. It is the peculiar product of migration and alienation—the ethnic group becoming strongly conscious of itself as a distinct ethnic entity only in the alien setting. What formerly was taken for granted is now actively pursued. The ethnic experience, however, is temporary and prepares the group for entry into the society. As such, it is ultimately integrative. It performs important psychological functions for its members, especially in buffering and muting the shock of displacement. It performs useful economic and social functions also, providing a familiar social context in the bewildering alien world of the host society and facilitating the search for employment. The assimilative host community of Rome, like America nearly 2000 years later, prepared the members of the ethnic group for entry and absorption into the total fabric of the host society.

Obviously adaptive ethnicity is only possible where the host society is essentially tolerant and inclusive of displaced minorites in its midst. In Greece, especially Athens, the host society with a large, freed slave population and large group of free aliens was strongly exclusive. Yet resident aliens in Greece, as far as the evidence tells us, did not develop ethnic groups. The Metic class was simply too heterogeneous to develop a strong sense of in-group solidarity. They were a collection of people derived from freedmen and migrants of almost every nationality in the Mediterranean. They constituted a substantial proportion of the total population of the Greek city-state, but no single group had a large enough number to form the basis of meaningful ethnic communities.

In Rome, on the other hand, aliens, slaves and free from the same areas of origin were in given localities in significant numbers. Only in the Laurium mines did Greece import people in quantities sufficient for the existence of significant tribal clusters. But ethnicity could not have developed here, since in these mines life was nasty, brutish, and short. Evidence exists of alien cult worship among the Metics of Greece, but there is nothing to suggest that membership in these cults was coterminous with ethnic solidarity. At the very most there were religious sanctuaries, such as the Citian sanctuary of Aphrodite or the Egyptian sanctuary of Isis. A sanctuary, by its very nature, was not a community; but an institution made necessary by the absence of community.

But what of the ability of human beings to create myths about their identity? Did we not observe earlier that social consciousness could generate social being, that all people needed was the will to ethnic unity to create the basis of such unity? People do not develop a sense of ethnic unity, however, just for the sake of it or out of any instinctive primordial drive; nor is it enough to be oppressed along with others in an alien setting for that will to unity to be stimulated. If no good reason, more particularly, no sound economic reason exists for such unity, it will not develop. Although the Greeks were ethnic chauvinists, they were not economic monopolists. They allowed the Metic elements to compete equally, even to dominate their trade. And their peculiar attitude to labor which involved a contempt not for manual labor but for subservience to anyone, allowed for equal access for all, Greek and non-Greek alike.[26] Almost all occupations except political offices were open to them. Some of the wealthiest bankers, financiers, and traders were Metics, Pasion being perhaps the most famous. The freedmen and aliens did as well as their talents permitted within the framework of the Greek economy, so there was no economic motivation to generate any kind of ethnic solidarity even if cultural unity had made this possible.

Ethnicity is basically a function of economic interests. There is nothing automatic or inevitable about it. I shall have more to say on this later, since it is a view not shared by the vast majority of social scientists who work in this area.

Ethnic solidarity for segments of the Metic class in Greece would also have been discouraged by the open hostility of the host community to it. The Greeks would not tolerate such solidarity. They were not only a strongly ethnic people but cultural absolutists. An ethnically distinct ruling class will only tolerate distinct ethnic minorities if their intellectual tradition tends toward syncretic universalism and inclusiveness, or if the dominant group is committed to a relativistic social dogma. In relations between conquerors and conquered in the early Mesopotamian empires, later in the Roman empire and, still later, in several of the Islamic empires there was a universalist tradition. The Greeks in the Hellenistic world, becoming the dominant group in alien lands, were encouraged by expediency, but also to a degree by the exceptional universalism of Alexander and his intellectual heritage, to adopt a relativistic social dogma as the racist ruling class in South Africa has today. The Greeks, in their homeland, had to make no such compromises. Their ethnicity was more akin to modern German ethnicity. We are not surprised to learn that the Jews, who had the misfortune of living under both regimes, were as intensely disliked in antiquity by the Greeks as they were later to be by the Nazis.

Ethnicity, especially its adaptive form, will emerge only in an inclusive, territorially based, society committed to universalist principles. Adaptive ethnicity, the most common form of ethnicity in the Roman world, largely disappeared in the Western world with the collapse of that empire and the emergence of the medieval world order. Fourteen hundred years later the form was to reappear in full flowering in the United States during the early twentieth century. Adaptive ethnic groups rose and disappeared in their usual transitory way throughout the Islamic world during the Middle Ages, especially in Iraq during the period of the Abbasid Caliphate.

A third type of ethnic group is what may be called the *revivalist ethnic group*. Such groups bear a special relationship to the adaptive ethnic group. Revivalist movements usually come about during the last stages of complete absorption by the dominant society when all that remains are fragmentary and largely sentimental cultural patterns with little vitality or relevance to the absorbed group. The symbols are what Schneider has called "empty symbols"—they lack potency and structural meaning, are simply part of the group's folklore. Revivalist ethnic groups also develop among native peoples who have been conquered by an alien successor elite. The symbols and language of the conquered group may maintain their cultural potency while lacking social relevance or status. Thus the traditional religion may have been replaced as the official state religion by the alien elite. Revivalist ethnic groups use cultural symbols to express grievances. The reinvestment of cultural potency to the empty symbols, or the restoration of social status to the displaced native culture, become the means of expressing discontent, the true sources of which may be economic, political, or psychological insecurity. Often they focus on the rise of charismatic leaders who lament the loss of cultural potency or the social status of the native culture as a means of whipping up group anger and solidarity. Revivalist ethnicity is typically found in the early stages of anticolonial movements, and one version of it (involving the reinvestment of cultural potency) exists today in the emerging ethnicity of the so-called white ethnics of the United States. But it is not peculiar to the modern world. Such ethnic movements existed in several of the Islamic empires, especially during the period of the Abbasid dynasty. Thus, there were the movements of Bibafarid in the middle of the eighth century, the revolt of the Persian heretic Muganna later in the same century, and of Babak in the early ninth century. Bernard Lewis, in his review of these movements, points out that they were mainly "economic and social in origin, some with national coloring." They were almost all articulated in religious terms, but while principally Persian in origin, the religious revival was not the old Zoroastrian state cult, but the "old Iranian heresies" of the peasant class.[27] They were essentially peasant movements expressed in ethnic and religious terms. These movements were joined by the displaced, downwardly mobile Persian middle classes (though not the old Persian aristocracy, which adapted itself nicely to the Arab conquerors). This conjunction of displaced or discontented middle and/or elite elements and lower-class masses through the revival of shared and threatened symbols, the major characteristic of revivalist ethnic groups, often accounts for their conservatism. This is as true of the ethnic revolts against Islam as it is of the white ethnic movements of the United States and the contemporary Celtic revivalist movements of Wales, Scotland, and Brittany.

These movements are also ideologically ambiguous. On the one hand, there are radical economic leanings in the demand of the mass of lower-class followers for better economic conditions or the preservation of insecurely held and threatened economic status. On the other hand, these radical economic tendencies are undermined by conservative elements who soon usurp leadership and whose main goal is the restoration of the old antiegalitarian order or, as in the United States, in the curtailing of the egalitarian thrust of the society. This ideological tension often accounts for the failure of such groups. (In the few cases where they do succeed, reactionary social policies invariably follow.) Several of the movements in the Arab middle ages, for example, openly avowed the communist ideology of the sixth-century revolutionary Mazdak, yet the societies they set up during their brief periods of success were anything but communistic. Perhaps the classic case in point was the Zandj state, set up in late ninth-century Iraq by rebel East African slaves under their Persian leader Muhamad b. Ali. The Zandj state, in spite of the proclaimed communistic ideology of its leader, was not only hierarchic in nature, but actually maintained the institution of slavery, with the former masters and several of the local peasant communities reduced to slavery. Alexander Popovic, who has done the most thorough study of the Zandj, concludes by saying that the failure of the revolt was due to the opportunism of its charismatic leader and to the "absence of a definite plan and of a social programme." [28] Exactly the same judgment can be passed on many of the Maroon societies of the Caribbean during the eighteenth century after the successful slave revolts of mainly Akan-Ashanti revivalist ethnic movements.[29] We find almost exact parallels in the Celtic fringe ethnic revivalist movements in Britain today, where there is a similar ideological confusion between the radical working class and unemployed elements and their middle- and upper-class supporters, especially in Scotland after the discovery of North Sea oil.[30]

A fourth type of ethnic group also appeared in the ancient world, the *colonial ethnic group,* those segments of the imperial power which colonized and became resident in the conquered regions. Before the Persian empire most imperial elites allowed their conquered societies to rule themselves in their internal affairs, subject to the payments of certain forms of tribute and conformity to the policy of the imperial power in foreign affairs. Conquering elites who were alien groups soon became rapidly absorbed by the native culture, as were most of the succession of imperial states in Mesopotamia. If the conquering group remained distinct, its distinctiveness rested in its class hegemony, not in any form of conscious ethnic identity distinct from the conquered peoples. An important change was to take place in the first Persian empire. The Persians found parts of their conquered regions more attractive to live in than their home base. The satrapies and their courts formed the initial colonial elite, soon followed by nonaristocratic Persians. By the beginning of the fifth century, hardly forty years after the conquest, we find what Olmstead calls "a veritable invasion of Babylonia by Iranian settlers." Persian ethnic tolerance soon led to an extremely pluralistic society in Babylonia. The Persians, however, could not help becoming ethnically conscious in this setting. They formed a distinct ethnic elite above the pluralistic collection of Egyptians, Syrians, Kashshites, Nabataeans, Kurds, and Jews who flourished in the Satrapy.[31]

The Greek conquerors in the Hellenistic empires continued this tradition, having an even stronger sense of ethnic exclusiveness, although, out of imperial expediency, they too were forced to become more tolerant than they were used to in the Greek heartland. With the Romans we return to an imperial power which, like the Persians, was unusually tolerant in dealing with conquered native peoples. The Romans had a far more highly developed policy of colonization than the rulers of previous empires, and the colonial ethnic elites they formed more closely resemble similar elites in the modern imperial states. Caesar, who pursued his colonial policy for mainly economic and social reasons, drew mainly upon the proletarii for his colonists, whereas Augustus, whose colonial policy was motivated more by militaristic factors, tended to draw his colonists mainly from among the veterans. To some extent this difference in policy was reflected in the nature and fate of the colonial elites that resulted. Caesar's colonists tended to assimilate more and were less ethnically conscious. In some parts of the Roman empire the Italian elite quickly abandoned its ethnic exclusiveness, intermarried with the local aristocracy, and formed a new hybrid ruling class. This was certainly the case in Spain, especially Emporiae and several African colonies.[32] Augustus' colonists tended to remain more exclusive and became, from an earlier period, ethnically conscious.

Yet we must agree with Brunt that the Romans were less generous with the grantings of citizenship than some earlier authorities would lead us to believe. Compared to the Greeks, the Romans seem a model of imperial tolerance and generosity, but almost any group of people would appear favorable in comparison with the Greeks in ethnic matters. The Romans in the provinces, however, formed a distinct ethnic group, incorporating to only a very limited degree cooperating elements of the displaced native elite.

Even so, Roman ethnicity was always very weak, reaching its height during the period of the last century B.C. and the first century A.D., the period in which Latin civilization flourished and a certain chauvinistic pressure was exerted on native authorities to learn Latin and Roman law. Such pressures soon gave way under the conquest of the Roman world by Greek culture. The rise and decline of Roman colonial ethnicity is revealed in the history of Antioch during this period. The Romans developed quite a fondness for the place and it is here, more than anywhere else, that, for a sustained period, they made the acquisition of Latin culture a prerequisite for advancement. And yet, even here, Roman colonial ethnicity never descended to the gratuitous chauvinistic indecencies of modern European colonial elites. The rival Roman studies—shorthand, Latin, and Roman law—never displaced Greek rhetoric and made no demands whatever on the native Syriac culture. Upwardly mobile native elements felt a sense of shame about their native culture only in their attempts to assimilate Greek culture, as with what Liebeschuetz calls the "shamefaced bilingualism" of Theodoret, the Syrian bishop of Cyrrubus.[33]

The main sociological role of the colonial ethnic elite is, of course, its reinforcement of the authority of the imperial power center and its promotion of a more efficient exploitation of the resources of the subjected people. What is even more interesting is the role of the colonial ethnic elite in forging and maintaining new societies on the periphery of empire or in harmonizing relations between formerly hostile groups within newly demarcated provincial boundaries. Thus the colonial provinces formed by the Romans often constituted the first form of unity, albeit one superimposed from above, experienced by the subject peoples. The same pattern was to be repeated by the modern colonial empires. The degree to which this unity persists after the removal of the colonial ethnic group will often depend on the degree to which this elite had succeeded, as a byproduct of its rule, in establishing integrative institutions during the period of its sovereignty.

The integrative and society-forming role of the colonial ethnic elite has been given insufficient attention by students of imperial history. It obviously varies with the type of colony and the degree of exclusiveness of the colonial elite. Clearly no such role exists in the so-called colonies of settlement, wholly new societies in which the colonizing groups rapidly become demographically dominant. In other types of colonies, however—colonies of occupation such as Roman Britain, British India, and the Dutch and French East Indies; mixed colonial settlements such as the French in Algeria, Spanish Central America, and Ptolemaic Alexandria; and plantation colonies such as those of the French, English, and Dutch in the Caribbean, in all of which the colonial group constituted a small ethnic minority—the social and cultural relationship between the dominant ethnic group and the native population was often a crucial factor in the nature and development of these societies, even during the postcolonial period.

The enormous success of the British colonial elite in India in imposing a centralized bureaucracy, a unified legal system, army, police force, and minimal infrastructure on what was formerly a politically fragmented subcontinent, and in the cultural sphere its success in creating a native Indian elite along the lines laid down by Macaulay with typical imperial candor,—"a class of persons Indian in color and blood, but English in tastes, in opinions, in morals and in intellect" [34] —must all be taken into account in explaining the relative stability of the subcontinent during the late colonial period and after independence. On the other hand, the Dutch political economist Furnival, one of the few scholars to examine the role of the colonial ethnic elite systematically, has shown how the failure of the Dutch East India elite to develop such integrative mechanisms was an important factor in the instability of their pluralistic colonial polities.[35]

The social and cultural practices of the colonial elite alone could not explain the course of development of these societies. I am not suggesting that there was any relation between overtly declared imperial policy and actual practice. The celebrated French policy of assimilation was nothing more than a typical piece of Gallic rationalistic propaganda, meant entirely for home consumption. Even in Algeria with its relatively large French population the policy failed miserably. Still, the cultural and social practices of the colonial ethnic elites may usefully be examined in order to refine, reinforce, and complete a necessarily structural analysis of the dynamics of imperial systems.

A fifth type of ethnic group I call the *symbiotic ethnic group*. Like the adaptive ethnic group such communities are found as aliens in a wider host society, but here the similarity ends. Such groups have an entirely different origin and they are persistent, not transitory groups.

Symbiotic ethnic groups developed as pristine states or were originally part of a social order with a highly developed sense of ethnic cohesiveness. Misfortune in war or economic necessity forced significant segments of such groups to migrate either to the center of the expansionist state or, very often, to the recently conquered provinces of the empire. They proceeded to perform crucial middlemen roles in the new setting, performing tasks the host society and its members considered contemptible or polluting (especially where they are at the center of the empire) or tasks the ruling class is reluctant to undertake and which the conquered native group is either not resourceful or skilled enough to perform: tasks such as slave trading, usury, small-scale shopkeeping, or various skilled crafts.

The ethnic group performs a valuable role for the dominant elite. Economic forces are critical for the survival of the symbiotic ethnic group, which finds its ethnicity in its own best economic interest. Where it does not, I contend once again against the weight of sociological thought on the subject, the group either withdraws from the society or disappears through absorption.

Because the symbiotic ethnic group originates as an ethnic group before its entry into the host society and enters the host society as part of a wider diaspora, such groups are trans-sovereignal. Very often such groups can take advantage of their international networks to serve both their own ends and the ends of their host societies. It is no accident, then, that most such groups tend to specialize in trade and commerce.

The classic case of the symbiotic ethnic group are the Jews.

Unlike the adaptive ethnicity of the Roman empire, Jewish ethnicity, like Greek symbiotic ethnicity in the post-Hellenistic Mediterranean world, was long born in the kin-hegemonic pristine state of the group. It was sustained by the special economic roles Jews became skilled at performing in the center and periphery of early imperial states. Long before the Persian conquest exilic Jews played a critical role in the development of Babylonian banking. In the less tolerant Seleucid period the names of prominent Jewish banking families dutifully celebrated the Babylonian religious Lord, but in the later, more tolerant Persian climate the leading Jewish banking family was named Bel-iau, Olmstead wittily informs us, an open "challenge to paganism," since it means: "Our God Yaweh is the true Lord (and not your alleged lord Marduk!)." [36]

In accounting for the nature and persistence of Jewish ethnicity and its relationship to Jewish economic roles and relative prosperity, it seems to me not that Jewish ethnicity explains Jewish economic status and role, but that its status and role account for the persistence of its ethnicity. My reading of Jewish history suggests no mystery in accounting for its persistence, once one understands the interplay of economic forces and the symbiotic adaptation of the group. Part of the false mystique about the persistence of Jewish ethnicity is due to the tendency of most Gentile, and not a few Jewish historians, to assert, in the face of contradictory evidence, that the Jews were always a suffering group of people, a kind of damned pariah class. This conception of Jewish history, as Baron has noted,[37] is sheer nonsense, put abroad partly by Gentile historians under the influence of a thinly disguised anti-Semitism, and by Jewish scholars who find it difficult to resist self-pity or the image of the suffering Jew in their writings. Jews have generally been a fairly prosperous element in the Western host societies in which they have lived. Their standard of living has generally been well above the mass of the population of such societies, and their standard of health better than the upper classes. Once we understand this all mystery about the persistence of the group vanishes. The explanation becomes ridiculously simple: it made good sense to be Jewish.

The Jews, however, were not the only symbiotic ethnic group of the ancient world; they were not even the most successful. In the Roman empire, the Jews, as Max Radin has pointed out, "were only to a very slight extent merchants or money-lenders." [38] They were mainly artisans. The roles of merchant and financier were monopolized by Greeks and Syrians. And after the collapse of Carthage there was a Phoenecian diaspora all over the Mediterranean and the Phoenecians adapted their traditional trading skills to the demands of their new role as symbiotic ethnic group. The diaspora Phoenecians saw so much in common between themselves and the diaspora Jews that they began to identify with them and a considerable number of the converts to Judaism during the period of Jewish expansion were from this group of people.

In saying that economic factors explain the persistence of the symbiotic ethnic group, I am not advocating any crude form of economic determinism. Such factors do not explain the *origin* of such groups; nor do they explain sufficiently or completely the persistence of such groups. Preexisting cultural factors may have dovetailed with and reinforced the new economic role of the group. The this-worldliness of Judaism and its unusual association of the idea of calling with vocation (in marked contrast with the Christian conception of calling), reinforce the adaptive tendency toward the acquisition of useful skills. And one sees how, in the case of other symbiotic ethnic groups, cultural patterns after a time would begin to be selected, emphasized, and developed so as to reinforce the most economically adaptive roles. In this way the culture of the group becomes causal in its superstructural feedback on the economic life of the group. In a later chapter I shall examine, in depth, the reinforcing relationship between ethnicity and class in a typical modern symbiotic ethnic group.

But it is not only in purely economic terms that a group can establish a symbiotic ethnic relationship with a host society. The Greeks, in addition to being traders, came to dominate Roman intellectual life and art. The Jews were most responsible for keeping the West in contact with the commercial and cultural aspects of Islamic civilization; in a remarkable geographical and historical convergence, they acted as middlemen in keeping the

West in touch with its own classical heritage via the Jewish contact with Islam. The works of Aristotle were revived in the late Middle Ages through the translations of the famous Sephardic Jewish family, Ibn Tibbon, which came in contact with Greek culture through its associations with the Moors of Spain.

The symbiosis, finally, can be of the most profound psychological and philosophical significance. In the last section of this work I hope to show how the Hebraic vision of man, the special crisis it confronts, and its way of resolving this crisis, has acquired a very special meaning not only for Jews but for all members of Western civilization, especially since the end of the eighteenth century.

The sixth and final type of ethnic group is unique in one important respect. With no counterpart in the ancient or medieval world, it is entirely the product of the modern world. It is the ethnic group which has had the greatest impact on the course of human history. We have come to call it the nation-state and its driving force is nationalism.

CHAPTER 3

The Nation-State

Few subjects are more confused and intellectually misunderstood than the problems of nationalism and the nature of the nation-state.[1] Many political and social analysts have defined the term "nation-state" so inclusively that it has come to mean the same thing as the more generic term "state." Attempts at defining nationalism have been no better. Almost every form of group behavior or expression of group sentiment is now referred to as nationalism, so much so that the only remaining meaning of the term is: the expression of group solidarity. In the United States, for example, black ethnicity, which is overwhelmingly an expression of the desire for equality and inclusion in the American state (the call for a separate state being advocated only by a tiny minority, and the call for an independent state being restricted to the insignificant lunatic fringe), has been described by American commentators and social scientists as "black nationalism" or black "nation-building."

The present connotation of the term "nation" came into the English language rather late. The Middle English usage of the term (its earliest English derivation) referred simply to a collection of people from a special locality or simply an aggregation of human or animal individuals. The term, referring in its modern usage to a group of individuals with a consciously shared set of cultural patterns belonging to a single state, is of French origin.

As J. D. Mabbott has argued, to the English ear the term nation-state has always sounded redundant. Nation is often used as a synonym for state by the English. It has never acquired the special meaning it holds among continental and American scholars. The English, with respect to their own political order, have never found the term nation useful, because they have never developed the entity. The United Kingdom of Great Britain and Ireland is not a nation-state. Nor was the English state before the union. Nor, for that matter, were any of the states of the Anglo-Saxon heptarchy. What is true of Great Britain is also true of the United States. Dewey and other American social theorists with some respect for the English language, the aims of the founding fathers, and the reality of the American political experience, have pointed out that the separation of state from nationality is one of the most salient features of the United States, a feature which may be seen as the most important Anglo-Saxon continuity in the country's political system.

The continental Europeans did develop a peculiar version of the modern state which necessitated the use of the compound term "nation-state." Among Europeans there has never been any confusion on this point. The confusion of the Anglo-American mind is due, I suspect, to the dual origins of its own political philosophy. From England it borrowed its theory of the state. From Europe it borrowed its definition of the philosophical foundations and objectives of state action, its "self-evident truths." As is so frequently the case with all intellectual migrations, the unwanted baggage of continental nationalism crept into the American political consciousness with the desired and consciously bought goods of the European Enlightenment.

The reasons for the peculiar disjunction in the development of modern European society—between the Anglo-Saxons on the one hand and the Continentals on the other—reflect the true nature of the ethnic group we call the nation-state.

One way of bringing into relief the distinctive properties and

uniquely modern quality of the nation-state is to distinguish it
from the kin-hegemonic pristine state which it resembles, but with
which it is by no means identical. The Greeks, aware of
themselves as a distinct people with a separate culture, certainly
had what today we would call a stong sense of nationality. They
never developed a nation state, however, and rarely felt the need
to. There was never an identification of the state with the entire
Greek people. State boundaries cut across nationality boundaries
and each city-state jealously guarded its independence, as jealously as the Greek people as a whole guarded and prized the
purity and superiority of their culture vis-à-vis the barbarians.
While some concession was made to nationality or ethnicity in the
somewhat more favorable treatment of fellow Greeks—Greeks,
for example, were usually, though certainly not always, reluctant
to enslave fellow Greeks during times of peace—on the whole
there was no automatic granting of citizenship to Greeks from
other city-states. A substantial number of the Metic class in
Athens were Greeks from other states, and they were subject to
the same rules of alienage as other Metics. The average Greek
would have been thoroughly scandalized by the modern idea that
because he shared a common culture with fellow Greeks he
should share a common state with them. The Greek world had a
cantankerous independence. Their violent, fratricidal wars were
more frequent than their few lame attempts at federation.
Attempts at imposed unity through the imperial expansion of
Athens or Sparta merely created a great deal of bad blood and
resentment. Here and there nationalistic voices called for the
formation of a pan-Hellenic nation-state. There is something
revealingly and chillingly modern in Isocrates' call for such a
union, with its suggestion that the best way to forge such a union
would be to intensify the Greek view of the barbarian as a natural
enemy, with the concentration of this out-group hostility on the
hereditary enemy, the Persians. The average Greek did not take
such ideas seriously. Isocrates was a couple millennia before his
times. Ehrenberg has pointed out: "State autonomy meant a
splitting up, a division that ruled out all possibility of unifying all

Greek states, even of establishing common peace between them. The idea of political unity never occurred to the Greeks." [2]

The Greeks at least had the idea of nationality. But there was not even the idea of nationality and certainly not the conception, much less the realization, of the nation-state in the empires and states of the ancient Oriental world. Ancient Egyptian society had an incredibly uniform culture and a postdynastic history of some 3000 years. There was a single, highly centralized state. The Egyptians were notoriously conservative about their culture, in this respect greatly resembling the Chinese. The tremendous development of ancestor worship among both peoples is not accidental. The Egyptians, however, never developed the idea that the state was based on, or should be based on, their common cultural heritage. A cultural group is not an ethnic group. At no time in their long history was there ever any doubt concerning the idea and nature of the state: It was an entity embodied in the person of the Pharoah, who ruled not by divine authority but through his own divine authority since he was god incarnate. Cultural chauvinism was unnecessary as a prop or rationale for such a state. The very idea was unthinkable. In a perceptive comment on the Egyptian dynastic state Jon Manchip White has written:

They can claim to have been one of the least neurotic civilizations that the world has seen. Their geographical isolation was so extreme that until a late stage in their history they were spared the ordeal of constant foreign invasion; and coupled with the absence of anxiety that goes with freedom from being conquered they lacked the miserable sense of guilt that blights the spirit of the conqueror. [3]

I can think of few better descriptions of the antithesis of nationalism than this passage from White. In a real sense nationalism is born in the collective anxiety that comes from a too great awareness of one's separateness vis-à-vis other peoples, and beneath all nationalisms is the acute neurosis which is expressed on the one hand in the fear of being less than others and on the other hand in the compensatory claim of being more than they are. As David Riesman once observed, "To participate as a citizen in national purpose is perhaps not inevitably a form of alienation." [4]

The other Eastern Mediterranean states and empires, as well as the Hellenistic and Roman empires, either cut across or were incorporated into wider political boundaries, cultural, and nationality groups. The medieval world order was also a peculiarly nonethnic system. With the collapse of the Roman empire in the West and the emergence of that strange process of cultural metamorphosis we have come to call feudalism, only two types of allegiances were possible. The most important was allegiance to the local manorial domain existing within the framework of the fragile feudal state, the other to the universal world order of Christendom. The local branch of the Catholic church was the only intermediary between the two. The average medieval individual lived through a daily routine circumscribed by the village with its economic base in the land. It was quintessentially a rural civilization, removed from the highly urbanized Graeco-Roman civilization that preceded it. "Socially," William Carroll Bark points out, "men bade farewell either wittingly or unwittingly, to the greater freedom, prosperity, and complexity of civilization known to some of their predecessors, and entered a state of subservience to overlords who owned or controlled vast estates by virture of their military power." [5]

What black Americans today call "the man" and their definition of subservience as being "the man" of another man, is almost identical, as Marc Bloch has told us, to the basic relationship that underlay the feudal system: "To be the "man" of another man: in the vocabulary of feudalism, no combination of words was more widely used or more comprehensive in meaning." [6] The political framework of their order was, ideally, a set of concentric status allegiances ranging from that between the local manorial lord and his men, and between the local lord and greater lord, whose man he was, up to the biggest man of all: the man himself, the king. Beyond his own local feudal lord, however, the serf or peasant knew nothing and cared even less. Nothing, that is, except the church, which demanded from him loyalty to a Christian order which in theory encompassed, potentially, all mankind. Nowhere in this extraordinary synthesis of the materially and socially particular and the spiritually universal (though how meaningful Christian universalism was to the medieval layman is a moot point) was there room for allegiance to anything remotely resembling an ethnic group.

Ethnic allegiance—and here we come upon one of its many ironies—involves and requires a certain kind of freedom. It implies, at least, the right to be, and to be consciously, something other than what "the man" wants you to be. It implies other loyalties, and neither the church nor the state would tolerate the "greater freedom" that made this possible. Almost all ethnic movements and groups, and especially the nation-state in its development, wave the banner of freedom:—the freedom from the constraint on their emergence, and the freedom to realize their destiny. The tragedy is that so many of them can only realize their freedom by denying the rights of others. "Nationalism," Ehrenberg wrote in his last work with that humane wisdom which comes only after a lifetime of scholarship and reflection, "is a child of freedom, but it can happen that the child kills its mother." [7] The medieval world was too cautious and constraining a cosmos to make possible such intellectual matricide. People were, of course, aware of each other and of themselves as Englishmen, Normans, Welshmen, Scotsmen, Danes, and the like. And there was always the infidel knocking on and here and there knocking down the doors of Christendom. But such terms had little but descriptive value. Occasionally one finds the rare, travel-weary noble, especially during the Crusades, boasting about the virtues of his own culture, but no one took this seriously, least of all the nobles involved. For as Lord Acton had pointed out, "In the old European system the rights of nationalities were neither recognized nor asserted by the people. The interest of the reigning families, not those of the nations, regulated the frontiers; and the administration was conducted generally without any reference to popular desires." [8] This is why Acton goes on to trace the beginnings of modern nationalism to the partition of Poland, arguing that the Polish decision to choose their kings on national grounds so outraged the ruling families of Europe that the Polish state was considered a delinquent open for grabs by the other European states. Acton has a point, to be sure, but his elitist conception of the course of Western history gets the better of him.

The important issue here is that political reality during the Middle Ages reflected no dependence of state on common cultural heritage; and political theory was monotonously centered on Christendom as the ideal imperial polity. This is so even with the secular thinkers who began to emerge in the thirteenth century. It is an amusing commentary on the a-nationalism of the medieval mind that Pierre Du Bois, a late-thirteenth-century lawyer in the court of Philip the Fair, and one of the first secular theorists of royal absolutism as well as of French imperialism had so little sense of ethnic or national pride in his women (and we know how closely nationalism is associated with sexual chauvinism and possessive claims on "our women") that he proposed as part of his imperial designs on the Islamic world the education of French women who would be married off to Muslim men and, in that role, convert the heathens to Christianity and French power.[9]

The medieval state was essentially a territorially circumscribed network of stratified political allegiances between highly autonomous seignioral nodes centered on a connecting monarchial axis. This political order persisted with remarkable tenacity up to the end of the thirteenth century, at which point cracks began to appear in the seams of the hoary structure. According to Norman F. Cantor these cracks were the first signs of what he calls "the neurotic death wish of medieval society." This is a fine phrase, but since I earn my living, sometimes, as a social scientist, I cannot afford to condone it. Less mystical is his description of what happened:

The creativity of the twelfth century has posited certain conflicts of the most fundamental kind which have never been resolved in human society and thought: the conflict between revelation and science, the conflict between sacerdotal authority and the freedom of individual religious experience, the conflict between hierocratic authority and the sovereign state.[10]

The transformation from feudalism to the modern absolutist state was twofold and countervailing. Fissionary manorial autonomy and fusionary papal imperialism both had to be suppressed. Both tasks were achieved by that interfacing node in the world system which had most to gain—the monarchy. In destroying the power of the nobility the newly emerging middle classes (partly brought into being for that purpose) came to the aid of the royal authority in their role as councillors and bureaucrats in the expanding, centralizing state, as secular intellectuals and ideologists of royal power, and as theologians of the new, antipapal religion. The Renaissance and the Reformation were the necessary reinforcements of the new structural thrust toward the concentration of economic and political power.

What is still not commonly recognized, however, is the fundamental difference in the way the Anglo-Saxons and the Continentals went about the task. For the English crown the development of the absolutist state was first and foremost a political affair. The Tudor kings sought to be absolute rulers of their own land, and nothing more. To the English king the modern state was a political creation concerned strictly with that cluster of activities which came to the Roman mind when the term *res publica* was used: the land, the laws, a well-stocked treasury, a strong loyal army, and dependable allies. It had nothing to do with the *res gestae,* that is to say, it was in no way related to the idea of a common nationality. There is absolutely nothing in early modern English thought to suggest that the English ever sought to unify themselves or to assert their sovereignty on the basis of a distinct tribal or cultural heritage.

There were many good reasons why the early modern British ruling class never resorted to this expedient. For one thing, it would have been unrealistic under the social conditions then prevailing. Britain was never a unified tribal or cultural entity. Its history up to that point was the product of the periodic invasions and infusions of a considerable number of foreign peoples, ranging from the Angles and Saxons to the Danes and Normans. The pre-Romanic Celtic population was still culturally vibrant and troublesome on the fringes.

Second, the historical origins of the Tudor house made such an appeal to national ethnicity, even on the mythical level, politically risky. Henry VII was the son of a nonaristocratic Welshman who had slept his way into the English royal family, and was a bastard to boot. Insecure about his own aristocratic ancestry and questionably ethnic background, Henry VII was hardly likely to exalt the power of his state on the basis of its cultural glory and distinctiveness, even though, as Tillyard has pointed out in his fine study of myth and the English mind, he did make a desperate though only partly successful effort to legitimize his authority in mythical ancestral re-creations.[11] It was descent which bothered him, not culture.

The nonethnic character of the modern British state at its inception was to carry through right down to late modern times. None of the British rulers ever found the appeal to nationality to be in their own best interests. Elizabethan patriotism, was peculiarly nonethnic. It was not British culture which was being celebrated, or British art, or music, or customs, or language. It was the very practical and enriching deeds of a bunch of pirates and desperadoes who had stolen successfully from the Spanish, and the heroic defense of the fatherland from the understandably outraged Spaniards. And Shakespeare certainly knew his audience when he selected his heroes. Nor is it chance that so many of the major plays of this greatest of English writers should have been set in foreign lands. Like his Tudor audience, it was not the celebration of British cultural distinctiveness which was of central concern to Shakespeare but the nature and problems of power, the loneliness and deep unease of authority, the integrity of the state, and the legitimacy of the crown. To show how these problems and experiences express in heroic terms the eternal problems of ordinary mortals was the great achievement of Shakespeare's genius.

It was Francis Bacon, that most British of British thinkers, who declared: "a retention of custom is as turbulent a thing as an innovation, and they that reverence too much old-times are but a scorn to the new." [12] Hobbes' view of the state was also a peculiarly British view of political reality. So, at the other, liberal, extreme was Locke's. Indeed, Locke went out of his way to point out that by the term "commonwealth" he meant that "which the Latins signified by the word *civitas,* to which the word which best answers in our language is "commonwealth," and most properly expresses such a society of men which 'community' does not (for their may be subordinate communities in a government), and 'city' much less." [13] The only British philosopher who came anywhere close to an expression of ethnic sentiments was Edmund Burke, and he was the exception that proved the rule. His contribution to the history of British political thought is as small as his contribution to the development of European romantic political thought is great. It is no accident that the German and French romantics loved him. And we can understand now the bemusement of certain of his German admirers at the fact that his countrymen so studiously neglected him.

The emergence of the modern French state is quite different. France, unlike England, had a remarkably unified cultural and historical tradition. We have all heard about Charles the Hammer and how he saved us all from a fate worse than death. The Gallic tradition has deep roots both in the unity of its pre-Roman Celtic substratum and in the transformation of this barbarian base into the most romanized province of the western empire. The product of this cultural synthesis was to become the most viable and continuous bastion of post-Roman Christian civilization in the Western world, so that the received tradition of the fourteenth and fifteenth centuries was a social order which, while as feudal as the rest of Europe, was unique in its cultural uniformity and continuity.

The French monarch, unlike his Anglo-Saxon counterpart, had an added latent force which could be used in his drive toward centralization and absolutism: the common culture of his state. But like the tribe that preceded the pristine state, medieval French culture was only protoethnic. There was genuine existential solidarity, but relatively little consciousness about this solidarity. It was inevitable that the French crown would exploit this latent force. One detects signs of an awareness of its potential in the writings of some of the early modern French men of letters. The Duc de Sully comes immediately to mind.

The decision to exploit this latent cultural force came slowly. For the first three hundred years of the modern French state strong countervailing forces worked against a too blatant use of ethnic particularism by the French crown. These forces centered on France's peculiar role as the leading Catholic state and its continued commitment to papal authority in spiritual matters. France continued to view her role in continental rather than purely national terms. Ethnicity thrives on the overt hostility of other peoples and the culture of the ancient regime inspired most ungrudging admiration from all other peoples in continental Europe, even temporary political enemies. Everywhere, not only the pageantry and splendor of the court of the sun-king, but the wider cultural elaborations of French language, literature, and arts were the objects of wonder and emulation.

Under such conditions a people become proud, but not chauvinistic; superior, but not jingoistic. The tenuous virtue of magnanimity mutes the latent vice of ethnocentrism. The same kind of adulation, during the Hellenistic period, mellowed and toned down somewhat the formerly aggressive chauvinism of the Greeks.

It is ironic that the latent force of French nationalism was first exploited not by the Crown, but by religious nonconformists in conflict with it. It is extremely revealing to contrast the intellectual strategies of the French monarchomachs, especially Francis Hotman, with their British counterpart a little earlier, especially the Marion exiles such as John Knox, William Wittingham, and

Christopher Goodman. While both groups were in opposition to the crown for religious reasons, the Marion exiles made their case on purely religious and legal grounds. Hotman objected to royal absolutism on the grounds that it violated the traditional source of legitimacy for the French constitution, which, he claimed—and in so doing produced one of the first truly nationalist treatises on the nature of the state—was rooted in the soil, heritage, and original community of the French people.[14]

All this was to change with that catastrophic bourgeois pretension we call the French Revolution. If the nation-state was conceived in the emergence of the modern French state, it came to a violent birth in its revolution. Its handmaiden was the bourgeoisie. On this point all major students of the revolution—Labrousse, Lefebvre, Cobban, to list a few—agree: The middle classes, and especially the upwardly mobile petit bourgeoisie, from now on here and in other places and other times, found in the peculiar configuration of intense national pride, industrial expansion, and libertarian values the apotheosis of human progress. And it is in this sense only that we can agree with Alfred Cobban that the eighteenth century was *"above all in France,* the nursery of the modern world"* (emphasis added).

It is not difficult to understand the logic of this development. The nation, the culture, and traditions of the fatherland were the perfect substitutes for that which was unattainable: the high culture and status of the nobility. Up to this moment history was the history of the ruling class, the antics and ancestry of the ruling families. There was no place in it for an aspiring group of petty bureaucrats and middle-class upstarts. To solve the problem a new conception of history was developed, one that emphasized the people and their culture rather than a clan and its doings. People replaces clan; culture, the doings of the people, replaces the dynastic activities of the ruling clan.

And who were the group of people best qualified to interpret this cultural heritage and to take pride in its achievements? Who else but those who had had their roots in the folk and who had become the embodiment and protector of its tradition? Who else but the bourgeoisie? When one adds to this the idea that the nation was the true basis of the state, that the will of the people was the will of the state, and that the group best able to interpret this will was that one which had just emerged from the people, hovering like a pack of Melanesian Sir Ghosts between the living reality of the fold and the hallowed ancestral heritage of its past, one sees immediately how powerful a legitimizing force nationalism was for the Jacobins and their followers.

Nationalism, the idea of the nation-state, was the most important consequence of the French Revolution. The French and their Anglo-American admirers have convinced themselves by sheer repetition that some disembodied intellectual force called "liberty" was magically let loose upon the world after the revolution, that this force somehow "captured the imagination," shook the foundations of countless nations, and inspired otherwise complacent men and women in lands unknown and cultures never heard of, to awake to the true realization of their human destiny. And for this, the world should forever remain in debt to a band of fanatical petit-bourgeois cut-throats, jingoists, slavemongers, and imperialists. Surely, if the pun be pardoned (which it isn't really when we trace the root of the word), in all the lively pretensions of European historiography nothing can match this piece of mythology for sheer gall.

The one lasting and dubious effect of the French Revolution for the rest of the world was, rather, the invention of the idea and reality of the nation-state. The paradoxical manner in which this principle was transferred across Europe with the imperial expansion of France need not concern us here. Nor is there any need to dwell upon the sometimes benign, more frequently tragic, consequences of this development in every area of Europe where it has taken root. The term nation-state has a precise meaning; it is, simply, the state which is based on, and identified with, a single ethnic group.

The idea of the nation-state is the view that a state ought to consist of a group of people who consciously share a common culture. Objectively, the members of a nation-state or aspiring nation-state may or may not share a single unified cultural tradition, and while the degree to which they actually do is of some consequence, the important issue is the degree to which they believe they do. The role of consciousness in defining ethnicity is nowhere more true than in the case of the ethnic group which is the nation-state. Max Weber has noted, "Any community can create customs, and it can also effect, in certain circumstances decisively, the selection of anthropological types . . . Any aspect or cultural trait, no matter how superficial, can serve as a starting point for the familiar tendency to monopolistic closure." [15]

As I have defined it, very few states are actually nation-states, although a great many states aspire to it. Britain, the United States, Canada, and Switzerland are not nation-states. Ireland, France, and most of the other European states are nation-states; so is Japan. Russia and China exhibit nationalistic tendencies, especially the former, but neither are nation-states, although Russia during the Stalinist period did aspire to become one. Chinese political traditions work against the idea of the nation-state, as does its current Marxist ideology. Most of the Latin American republics are nation-states or try hard to be, and all of them are nationalistic. The Arab world presents some fascinating problems. Are the Arab states really nation-states? To the average layman who reads the newspaper daily where foreign journalists explain with monotonous regularity every new event in terms of that dreaded explanatory catch-all, Arab nationalism, it might seem almost foolish to ask such a question. And yet, I can find little evidence that the Arab states are really nation-states, or even that they are fully committed to the idea of the nation-state. If it seems like an astonishing remark, it might be the astonishment that comes with the erosion of stereotypic thinking. The Arab states do have distinctive cultural heritages (although the degree of uniformity in each can be exaggerated). Arabs may be no less inclined to chauvinism than other peoples. Still, the specific political configuration which defines a nation-state seems remarkably absent here. On the one hand, there seems to be a weak tendency to identify the state with the specific culture within its boundaries, and on the other hand, chauvinistic feelings of the type often association with nationalism tend to transcend state lines. In many respects the Arab states, politically, remind one of the Greek states during the classical period. There is the same intense transsovereignal chauvinism centered on a common culture, especially a common religion with its concomitant values, laws, and customs. The infidel among the Arabs replaces the barbarians among the Greeks. There is also the same incapacity to federate in spite of repeated efforts, the same occasional outbreaks of fratricidal quarrels, the same strong tendency toward political autonomy and jealous protection of separate political boundaries. The Arab states possess something, however, which the Greeks did not. They espouse a creed which is both monotheistic and universalistic. The religious culture which unites them, and which is the source of their chauvinism, is not exclusive—as was Greek religious culture—but inclusive. The Arab world is no less universalist than was the late Roman world, and any comparison of Islam with Christianity must conclude that Islam is a great deal more tolerant as a creed than is Christianity.

What kind of states, then, are the Arab states? Quite frankly, I don't know what to call them. This is a problem I happily hand over to the student of comparative politics. Sufficient for the purposes of this work is the fact that the Arab states are not strictly nation-states.

The new states of the so-called Third World, the postcolonial states of Africa, Asia, and the Caribbean, have almost all adopted uncritically the idea of the nation-state as the ideal model for state construction. The tragedy of this adoption is, of course, the fact that very few have the cultural basis for its implementation. Everywhere the cry is the same: "We must build a nation! We must redeem our past, revive our heritage which the imperialists have brutally assaulted!" And everywhere reality has responded: With what?

India, with its scores of peoples and languages? Nigeria, Kenya,

Senegal, with their warring tribes and traditional enmities?
Malaysia, with its hostile ethnic groups? Trinidad, Jamaica,
Guyana, split a hundred ways between whites and non-whites,
Blacks and Indians, not to mention Chinese, Syrians and Jews, not
to mention peasants and urbanites, not to mention British-
oriented middle class and Afro-West Indian lower classes? How,
one wants to know, was it possible for so manifestly foolish an
idea to "capture the imagination" of so many peoples? Human
beings are capable of generating symbols of unity where few such
symbols exist in reality; the problem of the new states of the Third
World is often not a poverty of symbols but an embarrassment of
symbolic riches. It is not out of want of culture that many of these
states face chaos, but the assertion of too many cultures. This is
why the idea of the nation-state was such an astonishingly stupid
one in these states. For it was like fighting fire with fire in an
already dry and barren political landscape. If one gives a child of
six years ten cubes, each with a different color and asks him or her
to find some common principle uniting them, such a child would
immediately search for the required principle in the size, or the
weight, or the shape, or the value of the cubes. The last principle
the child would select unless terribly retarded is color. Yet,
amazingly, this most infantile error is being made by the leaders
of the Third World almost everywhere.

I find it hard to accept the view that so many leaders in so many
places could have been so wholly bereft of imagination and plain
good sense. They must have known what they were doing. Why
then did they do it? Why the nation-state, of all things? The
answer, sadly, is that they did it for the same reason that the
French and other continental nationalists did it. They were the
same kind of people—the bourgeoisie—and they had the same
kind of objectives: to replace a degenerate elite. The liberation of
the Third World, we now know, was, with the exception of
support by those leaders who had to fight for their freedom (and
not all of them, as Kenya shows), essentially a bourgeois
revolution, a thing wrought by bureaucracts, lawyers, and ex-

colonial clerks. The occupations and status of the passing colonial
ethnic elites were what they were after. The control of their states
was the necessary vehicle for their aggrandizement and the hoary
ideology of nationalism would provide the basis for both achievement and legitimacy.

The fact that with a few notable exceptions, most of them have
attained little real independence, that the economies of many are
still controlled by the metropolitan multinationals, that the
sovereignty of their states is still at the mercy of the regional desks
of other nations' offices of security, and that their peoples still
starve and face daily the humiliation of unemployment, matter
little. For whatever the reality, they are now part of the family of
nations. They have willed, however unsuccessfully, a common
culture, one people, and barring the occasional civil war or tribal
factionalism (always, of course, due to the manipulations of the
imperialists) they are free to pursue their own great little piece of
national destiny.

It is often claimed that nationalism was the only viable means
whereby the decolonizing native elites could achieve the social
momentum necessary for the overthrow of the imperial regime. If
an evil, it was a necessary evil, for only through nationalism could
the masses have been mobilized in the struggle for independence.
My response to this argument is that there are no theoretical or
empirical political reasons requiring the use of nationalism for the
attainment of independence. It is possible to conceive of and
develop a state in purely legal, economic, and territorial terms. If
it is argued that human beings need the charge of symbolic
appeals if they are to be moved to action, it can be responded that
such symbolic catalysts are not necessarily those of a national
culture. Sapir's distinction between referential and condensation
symbols, however "crude" as Firth described it, is nonetheless
useful.[16] Referential symbols are those which deal with objects
and problems of the external world; they are specific, economical,
and have clearly defined referents. A state's flag is such a symbol.
So are such symbols as a monarch, or titular head of state, or such

ritual symbols as independence day celebrations. Condensation symbols are those which relate to the internal aspects of human life; they resolve problems of the self, are diffuse modes of expression, and are often cathartic and sometimes generative. Such symbols are found in and often constitute the major component of living cultures: racial peculiarities, language, national heroes, myths, legends. Their greater potency is undeniable, which is why leaders find them so seductive, but precisely because they are vested in particular cultures they clearly become dangerous as a means of forging state unity, especially when the political boundaries enclose several cultures with several "dominant symbols," to use Victor Turner's term. The basic problems facing the decolonizing leaders were, on the one hand, the avoidance of the potentially divisive dominant symbols of the traditional cultures and, on the other hand, the creation of meaningful charters that went beyond the specificities of particular cultures and a particular moment in history, charters which could be communicated in their essentials through the temporary use of referential symbols, or what are better described as signs.

The failure of these leaders to do so must be interpreted as a failure both of imagination and intellect. It was a failure of imagination in that they proved themselves incapable of generating a new set of values specifically related to state formation, drawn from the more universal and generalizable symbols of the native culture yet going beyond them both in externality and specificity. And it was a failure of intellect in that the decision to draw on the dominant symbols of preexisting native cultures was a recipe for postcolonial disaster, since the fissiparous tendencies of such revived and relegitimized dominant symbols paved the way for ethnic divisiveness in these polities.

Since there was no real basis for the nation-state in the great majority of the Third World countries on the eve of independence but only the idea of nationalism, what was being created was not the nation-state but an impossible imitation of it. The idea and the model did not occur to them independently; they were diffusions from continental Europe. But of what value is an idea without a chance of realizing it? If there was absolutely no possibility of Nigeria's ever becoming a nation-state, in what sense can the idea of the nation-state have been useful in achieving its independence? Surely, is this not the same order of absurdity as a carpenter who is infused with the idea or model of a Chippendale chair trying to build such a chair when the only materials at his disposal are reeds and bamboo?

Human beings, through consciousness and will, can generate social being or unity, basing this unity on a mythologized reality. But no longer is nationalism the mobilizing force, rather it is a commitment to, or belief in, the idea of nationalism. It is claimed that the belief in the idea created the reality of unity, willed unity, a self-fulfilling prophecy which justified the belief in nationalism by creating it.

Such an argument is unacceptable on both theoretical and empirical grounds. Theoretically, it is unacceptable because there was a much simpler alternative. It would have been much simpler to have gone directly to the task of creating new and dominant state symbols. Nationalism and all its problems would have been circumvented. Tanzania's leaders pursued precisely this simpler and less problematic approach. Nyerere's emphasis on work and on the land beautifully illustrates how a set of charter and referential symbols can be forged which, while meaningful to traditional peasant farmers, go beyond their particular experience and direct behavior to a specific external task, that of building a prosperous state.

And empirically, the argument breaks down because the evidence on the decolonization of the Third World indicates that this is not what happened, but what the leaders tried to make happen, and what many misguided Western commentators reported as having happened. The question here is the actual level of involvement of the masses in the bourgeois decolonization movements which Western analysts have dubbed "nationalist" and by so naming have, in true Platonic fashion, persuaded themselves that the named thing existed. Foreign analysts have confused the staged mass rallies in the carefully selected capitals and provincial centers with the expression of total solidarity. But what of the silent majority of more than 90 per cent who stayed home? Can we assume that they were quietly involved? Can we assume that they cared one way or the other? I am convinced that we cannot.

For those of the masses who belonged to vulnerable minorities—ethnic enclaves, small tribes, or large but unwesternized tribes—the call to national unity may well have seemed like a thin disguise for subordinate unity under the group spearheading the so-called nationalist movement. For the incipient urban proletariat who stayed home, the call for unity may well have seemed too conspicuously shouted by the urban Western elite; and for the mass of the peasants the call for unity may simply have gone unheard in the daily grind of rural poverty.

To discuss what actually happened during the decolonization period of the Third World is well beyond the scope of this work. I suggest instead a classification of the ways in which the Third World leaders actually responded to the task of forging new independent states. There were five such responses, what I shall call the juridical, the syncretic, the transcendental, the nativistic, and the successor ethnic dominant. Of the five, only the juridical eschewed the idea of the nation-state. This, I argue, is in the long run the only sociologically, politically, and morally viable approach. It is the approach in which a new charter and attendant signs are created which are not cathartic or internal and which do not draw upon traditional dominant cultural symbols, but which are specifically aimed at purely political, economic, and territorial goals centered on the new state unity. Tanzania best exemplifies this approach. The little state of Barbados in the Caribbean is another, conservative example.

The other four approaches draw upon the idea of the nation-state, but in different ways, depending on the available cultural resources and tribal and/or ethnic situation existing prior to the decolonization movement. The approach of successor ethnic domination involves the domination of the decolonization movement by one ethnic group which, while claiming to strive for national unity, exploits either its greater level of westernization or its plurality to achieve domination over the other ethnic and/or tribal groups once it replaces the colonial ethnic elite. This is what happened in Nigeria, Malaysia and, to a lesser extent, in Kenya and Uganda. The potential for conflict and even chaos inherent in this approach has been borne out by the facts of their postcolonial history.

Syncretic nationalism is the least dangerous of the four nationalist approaches. The United States was the first state to adopt this approach and it is best summed up in the ideology often referred to as the melting pot. The American version of the melting pot approach, however, was a poor metaphor for describing not one but two techniques of state building. There was a genuine attempt at juridical unity in the United States, that is, an attempt was made to create a state which was not related to the specific cultural experiences of particular groups, but aimed at new ideals to which all Americans could strive, centering specifically on the goals of liberty and equality and the creation of a new cosmopolitanism. This approach, however, became confused with the cultural version of the melting pot creed; conservative elements in the United States, in successfully attacking the drawbacks of cultural syncretism, linked the fate of cosmopolitanism with that of the cultural version of the melting pot.

The Third World societies which adopted the syncretic approach to state building had no such second juridical version. They attempted the task of building a nation-state based on a synthesis of the different cultural segments within the colonial polity. The best examples of this approach are found in the Commonwealth Caribbean states, many of which have adopted as their national motto the "out-of-many-one" credo of the United States. It is impossible to rule out the direct influence of the United States in the adoption of this approach by the bourgeois nationalist leaders of the Commonwealth Caribbean.

Syncretic nationalism suffers from three basic problems. The first is the problem of credibility. It often turns out that only the neocolonial elite advocating the melting pot are truly melted, or, to use the West Indian term, creolized, with the mass of the population firmly entrenched in separate enclaves. Thus while the Blacks, Europeans, Chinese, Indians, Jews, Portuguese, and Syrians who make up the various West Indian elites can be said to share a truly syncretic culture, their claim that this is true of the entire population stands in stark and absurd contradiction to the facts of West Indian life. These elites have lately been forced to face reality as the various ethnic groups have gone through a postindependence revival often resulting in violent conflicts. They have shifted their ground and now claim that the melting pot ideology is an ideal to be strived for, not a reality, except for the fortunate, creolized few.

The second criticism of all cultural versions of the melting pot approach to nation building is the simple fact that even if they work, there is no guarantee that what comes out of the melting is most desirable. As any good cook knows, the best way to ruin a stew is to throw everything into the pot indiscriminately. Having no control over the eventual outcome, there is no way of restraining the emergence of cultural emphases or of dominant cultural symbols which contradict the proclaimed ideal of economic development.

My final criticism of syncretic nationalism is a more philosophical one. Even it it does work, and even if the dominant symbols that emerge are consistent with the aims of all the people, it would still be a nation-state.

Transcendental nationalism develops where a decolonizing or new elite in an old state tries to create unity around a set of dominant symbols which are, essentially, "condensation symbols," that is, symbols which have powerful internal, personal, and indeed physical and racial potency. Nativistic nationalism does the same thing. The critical difference between the two lies in their cultural base. The transcendental nationalist states often have a plural ethnic base and seek to transcend this plural divisiveness by drawing on the most powerful common condensation symbols, such as race and language of the different groups. Often the problem is one of a weak cultural base, in which there is an atavistic reinvestment of potency to the traditional dominant condensation symbols. In the nativist nationalist states there is a preexisting cultural unity which simply needs revival. Often there was a decline in the status of the traditional culture under the impact of foreign invaders, and the nationalist movement focuses on the reinvestment not so much of potency but of status to the traditional culture. There is a close relationship between these two forms of nationalisms and the two versions of revivalist ethnic groups. Actually, the resemblance to transcendental nationalism is superficial, while such ethnic groups bear an intrinsic relationship to the nativistic nationalist movement.

The basic problem of transcendental nationalism is a poverty of dominant symbols, not an overabundance, and a preexisting disunity of potential members based on class differences and political cleavages. The nationalist elite in such cases emphasizes the few powerful symbols such as race and language that can bring the potential nation together. These are then used to generate a new mythology aggrandizing the presumed glories of the race in the past and its manifest destiny. The claim of a unique national temperament or national character becomes a central part of the new mythology, enhancing the intensely personal nature of such movements and at the same time linking the resolution of private, individual anxieties to those of the state. If the conclusion has already been drawn that such movements are inherently fascist, the conclusion is correct.

And like all fascist nationalist states there is a strong tendency toward aggressive expansionism. Such expansionism has two sources. First, the condensation symbols selected—especially race and language—invariably cut across preexisting state boundaries. The call for national unity, then, inevitably leads to the call for the liberation of fellow nationals who suffer under the yoke of other states and, as such, are incapable of achieving their true raciocultural destiny.

Secondly, because transcendental nationalist movements develop to compensate for a fragmentary and weak condition the leaders of such states usually harbor strong feelings of inferiority which must be resolved by proving the superiority of the newly forged nation through the conquest of other states, especially those viewed as traditional enemies. Victory proves the claim of racial and cultural superiority can indeed be the only proof.

Additionally, the class origins of the leaders of such movements simply reinforce their compensatory will to power. Such movements tend to be dominated by leaders drawn from the petit bourgeois, who exhibit the chronic insecurities and inferiority complex of individuals with such backgrounds. Fascist or transcendental nationalism becomes for this group not only a means of reforming the system and of ensuring their mobility within it, but by transforming the state itself from one of lowly status to one of high, conquering status and by identifying their own personal destiny with the destiny of the state, political triumph becomes personal triumph and mass therapy.

Nazi Germany is the best-known example of the transcendental nationalist state. Peter Viereck has pointed out that glorification of "Kultur"

... became a rationalization of barbarism, an overcompensation for the inferiority complex of feeling less "Romanized" than the Mediterranean world. It became the easy side-step to the challenge of sanity, reason, and logic; in fact, a deliberate revolt not only against reason but against all moral and political restraints, a revolt against humanity, against universals, against internationalism on behalf of Volk and mother culture.[17]

None of the new states of the Third World have the resources either in communication, technology, or weaponry to match the Nazi movement, but here and there are clear signs of incipient fascism held in check only by economic backwardness and the retaliatory potential of neighboring states. The racial mysticism of Léopold Senghor, his confused theory of "Africanity," and his search for the "essence" of the black soul come dangerously close to the basic model of the fascist ideology. The fact that it is now harmlessly expressed in poetry should not console but alarm us, if the parallels with pre-Nazi Germany are to be taken seriously.

The same is true of postrevolutionary Haiti and several of the Latin American states with their perennial border disputes during the nineteenth and early twentieth centuries.

Nativistic nationalist movements develop in societies which already have a unified traditional culture, but have suffered loss of status from contact with invading powers. These movements bear an intrinsic relationship with revivalist ethnic movements. Brian Wilson maintains that such movements tend to "sanctify ethnicity," [18] that they "display distinct capacity for mutation," by which he meant that they are capable of being secularized and politicized. However, these mutations involve a departure from the original purpose and nature of such groups. Revivalist movements can generate pantribal ethnic solidarity, but of themselves they cannot become nationalist movements. Thus, while the Peyote cult played a crucial role in generating pan-Indian ethnicity, it never became truly nationalistic. As Wilson puts it:

Although the cult is the principal religious expression of Indian ethnicity, it has not played an active role in promoting this new sense of (Indian) identity, outside the confines of the cultists themselves. It is, indeed, a sanctification of ethnicity, and the ethnic way of salvation, but it is not the public manifestation of Indian ideology. It is a retreat into the ethnic enclave, rather than the promotion of Indian nationalism.[19]

Even when a revivalist ethnic group gets caught up with a nationalist movement it tends to remain distinct from it, sometimes providing its driving force, but always set apart and never identical with the nationalist objective. This is dramatically illustrated by the (Belgian) Congolese case where the Kimbangu movement and its messiah were used to invest the nationalist movement with legitimacy, but were not identified with it. Such movements either fade away with independence or become purely religious.

Nativistic nationalism, then, involves the routinization and secularization of, and separation from, the purely ethnic and religious base of a revivalist ethnic movement by politically

oriented leaders who use the ethnic base both as a driving force
and as a means of supernatural legitimation of their push for
independence and state building. Unlike transcendental nationalist movements such movements are not inherently expansionist.
They may or may not be, depending on their technological and
military capabilities. If they become imperialistic, the impulse is
either largely imitation, as with Italy, or for direct military and
economic gain, as was true of Japan and, to a much lesser extent,
Italy. If anything, such movements tend to be extremely insular,
even when pursuing a policy of imperial expansion, as Japan
clearly indicates. The leadership of nativistic nationalist movements, especially in the old states, tends to come from the upper
classes, incorporating a number of old aristocratic elements whose
status has been threatened by modernizing middle-class members
of their societies. Such leaders are not necessarily antimodernist.
They tend to oppose rather the control of the modernization
movement by newly emerged middle-class elements, the democratization of the political process, and the declining reverence for
certain of the traditional dominant symbols. It is because they
share with the peasantry the same reverence for the traditional
dominant symbols and the same fear of their demise that upper-
class leaders are able to join ranks with the conservative rural
lower classes in promoting the nativistic nationalist movement.

Spain, Italy, and Japan are the best examples of nativistic
nationalist movements in old societies; Zaire, Cambodia, and Iran
in the so-called Third World countries.

Even where the nation-state appeared to have been a viable
political entity in sociological and political terms I am still
opposed to it. I believe it to be a conception of statehood that is
inherently weak, contradictory, and dangerous.

The political theorist J. D. Mabbott defines the state as "an
association distinguished by (a) territorial limits, (b) inclusiveness
within these limits, (c) the power in its officers to exercise force
and the fear of force as instruments of policy, and (d) the
possession by its officers of ultimate legal authority." [20] With this

definition he then enquires into the ends of state action. He rejects completely the romantic and nationalist view that the state should achieve the end of stimulating the feeling of cooperation, sympathy, and solidarity among its citizens on the grounds that states usually achieve these objectives only in times of war, which is clearly too high a price to pay for them, especially when they can be more cheaply and safely achieved by other groups, such as the family, or by freely created communities which come together to satisfy their own special needs.

Mabbott rejects the nation-state in terms which are persuasive but stop short of sociological and purely logical conclusiveness. The nation-state, he argues, presents two problems: that of fellow nationals who are citizens of other states and that of citizens within the state who do not belong to the dominant national group—racial and ethnic minorities. Furthermore, the nation-state presents a threat to international peace in that "it is difficult to unify a people on behalf of a nationality, a religion or an economic creed without claiming intrinsic superiority for your nation or religion or creed." [21] Mabbott's inclusion of "economic creeds" is an unfortunate reflection of his anti-Marxist bias. Such "economic creeds" can be attacked, but they should not be confused with nationalist creeds. It is precisely this identification of Marxist ideology with nationalist ideology which undermines much of the work of Hannah Arendt and other right-wing critics of fascist totalitarianism. In Mabbott's case, however, it is a mere slip, as his own later elaboration of the purposes of state action indicates.

Mabbott's arguments are generally well taken, though as a critique of the nation-state they lack binding force. They are highly probable consequences of nationalism, but, as he states them, not necessary ones. Mabott's brief but penetrating work makes a brilliant case for the view, which I share fully, that the state can never be an end in itself, but must be a means to other ends. Moral action, he argues, can never be "identical with service of the state" because : (1) there are many actions which are intrinsically good, quite independent of their consequences, including their value to the state, (2) there are many actions which are aimed at intrinsically good ends which, however, can have nothing to do with the state since they are nonsocial, for example, the pursuit of beauty and truth, (3) there are many associations other than the state which can achieve good ends, and (4) even where the state is the best means of attaining certain good ends, these ends remain "intrinsically non-political." [22]

What then are the proper ends of the state? They are, Mabbott argues, provision of security, the policing of social conduct, the settlement of dispute, and the provision of conditions which will ensure adequate infrastructural services and an economic system that minimizes inequality and maximizes industrial income and employment opportunities. This definition of state ends is ideologically neutral; it makes no claims for or against either a capitalist or socialist political economy. One may choose to argue over which of these approaches is more efficient and least unfair in attaining the stated ends, but what is important here is that this definition of the nature of the state and the ends of state action in no way implies a nation-state and, indeed, strongly suggests that the nation-state both violates the idea of the state, as defined, and is the least efficient way of attaining the ends outlined.

What Mabbott merely implies and deals with in only a cursory way I want to develop into a direct critique of the nation-state. I have three criticisms of the nation-state which, I hope, will be sufficient to show that all such systems are webs of internal contradictions. The first may be called the anthropological critique. All cultures are, if not wholly, at least in good part, symbolic systems. Some of these symbols are dominant and it is these symbols which are mainly exploited in the political process. Firth, following C. Wright Mills and others, has pointed out that the dominant symbols are "instruments of control, or more bluntly, instruments of power." [23] Not only are they used as sources of legitimacy, but they can and are manipulated by persons in authority who wish to gain support for their policies or to transform the "subjective experience" of others.

The problem with symbols, however, is that they are an essentially irrational way of communicating and influencing other people. As a vehicle of expression the symbol "carries a load of meanings," to use Turner's term, meanings which are not often understood but felt. The main properties of symbols, as Turner sees them are "multivocality, complexity of association, ambiguity, open-endedness, primacy of feeling and willing over thinking in their semantics, their propensity to ramify into further semantic subsystems . . ." [24]

Dominant cultural symbols lend themselves not to a rational resolution of conflicts (which is the only sane way of ever resolving the conflicts of a complex modern state) but to the manipulation of the irrational by contending parties who compete with each other both in their interpretation of the true meaning of the symbols and for control over the powerful symbolic instruments. The fact that the same symbols can be used by different parties is in no way indicative of any unifying quality in such symbols, for the very "multivocality" and "primacy of feeling and willing over thinking" inherent in such symbols give all struggles deriving their psychic energies and rationale from them a certain life-or-death, all-or-nothing quality that is in the end destructive of all unity and compromise. Examples of such symbols are the Germanic conception of the Volk, the Gallic view of the general will, and the coronation ceremony in monarchial states.

My second criticism of the nation-state may be called the temporal argument, although it builds on the first criticism. It centers on the well-established sociohistorical fact that while both the cultural symbols and the social system of a social order change over time, they change at different rates and sometimes in different directions. Usually, there is a lag between the change in the cultural symbols and the social system. This lag is likely to be particularly great in rapidly modernizing societies, which is true of most if not all of the new states of the Third World. Where a culture at a particular moment in time (say the start of a nationalist movement) is taken as a charter both for legitimizing state authority and for defining the ultimate ends of state action, it will inevitably come about that the charter loses its relevance and meaning for the social reality to which it refers. It is true that dominant cultural symbols have what Turner calls an "orectic" pole, which, because they refer to "bodily experiences," possess a timeless quality, but this pole is not the one exploited in the political process; rather it is the other, "ideological" or "normative" pole which is so exploited, and it is precisely this pole which is most subject to cultural lag.[25]

Such lags can and often do generate tremendous social tension if there is a too close identification of the political order with the normative order of a given period. In terms of Parsonian systems analysis, the lag presents an irresolvable integrative failure. In the more realistic terms of the sociology of George Homans, which doggedly "brings men back" into all analyses, the lag will be reflected in a tension between those committed to the preservation of the old political order and the charter symbols that legitimized it, and those committed to the new order and the need to generate a new set of dominant symbols.

This last need is, however, a separate problem, for it is clearly an impossible situation where those most committed to the realities of change are obliged every two generations or so to redefine the cultural charter of their polity. Here the temporal critique joins with the anthropological critique. For not only will there be an irresolvable crisis generated by the conflict between the supporters of the old cultural charter and the new but there will be an equally intense crisis created by competition among the supporters of the new order over the right to define, control, and manipulate the new set of dominant symbols.

The obvious implication of the above two criticisms is that cultural symbols, especially dominant ones, should not be used to forge or legitimize state unity or to define the ends of state action. One is tempted to argue that the best kind of charter is no charter at all. This, as Bagehot tells us, is the "hidden secret" of the British constitution, the fact that it remains unwritten. Such an Anglicism, however, should be stoutly resisted. For whereas the British had the luxury of several hundred years to develop their unwritten conception of the state and its objectives, the major problem of all new states since the founding of the United States, the first new state (not "nation," as Lipset calls it), has been the shortage of time in which to construct the new polity and to define its aims. A written charter is clearly called for by all new states. The trouble with the constitutions of most of the new states is that they say both too much and too little. Too much, on the one hand, in the preliminary nonsense about cultural identity and national destiny, too much in the proclamation of time-specific and often irreconcilable ideals, and too little in the specification of rational means of conflict resolution. It is no wonder that almost all of them have been discarded. Sooner or later, however, civility and political good sense must prevail and, it is to be hoped, at such a time, the temporal and nonsymbolic nature of such charters will be recognized.

Only a small minority of the citizens of most new states now are literate. Written charters are therefore presently inaccessible to the mass of the population as points of subjectively meaningful political references. As a temporary expedient, I would provide not dominant symbols but signs as aids to communication in the political process. These signs are what were referred to earlier, following Sapir, as referential symbols. They are the only nonverbal means of communications permitted in a polity which takes the dangers of nationalism and the nation-state seriously. Signs are acceptable as a temporary device because, as Turner points out, "signs, besides tending to univocality, connect signifiers to signified by arbitrary, discretionary, conventional links. These are not the result of caprice but of rational thought . . ." 26 Turner, in a personal communication, drew my attention to a remarkable example of the rational use of signification by the Tanzanian government, one of the few governments of the new states which, it will be recalled, eschewed the nation-state as a model of state building. Party members adopted two signs in their electioneering: the sign of the Hoe and the sign of the House. Both these signs had direct, immediate meaning to the electors. There was no multivocality, no ambiguity or mysticism concerning what they

stood for. And when the Hoes won, the electors were clear and
articulate, even in the most illiterate regions, about their reasons
for electing their candidates. They voted for such candidates
because they stood for agricultural development, for economic
strength and for respect for the land. Absent from their responses
were all the irrational and inexpressible feelings bordering on the
mystical which characterize the responses of voters in other states
where dominant cultural symbols are exploited.[27]

Having said all this, it must still be emphasized that signs and
the technique of signification can be defended only as a temporary expedient in a semi-literate society. There is no room for
signification in a literate state. For even signs can be corrupted,
transformed into condensation symbols, and can acquire multivocality. Often too, their absence, or what they fail to say, can be
as important and potentially destructive as their presence or what
they do say. Thus the Statue of Liberty is, or once was, a powerful
sign. Originally it stood for, and to some extent still does, freedom
from political and economic constraints. Its fortuitous erection at
a time when America was receiving vast numbers of immigrants
from Europe brought it immediate identification with the
"Mother of exiles" among this segment of the American population. From the very beginning, there was a basic difference in the
meaning attributed to the statue by its American recipients and its
French donors. To the Americans it was a simple, noble sign of
liberty. To the French, with their romantic and nationalistic
traditions, it was not a sign but an extremely multivocal and
mystical condensation symbol. As Harold Rosenberg in his review
of Marvin Trachtenberg's book, *The Statue of Liberty,* points out:

Primarily, "Liberty Enlightening the World," as the sculpture was
originally entitled, was a piece of propaganda art designed to strengthen
Republicanism in France after the fall of the Second Empire and the
demolition of the Paris Commune. The light of liberty (the Statue was
conceived also as a lighthouse) was intended to direct its ray across the
ocean to sustain the cause of political freedom. In the imagination of
Bartholdi and his patrons, the "figure loomed so large and bright it could

be seen across the Atlantic"—apparently one of the less objectionable
ways of meddling in the internal affairs of a friendly nation.[28]

And in the same way that this originally simple sign had
different meanings to different people at the time of its erection,
so it has had different meanings to different generations of
Americans. It has been transformed over the years from a sign to
a condensation symbol. It has been corrupted in its role as
condensation symbol, becoming "an object of commercial and
political exploitation, a version of Miss America, and even of
derision." Now that it is a condensation symbol all the intense
passions surrounding such symbols have come into play. It was
with little surprise, then, that we learned from the F.B.I. a few
years ago that a group of young revolutionaries had been
apprehended on a Guy Faulkes mission to blow it up.

My third and final critique of the nation-state is sociological.
The state based on ethnic solidarity is internally inconsistent
because it accepts the principle of ethnicity not only as a desirable
form of social action but as the source of political power. But in so
doing it makes acceptable morally, and encourages sociologically,
not only the perpetuation of already existing nondominant ethnic
groups but the development of new ethnic groups among parties
whose (originally) purely political interests are not being served
by the state. A state that bases its existence on ethnic solidarity
encourages its citizens to express their political grievances in
ethnic terms, since, obviously, they have learned from the officers
of the state that political action is meaningless if it is not an
expression of ethnic interests.

Since no state can fully satisfy all interests, all states, including
nation-states, will have groups with grievances. Kenneth Arrow
has cogently argued in his *Limits of Organization,* that "the
incommensurability and incomplete communicability of human
wants and values" are such that no state can ever satisfy all the
needs of its citizens. The nation-state will always create fissiparous
forces through the subnational groups it generates by its own
example.

In response to such ethnic factionalism, the nation-state can do only one of two things. It can resort to brutal force in attempting to destroy the revitalized subnational ethnic group as in Spain with respect to the Basques or Israel with respect to its Arab minorities or it can allow them to exist and flourish as in the majority of new African and Asian states. But both alternatives are politically suicidal for the nation-state. If it resorts to force it morally concedes the nonexistence of its claimed ethnic unity, strengthens the solidarity of the subnational ethnic groups (which like all such groups thrive on opposition), and in the end weakens the body politic. If it allows the subnational ethnic groups to flourish, it eventually disintegrates into a gross and unworkable collection of competing ethnic factions.

The nation-state is a totally flawed model of statehood. The historical evidence on these states fully support this contention. Both the old and the new nation-states have exhibited a dismal incapacity to govern themselves except by means of the most brutal form of totalitarianism, the occasional breather of democratic France notwithstanding.

CHAPTER 4

The Nature and Classification of Ethnic Groups

My classification of ethnic groups is in no way evolutionary. No attempt was made to suggest any single path of development from the original ethnic group to all the different types isolated. I readily concede the possibility that other students of the subject may propose other kinds of classifications based on other sets of criteria. At the same time, in rejecting the evolutionary approach, I have not eschewed the exploration of historical and structural connections between the different types of groups discussed. The relationships, however, are complex, multilinear, and not necessarily unidirectional.

While I concede the possibility of other classifications, I believe the one I offer to be superior to most of those suggested in the literature so far, because it is based on the structural and dynamic aspects of ethnicity rather than on the symbolic content or cultural attributes of such groups. Ethnicity can only be understood in terms of a dynamic and contextural view of group allegiances. What is critical about an ethnic group is not the particular set of symbolic objects which distinguishes it but the social uses of these objects: Ethnic loyalties reflect, and are maintained by, the underlying socioeconomic interests of group members. A failure to recognize these facts explains why the use of this term in the sociological literature is unsatisfactory, indeed, often confused.

The term may be defined in two ways: one static and descriptive, the other dynamic and analytic. Most definitions of the term have been descriptive and static in an attempt to isolate a set of characteristics or traits by which the term may be delineated. Herein lies much of the confusion. Such definitions emphasize culture and tradition as the critical elements, and in so doing are so descriptive that they become analytically useless and often so inclusive that they are not even worthwhile as heuristic devices. Cultural attributes are of no intrinsic interest from a dynamic structural perspective. What is important about American Jews is not that they worship on Saturdays, or have certain unique rituals or patterns of socialization, but the functions of these rituals for the group—the ways in which they are used to maintain group cohesiveness, sustain and enhance identity, and establish social networks and communicative patterns that are important for the group's optimization of its socioeconomic position in the society. A theory of ethnic cultural elements and symbols is an absurdity, because these symbols are purely arbitrary and unique to each case.

Further, it is extremely important to understand that the context of an ethnic experience is critical to defining it. Once we understand this, we can begin to clear up a persistent error in the descriptive literature, the view that what is most critical about ethnic identity is the fact that it is involuntary and cannot be changed. This fallacy has an ancient heritage: The biblical refrain "Can the Ethiopian change his skin or the leopard his spots?" is one of its earliest recorded versions. Individuals are said to be born into such groups with no choice in the matter—one does not choose to be Jewish or Black or Chinese; the condition is chosen for one by fate.

If one emphasizes—as one should, to be analytic—not the symbolic and cultural objects but the structural significance of these objects, the irrelevance of such assertions is apparent. From a structural and contextual viewpoint, there is an important sense in which the significance of a given ethnic attribute can change and, as such, an individual can be said to have some choice in the matter, since the sociological and psychological significance of a trait can be selected. This is done simply by changing one's social context or seizing the opportunity offered by such a change over time.

Take the case of a black Jamaican who is a citizen of Jamaica and a permanent resident of the United States. He lives and works for eight months in the United States and four months in Jamaca. He travels between both countries twice a year. In Jamaica, which is 95 percent black, he belongs to the demographically dominant majority and is a member of the elite. In the United States he is a member of an ethnic group—the Blacks, although he holds a position of some status in that society. In one social context—Jamaica—the individual is not a member of any ethnic group; on the contrary, he is an elite member of the dominant group and his primary allegiance is to the state. In the other context, he is consciously a member of an ethnic group. He regards himself as a member of this group and he is so regarded by nonmembers of this group in America. Thus, while he does not change the color of his skin, there is a real and meaningful sense in which he changes his ethnic identity four times each year by changing his social context.

The many Puerto Ricans who migrate back and forth between Puerto Rico and New York are other similar cases. In Puerto Rico a black person might belong to the black ethnic group, in New York to the Puerto Rican ethnic group. Some highly Americanized black Puerto Ricans consciously manipulate different ethnic identities to serve their own best interests. In certain contexts (for example, running for local office or applying for a job in which affirmative action has created a black bias) he will emphasize his blackness. In other contexts (for example, personal relations with whites) he may mute the impact of his dark skin by emphasizing his Latin background, especially his Spanish accent. Or take the case of Sephardic Jews of Jamaica who travel to England or the United States. In the new social setting, some choose to maintain their Jewish allegiance, identifying with the Jews of the new host society; others choose to identify with the

Jamaican ethnic group; and still others abandon ethnicity, marry Gentile women, and blend into the host society. Similar range of choices are made by members of the Sephardic Jewish community from Curaçao living in Holland. Changes in the context of ethnic identification can take place by movement from one society to another in a particular period or over a course of time within a single society.

Ethnicity is, formally, that condition wherein some of all the members of a society, in a given social context, consciously choose to emphasize as their most meaningful basis of primary, extra-familial identity certain assumed or real cultural or somatic traits.

The groups formed in this way vary, of course, in size, duration, intensity of involvement, variety and number of shared traits, and in complexity of structure. Clearly there are numerous ways of classifying such groups, using these criteria, but such exercises are theoretically pointless. It is best to concentrate on the analytic qualities such groups have in common: namely, the fact that they are the structural expressions of primary, extrafamilial identity.

They resemble the family in the intensity of involvement of members and in the tendency to equate and rationalize relation-ships with other members in consanguineal terms—"kith and kin" is a term often used to describe members of one's ethnic group. But they are certainly not kinship groups, in spite of the ideological fiction among members to the contrary; nor are such groups necessarily endogamous.

An ethnic group exists only where members consider them-selves to belong to it; a conscious sense of belonging is critical. It implies that where all other criteria are met except this sense of belonging, the ethnic condition is not met—even where other members of the society may regard a group of individuals as an ethnic group. It also implies that where, in objective sociological terms, the assumed bases of group allegiance do not exist the salient condition of ethnicity is met when members subjectively assume the existence of such "mythical" bases.

This is why an ethnic group is not a cultural group. A cultural group is simply any group of people who share an identifiable complex of meanings, symbols, values, and norms. Such a group differs from an ethnic group in the following respects: First, there need not be any conscious awareness of belonging to a group on the part of the members of cultural groups, and usually no such conscious group identity exists. Second, a cultural group is an objectively verifiable social phenomenon. The meaning, symbols, values, and norms—in short, the tradition which they share—can be anthropologically observed, regardless of the ideological statements or expressed opinions of members about their tradition or their relationship with it. Third, a cultural group, or segments of it, may become an ethnic group, but only when the conditions of ethnicity are met. The fact that a segment of a cultural group becomes an ethnic group does not mean that all members of the cultural group thereby do.

Nor is an ethnic group a class, although closely related to it. We define class as an economic group determined by the relation of its members to the mode of production of a society. The term can be used in two senses, a distinction which goes back to Marx: in the abstract sense, as an arbitrary abstraction from reality based on certain objective criteria established by the analyst; and in the concrete sense, as an objectively real group existing independently of any arbitrarily defined instrumental criteria of definition. I tend to agree with Ralf Dahrendorf that it is possible to live with both these conceptions of class, using one or the other as one's intellectual needs demand.[1] I shall assume that classes are concrete, objectively observable groups and that they act in their own best interests, even if not consciously. Classes are, as I define them, economic groups determined by the productive forces of the society which, consciously or unconsciously, behave in such a way as to optimize their economic interest and position in the society.

Ethnic groups, for structural reasons, are either identified with the state, or cut across state boundaries, or are subgroups within it. Because the political context of ethnic groups is one of the most important factors bearing on the nature of such groups, we have chosen it as one of the basic criteria in our final classification. Finding a suitable adjective to describe the three kinds of

relationships between ethnic group and state, however, presents
something of a linguistic problem, since the most obvious term,
"national," is clearly inappropriate in view of the special meaning
we have given it. We will use the term "sovereignal" to describe
the three kinds of relationships between ethnic groups and states.
Our six kinds of ethnic groups will, at the widest level, be
subclassified as sovereignal, transsovereignal and subsovereignal
corresponding to groups which are identified with, cut across, or
exist within the boundaries of the state. The following table will
simplify matters.

TRANSSOVEREIGNAL	SOVEREIGNAL	SUBSOVEREIGNAL
1. *Colonial*	3. *Pristine*	5. *Adaptive*
Greeks in Hellenistic world.	Athens sixth century B.C.	Phrygians, Egyptians, in Imperial Rome.
Romans in provinces.	Ancient Palestine.	West Indians in U.K.
Europeans in Africa, Asia, Caribbean, etc.	Early Republican Rome.	Poles, Irish, Italians, etc., in U.S. up to 1930.
	Pre-Islamic Arabian states.	
	Ashanti, eighteenth century.	
2. *Symbiotic*	4. *National*	6. *Revivalist*
Diaspora Jews.	France.	Peyote Indian movement.
Diaspora Phoenicians.	Germany.	Celtic Nationalists.
Greeks, Syrians in Roman provinces.	Israel.	Iranian anti-Islam movements in medieval Iraq.
Chinese & Indians in Africa, Caribbean, S. E. Asia, etc.	Italy.	White ethnics in U.S. post 1965.
	Japan.	
	Iran.	
	Ireland.	

The two subtypes of the sovereignal ethnic group are the pristine state and the nation-state. The *kin-hegemonic pristine states* sometimes diverged quickly from the ethnic group. They were to generate other types of ethnicity and while, in some cases, ethnicity was to remain an important principle of political and social organization, it ceased to be a sufficient principle. Thus ethnicity always remained a necessary condition of Greek citizenship, but by Pericles' day the ethnic principle had spread beyond the boundaries of the Greek state and as a result ceased to be a sufficient condition. Pan-Hellenic ethnicity postdated the emergence of the Greek state.[2] The ancient Greeks, of course, thought just the opposite: They believed that their sense of identity as a people existed first and that only afterward did the separate state identities emerge. This inverted and erroneous conception of their history was reinforced by their intellectuals and poets. The significance of Homer for the Greeks lay mainly in this fact: He was the first ethnic ideologist who propounded the myth of a preexisting Greek identity. Such reinterpretation of history to conform with present ethnic reality is typical of all ethnic groups. The objective truth of Greek historical reality is that they were, before the emergence of the Greek pristine states, simply a cultural group with only a general awareness of linguistic similarity and cultural correspondences and little knowledge of the different waves of migrations by which they settled in the Mediterranean. It was the pristine state, the ethnicity it generated, and the civilization it made possible that together created Hellenic ethnicity.

The *nation-state* differs from the kin-hegemonic pristine state during its generative phase of identity with the ethnic group in several important respects. Most important is the fact that the nation-state is in principle permanently based on the ethnic group. The ethnic group is the entire culture group. To belong to such a group consciously is to belong to the state based on this group.

The nation-state differs from the pristine state also in that ethnicity almost always precedes the formation of such a state or,

at the very least, helps to define it in its final form. This is why
Poland, in the view of Lord Acton, was so unique in the history of
Europe. For it was Polish ethnicity that led the Poles to the view
that they should choose their own kings. And it was this utterly
alien view, in European terms, that so outraged the crowned
heads of Europe that they felt no compunction in carving Poland
up. Lord Acton declared:

Thenceforward there was a nation demanding to be united in a state,—a
soul, as it were, wandering in search of a body in which to begin life over
again; and for the first time a cry was heard that the arrangement of
states was unjust—that their limits were unnatural, and that a whole
people was deprived of its right to constitute an independent country.[3]

Adaptive ethnic groups, one of the two subtypes of subsovereignal ethnicity, are by their very nature temporary and exist partly
to buffer the shock of entry and adjustment to the new society,
partly to facilitate assimilation into the host society. The assimilation of the immigrant (and all modern ethnic ideologists must
heed this point) is never, however, a one-way process. The same
conditions that allow for assimilation also ensure, indeed demand,
that the immigrant influences the host as much as the host
influences the immigrant. This is true even when the immigrant is
a slave. It is to fly in the face of historical reality to deny the two-
way direction of such influences or to claim that there can ever be
such a thing as an "unmeltable" ethnic group.

Where objective reality departs from the ethnohistorical perception of reality one version of the *revivalist ethnic group*
emerges. Such ethnic groups are, on the intellectual level, a
desperate attempt to deny the reality of assimilation, to distort its
meaning with tendentious talk about cultural oppression, and to
reinvest the fragments of the past with a life it can barely sustain.
But this is merely the rationalization of a more sinister development. For, in fact, this version of the revivalist ethnic group, while
some may sincerely believe in it, is merely a disguise for the
conservatism of the economically insecure and the politically

opportunistic. It develops when groups, especially petit bourgeois groups which have achieved a tenuous hold on the lower steps of the good life, feel threatened by those beneath them who are clamoring for a place on the ladder. Politically, it provides a base for charlatans who, lacking all sense of human decency or commitment to the common good, would place their own personal advancement by means of the monopoly of their own little ethnic turf above the harmony of their society. And, psychologically, such ethnic revivals are pathetic attempts to enhance a doubted sense of dignity and honor at the expense of others less fortunate and more vulnerable. It was to this kind of ethnic group that Max Weber referred (though his remarks were aimed at all ethnic groups) when he wrote that: "The sense of ethnic honor is a specific honor of the masses for it is accessible to anyone who belongs to the subjectively believed community of descent—the social honor of the 'poor whites' was dependent upon the déclassement of the Negroes." 4

The second version of the revivalist ethnic group—that which involves the revival of status rather than potency—takes less liberties with reality, but is no less misguided. Such groups easily become the preys of romantic reactionaries who wish to revive the declassed culture; not to improve the condition of the materially exploited, as the mass of supporters hope but to restore the social order associated with the old culture, a social order which is invariably feudal or oppressive. This, as we have seen, was the tragedy of those ethnic groups which revolted against Islam during the Middle Ages, and the pattern is repeated today in the Celtic revival in Scotland.

The *colonial ethnic elite* group has played a crucial role in the history of ancient and modern imperial expansion. Such groups tend to withdraw with the empires that sustained them. But not always. For it sometimes happens that in adapting to the native people in order to exploit them more effectively, a colonial ethnic group will develop a peculiar ethnic culture which is neither native to the conquered group nor to its parent culture. When this happens, the colonial ethnic group faces a serious crisis at the end of empire. For home, or what they thought was home, turns out to be an alien place. And the emerging nationalist elite of the natives finds such a group an alien nuisance. This was the crisis faced by the whites of Kenya, South Africa, Algeria, and the West Indies during the decolonization period. It can sometimes result in desperate action, as in Rhodesia. South African white ethnic groups have been one of the few to maintain their control after the withdrawal of the imperial power. How long their success lasts will depend on the limits of their brutality, the cynicism of the world powers, and the patience of the Blacks. The French in Algeria tried the same thing and failed, but on their behalf it can at least be said that they did produce Camus.

Symbiotic ethnic groups survive because they perform vital functions for their host societies, either because the host is unwilling or incapable of performing them or does not have a sufficient number of persons to perform the required roles. The transsovereignal nature of such groups also gives them special adaptive advantages, especially in states which lack a well-developed international network. The symbiotic ethnic group, however, may be of economic value in a general way. Its members may perform the whole range of occupations in the society but do so at a level of competence well above the norm for the members of the host society. No special set of cultural factors accounts for such superior competence, although there may be some uniformity from one such ethnic group to another in the kinds of interpersonal and intellectual skills which specific elements of their cultural patterns emphasize. Thus Jewish and Japanese Americans have entirely different cultural patterns, so it is clearly foolish to account for their relative successes in American society in terms of the specificities of their cultures. Rather, such ethnic groups have a *common emphasis* on certain psychological patterns which induce high motivation and achievement. And such common emphases tend to emerge *only in certain contexts.* It is truly amazing how many people are incapable of seeing this simple point, preferring to emphasize the cultural contents of successful ethnic groups rather than their social context and special psychological conditioning within that context in explaining their success. One may "prove" the foolishness of all cultural explanations of the superior competence of symbiotic ethnic groups in a simple *ad hominem* way. If the Indians of East Africa and the Chinese of Southeast Asia owe their superior commercial and industrial competence to the cultures which they brought with them to the new setting, then their own parent societies made up of millions of people sharing nothing but this presumably superior capitalism and competence-inducing culture must be among the most advanced commercial and industrial civilizations in the world. Yet one is the poorest country in the world and the other is the most vehemently anticapitalistic. The cultural explanation of successful ethnic groups is by contradiction, an absurdity.

Some maintain that cultural distinctiveness explains the social separateness of an ethnic group. The opposite, is, in fact, the case. Groups maintain their separate cultural distinctiveness, where they choose to do so, because of their assessment of the advantages of social separation. The group does not exist because the culture exists, rather the culture continues to exist because the group finds it in its best interest to preserve it. When cultural patterns cease to be relevant, the history of ethnic groups suggests that they are ruthlessly discarded, although there will always be some cultural lag between the most innovative members of the ethnic group and the most conservative. Furthermore, discarding the irrelevant cultural baggage does not mean that the sense of ethnic identity will be discarded. An ethnic group is quite capable of existing without any distinctive ethnic culture. Nonreligious American Jews—the vast majority—constitute a classic example of such a group.

But it is also true that the sense of ethnic identity itself, like the culture that may once have sustained it, is dependent on the group's perception of its relevance. There is nothing primordial about either the cultural basis of an ethnic identity or the choice of ethnic identity. Thus the Welsh, when they migrated to the United States, did not find their culture or a sense of ethnic identity on any terms to be in their own best interest in the new context. They therefore promptly abandoned both. If we compare the Welsh with their Celtic cousins, the Irish, in their parent cultures, we find that of the two the Welsh had a more distinctive culture, for they did not suffer to the same degree the brutal dislocation of their traditional way of life as the Irish did under the impact of English colonization. Indeed, it is only among the Northern Welsh that a living Celtic language thrives. Irish is an artificially re-created and official language. In other areas, the manners and customs of the Welsh, in Wales, are as distinctive as those of the Irish. And it would be a poor and hopelessly biased student of religion who would fail to see that Welsh, chapel-based Calvinism is as distinct from English high church Anglicanism as is Irish Catholicism.

And yet, in the history and social structure of the Welsh and Irish in the United States we find little or no trace of Welsh ethnicity but a good deal of Irish ethnic allegiance. Those proethnic intellectuals who attempt to explain Irish ethnicity in terms of the "transmission" of a distinct and primordial Irish culture must first explain why their Celtic neighbors, the Welsh, with an equally pronounced and more vital aboriginal culture and a not entirely dissimilar experience of Anglo-Saxon domination did not converge in ethnic ghettos.

CHAPTER 5

Context and Choice
in Ethnic Allegiance:
the Chinese in the Caribbean

I have made several bold assertions. The position I hold and will attempt to substantiate may even strike some as outrageous, if not perverse. This is understandable, especially from those who are strong supporters of a particular ethnic group and, as such, of the principle of ethnicity in general. From the viewpoint of the insider, to belong to an ethnic group is to believe sincerely that one belongs for deep personal reasons which transcend socioeconomic interests. It is not possible to belong and at the same time recognize how one overtly exploits one's belonging. To recognize this is to commit heresy. Heresy is not what other people think, as someone once observed, nor is it even a category of forbidden thought; it is not a category of thought at all. Heresy is the willing suspension of belief, it is the error of looking into the area of protective ignorance that surrounds and seals every conscious group. This, incidentally, is the main reason why the members of strongly defined ethnic groups often resent being studied or even questioned about their ethnicity, especially by outsiders, and this includes ethnic groups whose members have not exhibited any marked reluctance to study other such groups.

But as Max Weber pointed out years ago the ways in which individuals rationalize their behavior, while a vital clue to an understanding of their actions, is not to be confused with the rational choices they make in enhancing their own interests. Such a confusion amounts to sociological navieté, of which there is a great deal in modern ethnic studies. And yet, it is possible to go too far in the Weberian direction. The sociologist holds no special Godlike detachment in his examination of human groups. Detachment is a relative business and taken too far it easily descends into cynicism or mindless sociologism. Human beings, in the final analysis, are rational animals. The ways in which they rationalize their actions have as much right to be taken seriously as the ways in which the sociologist thinks about their actions. This is true even among primitive peoples, as Lévi-Strauss has shown us. It is likely to be at least as true, and indeed very much more so, among civilized groups whose rationalizers are men and women with powerful intellects. I take these rationalizations seriously.

Before we get to the intellectual roots of ethnicity, we must add depth to our sociohistorical analysis. A case study of the Chinese in the Caribbean will allow us to do so. If the traditional view of ethnicity is correct, we should expect that groups, once they become conscious of their ethnic identity, will struggle to preserve these so-called primordial ties at all costs. We will not expect to find them using these almost sacred ties to promote something as base as their material self-interests. Rather, we will expect them to put the interests of their group and their ethnic loyalties above such interests.

I have chosen two symbiotic ethnic groups because it is to this kind of ethnic group that most people point when making the case for the primacy of ethnic interests. I have, further, adopted the technique of selecting an example which stacks the argument against my own. That is, in selecting the Chinese to prove my argument, I have selected a group which my opponents agree is among the most culturally bound, intensely ethnic, and exclusive in the world. In choosing two Chinese communities in the Caribbean I have selected what Robert Merton called the "limiting case." Using such a case compensates considerably, though not wholly, for substantive exhaustiveness or statistical

CONTEXT AND CHOICE IN ETHNIC ALLEGIANCE

sampling, for it will generally be agreed that if my argument holds on the limits, as it were, it should hold for all "easier," less limiting cases, presenting fewer challenges to my argument.

In precise and more formal terms these are the principles of social action which underlie my thinking. I propose to argue that three basic principles determine the relative choice of allegiances, including ethnic allegiances: the principle of reconciliation (or least conflict) of interest, the principle of optimization of interest, and the principle of the primacy of class interest.

The first principle proposes that individuals with several allegiances will, whenever possible, seek to reconcile the varying interests implied in their separate allegiances. Thus an individual will, ideally, want his class, cultural, ethnic, and status interests to harmonize with each other and, wherever possible (although the principle of reconciliation does not require it), to complement each other. I am not arguing that individuals seek to equalize or identify their varying interests or even that they actively seek to have one complement the other. The East Boston Italian construction worker thinks in class terms on his job and in trade negotiations, and he thinks in ethnic terms in community affairs. He does not expect trade union negotiations on his behalf to have any necessary direct impact on his community, but he does expect that his class activity will not actively conflict with his community activity. This is why the principle of reconciliation is perhaps best described as the principle of least conflict.

The principle of optimization posits that in all those instances where interests cannot be reconciled—that is, where inevitable conflict of interest is implied in the individual's varying allegiances—there will be a tendency to choose that set of allegiances which maximizes material and social gains in the society at large and minimizes survival risks. This may be a roundabout way of saying that individuals tend to act in their own best interests. We state it as a basic principle because, while it may appear obvious to some, it is by no means obvious to all sociologists, and it seems least obvious to precisely that group of social scientists who work in the area of ethnicity. A truism becomes worthy of the status of a principle, or law of action, when it ceases to be or is no longer regarded as a truism.

Students of ethnicity tend to emphasize the nonrational implications of ethnic behavior as one of its critical attributes. Harold Isaacs, for example, thinks that the quintessence of ethnicity is the primordiality and near primeval intensity of involvement with and allegiance to one's ethnic group.[1] As such, it becomes highly possible that where there is a clash between ethnic and other interests, the individual will act against his other interests in favor of the integrity of his ethnic allegiance. It is one of my major contentions that such a view is false; I do not think that primordiality and intensity of involvement are distinguishing features of ethnicity. This is not to say that such involvement does not sometimes characterize ethnic allegiance; it often does. But it is not peculiar to ethnic allegiance and is not required by it.

Individuals will be most intensely involved with those allegiances that are in their own best social and economic interests. Where ethnic allegiance is in individuals' own best interests, intense feelings will be attached to it. This is true, for example, of a persecuted ethnic group faced with a genocidal or otherwise hostile majority, or a group which so perceives its position. It is also true of those individuals whose survival and best interests are threatened on a class or religious basis. In such cases people are quite prepared to abandon their ethnic allegiance in favor of their class allegiance, and attach to the latter the same kind of "primordial" intensity which is exclusively associated in the vulgar sociological imagination with ethnic allegiance.

This brings us to our third principle. Where a plurality of allegiances involves a conflict between class interests and other interests, individuals *in the long run* will choose class allegiance over all other allegiances, including ethnic allegiance. I say "in the long run," because this takes account of those special situations in which individuals face severe survival risks or so perceive their situation, on bases other than class. As I indicated above, individuals whose very existence is threatened by a hostile majority on purely ethnic terms will, in such crisis situations, temporarily suspend all other allegiances in favor of the one in which they are being threatened. Such situations, however, are by their very nature short-term; no group of people can continue to live in a society which constantly threatens their existence. Either the majority group withdraws the threat or the threatened group withdraws from the society, or the dominant group exercises its threat and destroys the group, or, finally, if this is possible, individuals may abolish the basis of their allegiance to the group which offends the hostile majority, solving the problem by destroying the group in order to ensure the survival . of its members.

In the short run, then, we readily concede that survival threats may create situations in which other allegiances may take primacy over class interests, but in the long run—and it is only in the long run that sociological generalizations are viable—there is definitely a tendency for class membership and its implied interests to assert primacy over all other allegiances.

I shall test my hypotheses with the comparative case study of two Chinese communities in the Caribbean: the Chinese of Jamaica and Guyana. I begin with the social context of Caribbean societies in which this minority lives.

The societies of the Caribbean area are Latin and Afro-Caribbean.[2] The Latin area, which will not concern us, is distinguished by the overwhelming presence of the New World version of Iberian culture, by its greater cultural homogeneity, by its larger size, and by differing political experiences and structures. The Afro-Caribbean societies are characterized by the over-whelming presence of people of African descent, by a common colonial experience, by the prolonged historical experience of slavery on a large scale, by their relatively small size, and by their continued economic dependence on the former European colonizing powers.

Jamaica and Guyana, like all Afro-Caribbean societies, have a similar pattern of sociocultural development. An early phase of discovery and European settlement, which lasted from the beginning of the sixteenth century to the latter part of the seventeenth century, saw attempts at establishing white settlement colonies. The attempts were only partly successful. When the Spanish were displaced by the North Europeans, the attempt was repeated for a brief period of about forty years but finally failed, as the North Europeans shifted to large-scale plantation agriculture, concentrating on a single crop—sugar.

This shift in economic base ushered in the second phase of the development of Afro-Caribbean societies. The sugar plantations, which became all-important by the turn of the eighteenth century, made the Afro-Caribbean societies among the richest areas of the world,[3] and set the basic social structure and tone of these societies. African slaves were brought in on a large scale, resulting in the early demographic dominance of black people. Ruling them was a small minority of white planters, many of whom were later in the century to become absentee landlords, their estates being managed by attorneys and overseers with little commitment to the societies they managed.[4]

Between masters and slaves a third group soon emerged—the coloreds, or people of mixed ancestry. This group formed a useful racial and sociocultural buffer between the whites and blacks.[5] By the end of the eighteenth century a substantial number of them were freedmen, and in Jamaica these freedmen were sufficiently influential to win full civil liberties, along with the small Sephardic Jewish minority, from the white ruling class a little before the emancipation.[6]

While the pattern was similar, Guyana lagged behind in the development of its plantation-based economy, partly because of the enormous geographical difficulties which its low-lying coastal terrain presented, partly because of its peculiar political situation of being a Dutch-controlled territory with a majority of British settlers, and partly because of the lateness of the critical decision to shift from the river bank areas to the coastal strip.[7] Its period of economic expansion really moved into full swing after the British occupation in 1803, at a time when Jamaica's was already on the decline.[8]

The collapse of the slave-based economy with the complete

emancipation of the slaves by the British in 1838 paved the way for the third phase in the development of Afro-Caribbean societies. This phase was marked by rapid economic decline on the national and international levels, reflected in the general neglect of the area by the former colonial powers and a withdrawal of substantial segments of the former planter classes.[9] During the last two-thirds of the nineteenth century what may be called the segmentary Creole phase of Afro-Caribbean societies was to evolve from the precarious foundations which were laid during the period of slavery.[10]

The term creolization refers to the process whereby a group develops a way of life peculiar to a new locality distinct from the cultures of their homelands.[11] I make a distinction between two types of creolization: "segmentary creolization" and "synthetic creolization."

In segmentary creolization each group in the new setting creates its own peculiar version of a local culture. In Afro-Caribbean societies, two segmentary Creole cultures evolved. A peculiarly West Indian brand of the dominant metropolitan culture of the European ruling class developed. In form Euro-West Indian creole culture is almost wholly European; its institutions are direct borrowings. They are also largely European in content, but with substantial variations in emphasis and interpretation. It also involved new developments to meet the specific needs of the colonial area in architecture and dietary patterns. The most important difference, however, is style. There is no obvious difference in the form and content of the game cricket as played in England and in the West Indies, but there are numerous differences in the style, interpretation, and symbolic value of the game.[12]

Another important difference between Euro-West Indian Creole culture and its metropolitan counterpart is the high value placed on color—the "white bias," to use Henriques' phrase, [13] in all these societies. This is the peculiar product of a racially segmented society in which the ruling class of one race dominates a colonized group of a different race.

This white bias did not prevent the adoption of Euro-West

Indian culture by the mixed-race freedmen, later to become the middle class in the postemancipation society. In spite of the negative racial self-image it engendered, the new middle class vied with each other to emulate all things European.[14] They compensated to some extent for the negative racial self-image implied in the acculturation by turning it against those lower in the shade hierarchy and by lightening their own group by marrying "up," that is, by choosing spouses lighter than themselves.

The second type of segmentary creolization involved the development of a peculiarly West Indian peasant culture, forged partly out of the torn shreds and remnants of surviving African culture and out of a creative response to the exigencies of small-scale tropical peasant agriculture. We describe it as Afro-West Indian segmentary creolization. The ex-slaves of the Caribbean varied in their responses to the challenge of emancipation, depending mainly on the availability of land after emancipation. In Jamaica, the largest of the Commonwealth Caribbean islands, it was possible to retreat to the mountain backlands and to buy up abandoned estates. These areas formed the nuclei of the peasant communities which were to form the economic and social context of black peasant life in the country for the next century.[15] In Guyana, land was plentiful, but difficult to cultivate, so the attempt to form a largely self-contained peasantry was only partly successful and a substantial number of blacks continued to depend on the estates as the major source of their livelihood.[16]

In all these areas the new ex-slaves forged a culture distinctive in social organization, language, religion, attitude, and values. Like all peasant cultures, it was open to the influence of the urban high culture, in this case the Euro-West Indian segmentary Creole of the ruling class.

While the brown-skinned middle class tried its best to imitate the Euro-West Indian culture of the ruling planter group, this was not entirely possible, because this middle class lacked the educational and economic resources to sustain such a life style. Partly by default it created its own cultural patterns and finally developed a "synthetic Creole" culture. In segmentary creolization each group develops its own local culture; in synthetic creolization the group attempts to forge a local culture with elements from all the available cultural resources. Nothing more than a kind of poor man's Euro-West Indian Creole culture in the early period. With the growing influence of the middle classes there was an increased tendency to think in national terms rather than the earlier pathetic attempts to imitate the Europeans. The culture became more self-consciously synthetic. When the new middle class finally assumed complete control of the political system, it attempted to give an official seal to its culture, as reflected in the national motto in many of these Caribbean societies—"Out of many one people." [17]

Synthetic Creole draws heavily on Euro-West Indian culture for its instrumental component and on Afro-West Indian segmentary Creole for its expressive institutions and symbols. The political, economic, educational, and legal institutions of synthetic Creole are, essentially, slightly modified versions of Euro-West Indian segmentary Creole; its language, theater, music, dance, art, and literature are actively drawn from Afro-West Indian segmentary Creole sources.[18]

Caribbean societies are thus, today, best seen as neocolonial systems with enormous class cleavages and other cross-cutting cleavages based on race, color, ethnicity, and even urban-rural differences. Middle- and upper-class roles are increasingly occupied by upwardly mobile brown and black populations whose culture is synthetic Creole. At the same time, the economies are not expanding at a rate sufficient to allow for significant group mobility among the mass of the black lower classes. The elite view the system as highly fluid, since most of them are upwardly mobile, but the mass of the population views it as static and undemocratic, since the few who have moved up from their ranks are insignificant demographically.

This is clearly a volatile situation. Expanding educational facilities have succeeded more in increasing expectations than in providing the opportunities to satisfy these expectations. Urbanization has brought in its train a well-known set of problems. When, further, the rise of black racial consciousness has led to an interpretation of the color-class hierarchy, not as a residue of the old colonial system but as an active consequence of ongoing racist and imperialist policies, one begins to understand why, in recent years, this part of the world no longer reflects the sleepy, tropical paradise of travel agents' brochures but reveals increasing signs of impending social and political upheaval.[19]

If or when an upheaval takes place, the groups which stand to lose most and are most fearful of their interests are the members of the various ethnic and racial minorities, especially those who now occupy high-status positions out of all proportion to their numbers.

Most prominent among these groups are the Sephardic Jews, who came to the West Indies during the seventeenth century from northern Brazil after the Portuguese reclaimed that area from the Dutch.[20] Unlike their counterparts in Curaçao, the Jamaican Jews have slowly given up their ethnic identification in favor of middle- and upper-class allegiance and a growing identification with the white and light-skinned community at large. Today they are found in all parts of the country's life, including its economy, its political system (a former minister of National Security and Justice came from a prominent Jewish family), the professions, the arts, and recreational institutions. It is only a matter of time before the group will become completely absorbed into the Creole elite.[21]

The descendants of the nineteenth-century indentured East Indians now constitute over a third of the population of Trinidad and almost half of the population of Guyana. Descendants of Chinese and Portuguese migrants (the latter coming from Madeira in the mid-nineteenth century), small in numbers but great in influence and occupational status, now add to the ethnic complexity of Guyana. In Jamaica Indian indentured labor on a large scale was a failure, although less unsuccessful than the attempts to use Chinese laborers.[22] The descendants of these two immigrant groups make up small but highly visible—and in the case of the Chinese highly successful—ethnic groups in the islands.

(See Table 1 for a summary of data on the ethnic composition of Jamaica and Guyana.)

Table 1.
Some Basic Statistics on Guyana and Jamaica

COUNTRY	AREA (KM)	POPULATION	POLITICAL STATUS	PER CAPITA INCOME	ETHNIC COMPOSITION (BY PERCENT)	
Jamaica	11,425	1,800,000	Independent Member of British Commonwealth	$408(U.S.)1967	Blacks (including mixed) Indians Jews and other Whites Chinese	95.0 2.0 1.8 1.2
Guyana	210,000	714,000	Independent Republic of British Commonwealth	$200(U.S.)1964	Blacks Indians Amerindians Portuguese Chinese Mixed and others	34.0 50.0 4.0 .9 .6 10.5

Source: David Lowenthal, *West Indian Societies* (Oxford, Oxford University Press, 1972), pp. 78–79.

The Jamaican Chinese

Over a quarter of a century before the abolition of slavery in 1838, the possibility was raised of introducing Chinese indentured labor into the West Indies, and a small group did arrive in Trinidad as early as 1806.[23] It was not until the middle of the nineteenth century, however, when the labor problem became severe, that the Chinese began to arrive in the Caribbean in significant numbers.

The first set of migrants arrived in Guyana, Trinidad, and Jamaica between 1853 and 1854. This first scheme proved a disaster. There were enormous adjustment problems; the planters found the Chinese unruly laborers; and the physical condition of the migrants deteriorated rapidly. Most of this first batch ended their days in hospitals and alms houses, and died as paupers, vagrants, and beggars, and the entire group vanished with the death of the first generation. The disappointment of the planters together with the hostility of the native population dampened attempts at further immigration on a substantial scale for the next thirty years.

The labor shortage created by massive out migration of the Jamaican working class to Panama in the early 1880s revived interest in Chinese immigration, and in 1884 696 indentured servants arrived from Hong Kong. It was the last group to come directly from China under the indenture system. This second attempt at employing the Chinese as agricultural laborers was also a complete failure. By 1891 the vast majority of the Chinese were out of agriculture and into small trading activites.

Beginning in the 1890s, all new Chinese migrants were brought in by their compatriots to augment their numbers and to work in their growing commercial enterprises. The 1911 census shows a population of 2,111 but a sex ratio of 540 males for every 100 women.

In 1919, following further tensions aroused by the growing Chinese presence and their increasing domination of the grocery trade, the first restrictive immigration laws were passed. They were mild, almost absurd, however, and by 1921 the Chinese population had increased to 3,696. They had begun to expand out to the countryside once again, where they set up isolated retail shops; 52.8 percent now lived outside Kingston. The high ratio of Chinese males to females led to the growth of the colored Chinese—half-black, half-Chinese—population, the children of male Chinese shopkeepers and their black concubines and housekeepers.

The government stopped issuing passports to Chinese migrants in 1931, and in 1940 all Chinese, except diplomats, tourists, and students were barred. The Chinese population was still relatively small, but it had become demographically viable. By 1943 there were 12,394 persons of Chinese extraction on the island, of whom 6,879 were "pure Chinese" and 5,515 were colored Chinese. (See Tables 2 and 3.)

Table 2.

Characteristics of the Jamaican Chinese Population, 1871–1960

YEAR	TOTAL POPULATION	MALES	FEMALES	SEX RATIO M/100 F	PERCENT URBAN	PERCENT TOTAL POPULATION
1871	141	131	10	1,310	82.2	0.0
1881	99	n.a.	n.a.	n.a.	88.9	0.0
1891	481	373	108	345	63.2	0.1
1911	2,111	1,783	328	543	45.0	0.3
1921	3,696	n.a.	n.a.	n.a.	41.8	0.4
1943	12,394	6,922	5,472	126	50.3	1.0
1960	21,812	11,265	10,547	106	50.6	1.2

Table 3.

Characteristics of "Pure" and Colored Chinese Population, Jamaica, 1943, 1960

	"Pure" Chinese				Colored Chinese				All	
YEAR	MALES	FEMALES	SEX RATIO M/100 F	TOTAL	MALES	FEMALES	SEX RATIO M/100 F	TOTAL	TOTAL	PERCENT CHINA BORN
1943	4,338	2,541	171	6,879	2,584	2,931	89	5,515	12,394	22.8
1960	5,693	4,574	124	10,267	4,631	5,041	91	9,672	21,812	9.5

During the early period of settlement, 1854–1900, a time of inevitable tension of adjustment to a new society, the major problem was survival, not so much as a group, nor as culture carriers, but as individuals. This point cannot be too strongly emphasized. If our objective is to show how the Chinese developed as a group after coming to Jamaica, it would clearly be tautological to speak of them as if they were already a group on coming to the island. The Chinese who came to the Caribbean did have some rudimentary bases of group affiliation: their shared experience of crossing the ocean and the experience of being physically and culturally different in an alien land. These shared traits offered the opportunity for group allegiance, but there is no compelling nor "primordial" reason why they had to accept this opportunity. In Jamaica they did, but in Guyana they did not.

Those who came to Jamaica in the nineteenth century chose to use their shared social and cultural traits as the bases for establishing an ethnic group because it was in their best socioeconomic interest to do so. The postemancipation society to which they came had one glaring gap in its economy—there was almost no retail trade system. None had been necessary in the plantation-slave economy, in which each plantation was a self-contained world with master and slave providing for their mutual needs through domestic production and direct importation of goods and staples. With emancipation a more complex economy had evolved. There was an extensive peasantry alongside the surviving plantation system; there was a growing urban center, especially in Kingston.[24] Both the rural and the urban areas needed retail systems, and the Chinese immigrants quickly exploited the situation.

How could a struggling band of aliens take over, in so short a period of time, such a key sector of the host country's economy? The answer, quite simply, is this: They had no competition. And there was no competition because native members of the society who had skills and resources to develop the retail trade—the colored and the white middle and upper classes—had no interest in doing so.

Nor were the Jews interested. The status factor alone would have been critical for them, since precisely at this time they had begun to move into the upper echelons of white society from which they had been excluded for most of the period of slavery.

Like the British they had better and more lucrative things to do. Those who might have been interested—the black lower classes—lacked the resources.

The natural choice should have been the new middle class of coloreds, for whom emancipation offered enormous opportunities. But status was all important to them. The dominating, all-pervasive quality of their lives was their desperate and often pathetic attempts to identify with the white ruling class. More than any other group, they despised the blacks, with that self-destroying contempt characteristic of half-breed groups. Physically closer to the blacks than to the British and Jewish groups they were so eager to emulate, they found it vital to create even greater social distance between themselves and the black masses. A white man serving a black ex-slave was unthinkable. A colored gentleman serving an ex-slave, while thinkable to the whites and to the blacks, was to the coloreds a source of humiliation, outrage, and utter disgust, and was to be avoided at all costs.

The Chinese then found themselves with a remarkable opportunity. Like all immigrant groups, they could more easily forego the social activities requiring capital and time that full membership in a society demands. No questionable notions about greater initiative or resourcefulness are needed to explain their success.

At first, the Chinese responded to the opportunity individually. There was a rapid shift to the urban area by the scattered Chinese population. In Kingston they recognized their common interests and began to develop as a group. Soon the Chee Kung Tong Association was formed (a branch of the Hing Min Association); and in 1891, the Chinese Benevolent Society was organized, mainly to perform charitable work among the aged and the poor.

Toward the end of the nineteenth century, with a strong hold on the retail trade in Kingston, the Chinese traders began to move back to rural areas to take advantage of retail opportunites among the peasantry. The Chinese, only 0.4 percent of the total population, had all but conquered the entire retail trade on the island. Only after an economic base was secured did they begin to consolidate as an ethnic group. Before this, each family had kept to itself. There was only a vague sense of community in the common experience of being strangers in a strange land and out of certain common necessities. Collective activity seems to have come with some difficulty. Early attempts at ethnic consolidation during the first decades of the twentieth century were marred by bitter feuds and disputes among the more prominent Chinese. The Chinese Benevolent Society collapsed in 1916, although its services were desperately needed, given the extremely high dependency ratio of the population.

Race was never the most critical basis of group activity during this or the ensuing period, and for a simple reason: If the Chinese had tried to maintain their racial purity, they would have suffered the same fate as the earlier group—extinction with the first generation. With a desperate shortage of women, to survive the Chinese turned to the native population and took black women as concubines to bear their children. They rarely married these women, but it is unlikely that this was an expression of racial contempt, since black men did not marry them during their childbearing age either.[25] Further, the institution of concubinage which the Chinese found among the native population was by no means alien to their own Oriental experience. It was a nice situation of cultural congruence, and the Chinese took advantage of it. Out of these unions an interesting pattern emerged that was to persist through the second half of the century. There is no evidence that the Chinese ever considered this a problem or that they had any strong feelings of primordial loss. "Pure Chinese" had to take on a cultural rather than a racial meaning and this the Chinese achieved. The sons born to their black concubines, and later to the racially mixed women, were made over into the Chinese cultural mold, first by the fathers themselves. But as the Chinese gained prosperity, the half-breed sons were sent back to Hong Kong and China to be acculturated by their kinsmen.

The homeland kinsmen did their job of enculturation well. Having left Jamaica at the tender age of five or six, the children returned to the island in early manhood totally Chinese, many even monolingually so. Later, the tendency was for these grown-up male children to make a second and last journey to China to procure a wife, whom they would bring back to Jamaica with them.

The phase of ethnic consolidation began about the turn of the century, especially after the First World War, and continued until 1940. By then the Chinese had not only established themselves in Kingston but had fanned out to almost all the major and minor urban centers on the island. Only then, with complete economic security, did they turn in earnest to the task of forging a group identity.

The development of this identity was both caused and motivated by economic interests. Having taken over the retail sector of the economy, the Chinese began to move into the wholesale business after 1900 and took a firm hold there by 1920. Between 1920 and 1940, in the urban center of Kingston, the primary wholesalers who bought directly from the import agents were concentrated around the Chinese quarter. These primary wholesalers supplied secondary Chinese wholesalers who had, by now, spread out over the countryside. Secondary wholesalers combined wholesale selling to local businesses with their own retail outlets.

Prosperity made ethnic consolidation possible. It meant that there was enough surplus wealth to support charitable causes among themselves. Thus in 1921, after being defunct for five years, the Chinese Benevolent Society was revived, and from that time served the community continuously for the next half-century. Prosperity also encouraged the development of a Chinese-language press, *The Chinese Public News*. The press became an important instrument of community formation, keeping the scattered community informed not only of news abroad but of other members in Jamaica. With economic prosperity also came, in 1924, another important cohesive institution, the Chinese public school. Finally, prosperity permitted Chinese fathers to send even more of their sons on the expensive journey of enculturation to China and Hong Kong and, at the same time, to import more women, as well as other men, into the society. The cultural distinctiveness of the group was enhanced and its demographic position improved. With ethnic consolidation came a third stage in the racial composition of the Chinese population. In the earliest period, the group was pure Chinese but over-whelmingly male. During the first phase of adjustment there was a strong infusion of Negro "blood" into the group, creating a need to emphasize cultural factors rather than racial ones in group identification. This was followed by a reinfusion of Chinese genes through the importation of pure Chinese women from China, and through half-Chinese women who, while rejected as candidates for full enculturation, were preferred as mates, when they grew up, to produce more sons.

There were, however, still not enough "pure" or colored Chinese women to meet the biological and social needs of the male Chinese community. At no time could Chinese men on the island expect to find mates wholly from among purely Chinese women. The technique of defining pure Chinese in largely social and cultural terms, then, became entrenched among the Jamaican Chinese, so that today one hardly ever hears the distinction "Chinese colored." Whether or not a person is Chinese depends on whether he or she chooses to define himself or herself as Chinese (always, of course, with the constraint that the individual must have some vague resemblance to Chinese), and whether they are accepted as such by the Chinese community.

Economic factors made possible and encouraged the growth of Chinese ethnicity, and consolidation was stimulated because it was good for business. What, after all, is retail and wholesale trading but a network of people among whom there is a flow of goods and credit in one direction and a flow of profit in the other? Now that they were spread out over the country, it was to their economic advantage to consolidate into an ethnic group with excellent intragroup communications. The structure of the social network became one with the structure of the trading network. The strongest community organizations were also trade associa-tions—for example, the Wholesalers Association, the Chinese Retailers Association, and the Bakeries Association.

However much they may have tried to preserve the old culture, the Chinese were living in a host society to which they had to make some adjustments. They were totally dependent on this society for their livelihood; they were at its political mercy, and they depended on it for biological support. Though they were to remain, by and large, culturally exclusive and were to enrich their own cultural background through their prosperity during this period, one can detect the seeds of the segmentary Sino-Creole which was to develop later on. Dietary patterns had to change, if ever so slightly; some form of English had to be learned; adaptations had to be made to the black women (who had a highly developed sense of their own independence). Again, as the Chinese community grew larger, there was the problem of educating the young. The technique of sending their children to China to be educated could not go on forever; it was prohibitively expensive. As more years separated the first generation from the new, a return to China was becoming increasingly awkward. Prosperity and expanding business also brought problems in educating the young abroad. When businesses had been small-scale, being culturally Chinese and illiterate in the language of the host culture was no disadvantage. As business enterprise grew larger social skills in the host society became essential.

In this period of ethnic consolidation, the greatest adjustment to the host society was perhaps in religion. Chinese religion did not appear to survive long among the Chinese in Jamaica or among the Chinese elsewhere in the Caribbean. The Chinese during the early part of the century began to convert to Roman Catholicism.[26] The choice of Roman Catholicism, a small, minority religion in Jamaica, involved a cultural compromise but it maintained the social exclusiveness of the group, an exclusiveness the church was willing to respect.

As the Chinese community grew larger and more prosperous, and as a second and third generation emerged, cultural exclusiveness became less desirable. The younger generation was increasingly unwilling to be deprived of a Western education and in this way suffer a disadvantage vis-à-vis their fellow Jamaicans. Even within the Chinese community, the need for more Westernization was felt. The segmentary creolization period developed in 1940 to 1945 in consequence.

Once again, the Chinese had to make a fundamental choice critical to their own economic self-interest, a choice between continued prosperity or continued ethnic solidarity on the basis of cultural exclusiveness. A division emerged in the community. On the ethnically conservative side were the older generation of Chinese and the remaining China-born (many though not all of whom were older), and on the other side were the younger generation, mainly Jamaican born, who opted for a more progressive, less exclusive approach to the host society.

The younger generation of Chinese Jamaicans in the early 1940s was troubled by the first stages of fundamental change in the direction of independence in the colonial society. Dissatisfaction of the mass of people, especially on the sugar plantations, was echoed also by the brown middle classes, who were beginning to assert a claim to national leadership. The emerging middle class began to forge a national solidarity around the theme of an explicitly stated national culture that incorporated all elements of the society. This is the official version of the synthetic Creole I described above.[27]

In this attempt to legitimize the synthetic Creole, the Chinese began to attract serious attention. They were resented, not because they were despised or because there was any desire to keep them out but, on the contrary, because they were seen as aloof from the national effort. Many felt indignation at the refusal of the Chinese to accept the invitation to join in the movement toward nationhood and to share in the emerging synthetic Creole culture.[28] The younger generation took the statement seriously and their hands were strengthened by it.

The position of the older generation was weakened further by the Communist revolution and final takeover of the mainland. Immigration to Jamaica had been stopped completely by the 1940s; now, the possibility of returning to China, or of sustained contact, was gone. The Communist ideology of the new government in mainland China created a real crisis of allegiance for many of the older group of culturally conservative Chinese.

To maintain their cultural exclusiveness, the conservative Chinese would have had to support a government and an ideology (on the mainland) that was totally inconsistent with their position and implicit economic philosophy in Jamaica. In rejecting this contradiction, the older generation of Chinese moved to reconcile their economic interests with their cultural orientation. It marked a grudging acceptance of the fact that Jamaica would remain their homeland.

These developments were accompanied by a far more radical shift toward a greater adjustment to Jamaica by the younger generation of Jamaica-born Chinese, who insisted on having a Western education and, later, on sending their children to the local public schools. They established greater contact with members of the host society. In making these adjustments, they were met halfway by the less conservative members of the older and China-born generation. What emerged was an attempt at building a segmentary Sino-Creole society strongly Jamaican in emphasis with many of its institutional forms borrowed from the host society but directed exclusively at the Chinese community.

The effort came too late and did not go far enough. Jamaican society had passed the stage where it could tolerate or contain, without great social risk, a segmentary Creole society, especially of those who almost completely monopolized one sector of the island's economy. In the 1950s began the synthetic creolization period that continues to the present.

From a more theoretical perspective, segmentary and synthetic creolization are basically antithetical. Synthetic creolization seeks to unite all the different segmentary cultures into a unified national culture; it is, indeed, the dialectical synthesis of the various antithetical segmentary Creole cultures. Segmentary creolization, by its very nature, resists such unification. The two types of Creole culture can exist side by side only if the group which exercises total power is not committed to synthetic creolization and supports a segmentary Creole culture. This was the case during the colonial period, when the British exercised power over all other groups. Once the group that assumes power is committed to synthetic creolization, the synthetic cultural dialectic is likely to evolve as one way of resolving the potential tensions of decolonization in a multiethnic society. Sometimes a new postcolonial elite can commit itself to segmentary creolization, in this way legitimizing the existence of other such Creole cultures, as in Surinam and, to some extent, in Guyana. In Jamaica, however, the new elite was firmly committed to a national synthetic Creole culture.

This placed the Chinese in a dilemma. They could see that the synthetic national Creole culture was in their own interest, but unlike the other capitalist groups, whose ethnicity rested primarily on race and kinship, it meant abandoning not only earlier cultural exclusiveness, but the social exclusiveness and cultural distinctiveness of the hastily organized segmentary Creole culture of the post-1940 period. Precisely because cultural symbols rather than race formed the basis of their ethnic identification, the Chinese found it far more difficult than the white ethnics to make any generous concessions to the emerging synthetic Creole society.

But a choice had to be made. The position of the younger generation won out by the late 1950s. The decision was a radical one. It was also the decision that was in the group's best class interests.

Rapid and near complete dismantlement of their culture was accompanied by radical intersocial and intrasocial changes. The Chinese chose to move into the middle and upper-middle classes. They found an elite which was happy to have them. Even this change had a direct economic motivation. The native bourgeoisie had made a rapid shift in their residential and shopping patterns in both Kingston and Montego Bay. In Kingston they moved from the south, east, and center of the city to the new suburban regions of upper St. Andrews to the north of the city.[29] Prosperity and Americanization led to a preference for suburban shopping centers instead of the traditional Chinese groceries and open markets. The Chinese were quick to adapt to these changes in residential patterns and life styles. With a shift from emphasis on wholesaling to supermarkets, the base of the wholesale business was undercut, since supermarkets, because of their scale of operation, deal directly with the importer. The Chinese responded by going into the supermarket and shopping plaza business in a big way and also, for the first time, began to challenge the Middle Easterners and Jews in their traditional monopoly of the import-export business.

In response to economic developments, the Chinese moved out of Chinatown and the Chinese quarters and into the new middle-class housing and other residential areas of the main towns. There was a shift toward the professions and toward managerial, clerical, and sales positions in non-Chinese firms. They adopted the bourgeois life style of synthetic Creole culture with the same energy that characterized their takeover of the retail trade system.

Within a period of fifteen years, the Chinese ceased to be a culture group, and no longer defined their ethnicity in cultural terms; they have become instead an integral part of the bour-geoisie, with the synthetic Creole and middle-class life style of that group.

They did not, however, cease to be an ethnic group. Rather, they changed the basis of their ethnicity. Now culturally Jam-aican, the Chinese have been careful to maintain those patterns of behavior in and attitudes toward work and family which maintain group cohesion and are congruent with qualities that ensure high achievement in the society.

The nuclear and stem families replaced the extended family, a further move away from a distinctly Oriental pattern to one that was essentially middle-class Jamaican. There was an emphasis, however, on strong collateral ties that ensures the maintenance of community and kinship bonds and, at the same time, is ideal for economic success. The extended family was an ideal social unit for the economic success of the Chinatown wholesale establishments

or the isolated rural grocery; the nuclear family ensures the
flexibility required for competition in a complex modern
economy.[30]

Changes in attitude, especially toward parents, the work ethic,
and leisure, also reflect the same balance between synthetic
creolization, communal integrity, and economic achievement.[31]

There is, then, still a Chinese ethnic group in Jamaica. Somatic
and generalized kinship ties and a sense of shared experience
constitute their most meaningful bases of primary extrafamilial
identity. Still it would be inaccurate to say that all the Chinese in
Jamaica constitute an ethnic group. Some Chinese choose not to
make their somatic distinctiveness or their kinship and affinal ties
their most meaningful bases of extrafamilial identification. Those
who choose ethnic identification invariably make the choice the
parental generation made for them, because it is still in their own
best economic interest. Being "Chinese" gives one access to a
relatively substantial pool of capital; it ensures economic "breaks"
which might otherwise not have existed; it provides a wide range
of social and business contacts; it gives one access to valuable
business "intelligence"—who is on the up-and-up, who is secretly
bankrupt, who has the best real estate deals, and the like—and it
provides a supportive network in the otherwise harshly competitive business world. Only to the extent that this ethnic group
continues to be a useful economic network will the ethnic group
survive.

Many Chinese Jamaicans have found that their economic
interests do not require, or are not best served, by this network. It
is these Chinese—mainly those in the professions and those who
work for non-Chinese firms—who show the greatest tendency to
leave the ethnic group and often, though not always, seal their
withdrawal from the group by marrying non-Chinese.

Those who remain fully committed to the Chinese ethnic group
have, for the first time in their history in Jamaica, begun to shift to
somatic traits as the main basis for overt group identification.
With the erosion of what was formerly their main focus of group
identity, race is its only distinctive overt trait. But, this is the right

answer to the wrong question. The real questions are: Why do some Jamaican Chinese continue to maintain their ethnic ties? How does the choice of somatic features relate to the choice of ethnicity over assimilation?

What seems to have happened and is still taking place in the Chinese ethnic group in this: Choice of mate has become of vital importance for the maintenane of the continued congruence of the sets of social and economic networks which constitute the sociological *raison d'être* of the ethnic group. When black women were used to bear their children, male offspring were kept in the group for cultural training and women were not. Later on, as more and more Chinese colored women as well as pure Chinese women became available, there was a shift back to the pure Chinese racial type on the individual level, even though, on the group level, this was accompanied by a wider distribution of Negro blood. Fewer and fewer Chinese were "pure" Chinese racially, while more and more individuals who were defined as Chinese were getting closer to the pure Chinese racial type.

When the Chinese abandoned culture as the major basis of ethnic identification, race gained in significance as a basis of group identification, not because it was natural to choose race, but because an important economic factor favored the choice of race at precisely the time when culture was losing its significance. Over the years those Chinese who were most successful economically had been the very ones who had been most endogamous. Women have become the means whereby wealth is exchanged, shared, consolidated, and kept within the group, all this while performing the equally valuable task of perpetuating the group. As such, they have become highly valued and jealously guarded.

From a position in which the group was defined culturally and race was marginal, the Chinese shifted from cultural and social exclusiveness to complete cultural integration into the synthetic Creole Jamaican culture and to a consolidation of wealth accomplished through endogamy. This has resulted in the emergence of a tightly knit socioeconomic network which is increasingly homogeneous racially (though with fewer and fewer racially pure individuals) and which uses racial similarity to symbolize their distinctiveness and to sanction the all-important principle of endogamy. Jamaicans of Chinese ancestry who do nct choose ethnic identification are immediately absorbed into the non-Chinese community, since there are no cultural obstacles and no reluctance on the part of non-Chinese members to marry non-ethnic Chinese.

The Chinese ethnic group, then, is likely to grow smaller with the withdrawal of those who choose to marry outside of the group and choose the nation as their most meaningful basis of extra-familial identity. As it grows smaller, it will become more and more ethnically visible, more tightly knit, and will achieve more of the attributes of the corporate, racially defined ethnic group—a rather ominous development at a time when the overwhelming majority of the black population are themselves becoming racially conscious and are showing signs of rejecting the synthetic Creole compromise of the bourgeois elite for some as yet unspecified form of national "black power."

The Chinese in Guyana

In striking contrast to the pattern of development in Jamaica is the experience of the Chinese in Guyana. The Chinese were brought to Guyana to meet the same pressing labor needs that prevailed in Jamaica in the mid-nineteenth century; in fact, they were brought under the same scheme. Those who went to Guyana came from much the same areas of China as the Jamaican Chinese and, in some cases, were even recruited by the same agent.[32] By 1866, Guyana had the greatest number of Chinese in its history—approximately 10,000. A year later came rapid decline in the population.

The Chinese were brought into the colony as indentured agricultural laborers, but this scheme was abandoned in 1874 for much the same reasons as in Jamaica. More Chinese were to trickle into Guyana after the indenture period, but these were relatives and friends brought over by Chinese already in the colony, not by the planters. In all, approximately 700 more were to come from China after 1878. This postindenture immigration did not reverse the seemingly irrevocable downward trend of the Chinese population. In 1879 there was a total of only 6,000 Chinese in the colony, which meant that more than half had either died or left the colony during the 25 years since they first arrived. The population reached its lowest point in 1911, with only 2,118 Chinese. Thereafter there was a slow increase until 1947, when the population was 3,528. Between then and the census year of 1960, the Chinese population had grown to a total of only 3,600, making up 0.6 percent of the total Guyana population of 600,000.

Up to the end of the nineteenth century, there was little real difference between the pattern of adjustment of the Chinese in Guyana and their counterparts in Jamaica. Both groups refused to work on the estates, and their efforts at peasant farming were equally sporadic and unsuccessful. Both groups quickly headed for the urban areas and soon became among the most urbanized groups. By 1911, one third of the Chinese population in Guyana lived in the two urban centers of Georgetown and New Amsterdam, and at the present time more than 60 percent of them live in these two urban areas.[33]

After the turn of the century, however, one begins to detect fundamental differences in the choices made by Chinese in Jamaica and Guyana. The first was choice of livelihood. In Jamaica the Chinese were almost exclusively concerned with retail trading after rejecting agriculture; in Guyana they selected retailing as only one of several means of economic survival, although it was the main one. From the start, the Guyanese Chinese showed a willingness to select a wide range of occupations. And while it remained true that up to 1943 as many as 63 percent were in retail trade, only a small number made it in a big way in this industry and, as a group, they in no way monopolized either the retail or the wholesale trade as they did in Jamaica. Another ethnic group had this distinction.

A second important difference, deriving from the first, was that the Guyanese Chinese never went through a phase of ethnic consolidation; nor did they even attempt to any great degree to adjust through the technique of segmentary creolization. Instead, the Chinese in Guyana moved from their period of initial settlement and indenture straight into the evolving synthetic Creole culture of Guyana.

The transformation was truly remarkable. It began, in a way, the moment the Chinese landed in Guyana. From that time they broke their ties completely with the Chinese homeland. By the time Clementi studied the group in the first decade of the twentieth century, he found it possible to write that: "British Guyana possesses a Chinese society of which China knows nothing, and to which China is almost unknown." [34] Fried offers an explanation of his own, that a substantial number of early migrants came during the Taiping Rebellion and that kinship and locality ties were already broken as a result of this upheaval before leaving the Mainland.[35] The explanation makes some sense, but it applies only to a part of the Guyanese Chinese community.

The real answer to the problem of the radically different adjustment of the Chinese in Jamaica and Guyana lies in Fried's almost offhand reference to "the difficulties in making a living in British Guyana at the time." These were indeed difficult times for Guyana. It is in looking at the differences in the pattern of socioeconomic development in the two countries that we begin to understand why the Chinese in Jamaica chose ethnic consolidation based on cultural exclusiveness and the Chinese in Guyana chose to make a total cultural break with the homeland.

After emancipation, the sugar industry faced hard times in both Guyana and Jamaica, more so in the latter than in the former. In both areas the ex-slaves attempted to form a peasant sector, but were more successful in Jamaica than in Guyana. Guyana was highly successful in recruiting indentured laborers from India after the attempt with the Chinese and the Portuguese from Madeira had failed. Thus Guyana continued to be a monocrop, plantation-based economy with a relatively simple social and economic system, in which the mass of the population remained largely at the mercy of the planter class.

Jamaica, on the other hand, took a more complex course of development. In 1865, the Jamaican peasants, with a strong tradition of rebellion behind them, staged an uprising against their depressed conditions which so scared the white ruling minority that it committed what Mavis Campell called "politcal immolation"; that is, it voted its political constitution out of existence and asked the British goverment to impose direct rule.[36] There followed a period of relatively enlightened Crown colony government, in which basic infrastructural development took place and the economy was further diversified with the introduction of banana cultivation, mainly by the ever creative peasantry, who by now had also begun to control a sizable portion of the sugar cultivation on the island.

None of these developments took place in Guyana. The colony's economy paid a heavy price for its continued emphasis on the monocrop plantation system, especially after the British moved to free trade in sugar in 1874.[37] This prolonged crisis in the world price of sugar was reflected most tellingly in the depressing condition of the masses in Guyana.

It was to this kind of economy that the Chinese were introduced and in which they had to find a livelihood. Many tried retail trading and continue to do so. But here they found a major obstacle to quick prosperity or economic security. Another ethnic group—the Portuguese, who were recruited from Madeira in the late 1840s and '50s[38]—had taken over the retail trade. Actively encouraged by the European ruling class, they got preferential treatment for credit over their African and Chinese competitors, partly because they were Europeans, partly because they provided a useful class and cultural buffer between the planter class and the black masses. Although thus favored, the Portuguese were kept at a distance by the British Creole planters, who never saw them as quite "white," whether racially or culturally defined; nor did the blacks ever so regard them. The fact remains, however, that they were sufficiently favored and skilled to monopolize the colony's commercial life.[39] The many Chinese who worked in the retail trade had to be satisfied with the pickings left by the Portuguese traders.

In 1900, at a time when the Chinese in Jamaica were already economically secure and could begin to use their economic prosperity to consolidate an ethnic group through the development of institutions which supported the perpetuation of their culture, the Guyanese Chinese found it in their best economic and social interest to choose the opposite path. If they were to succeed in a wide range of occupations they had to creolize themselves.

There is a relationship between the nature and type of occupation and the propensity of a culturally alien immigrant group to isolate itself. Of all occupations, retail trading offers the best opportunity for such a group to maximize earnings while minimizing acculturation.[40] Where other choices have to be made, cultural obstacles must be overcome. For a Guyanese Chinese to choose a career in the colonial civil service, the professions, or even in occupations such as barbers or chauffeurs requiring a lower level of skills but a high level of ascriptive or diffuse interaction, it was imperative that the culture of the host society be mastered. The only alternatives were manual labor and peasant farming, both of which, while they avoided the cultural problem, provided little possibility of improvement. Both alternatives were tried by the Chinese in Guyana, who attempted life as indentured laborers and as pioneer farmers; both were rejected because of their limited possibilities. In rejecting these and choosing other occupations, the Chinese also chose to abandon the traditional culture and to adopt the evolving Guyanese Creole culture.

The Chinese in Guyana not only quickly and efficiently adopted the Guyanese creole culture but did it quite methodically and self-consciously. Their response to Christianity illustrates this. As early as 1875, even before they had mastered English, a Chinese-language branch of he Church of England was founded by them at their insistence. Soon the Chinese had become "devout

Christians," [41] almost forty years before the Chinese in Jamaica had made their decision to adopt Christianity.

But note here another significant difference between them and the Jamaican Chinese, who, when they decided to adopt Christianity in the early twentieth century, went into the Catholic church. The Guyanese Chinese avoided the Catholic church in Guyana, although by that time it was well-established there to serve the spiritual needs of the Portuguese and other Catholics and chose Protestantism, the religion to choose, obviously, if creolization was the major objective. So thoroughly creolized have the Chinese become that later they began joining not just the established Anglican church, but the Pentecostal sects of the blacks, and by the 1950s were themselves "holding revival meetings in the colony ... aimed at a general public and not specifically at other Chinese." [42]

The locally born Chinese, known as T'u-sheng, have given up any tendency to withdraw from the total society. In the bitter ethnic fighting between blacks and Indians which preceded independence, the Chinese emerged in a new role—that of mediators between the warring ethnic groups. Significantly, a Chinese was named the first president of the newly independent nation, a most extraordinary appointment for a minority group that numbers less than one percent of the population. It reflects as favorably on the successful creolization and broker role of the Chinese as it does unfavorably on the failure of the dominant groups to work out a genuinely transethnic society in Guyana.[43] The idea of a Chinese governor-general in Jamaica, on the other hand, is unthinkable. No Jamaican prime minister would be reckless enough to make such an appointment, and, were it made, it is unlikely that any Chinese would be foolhardy enough to accept.

In spite of the overt emphasis on endogamy, Fried found that in practice, "There is considerable mating across ethnic lines, both with and without formal marriage." [44] Significantly, the major loss through intermarriage is through female Chinese marrying non-

Chinese, quite the opposite of the present situation in Jamaica. As any student of endogamous groups knows, female outmarriage is the surest sign not only of the weakness of the endogamy principle but of the demographic decline of the group.

The second, much smaller, group consists of the China-born Chinese who migrated to the island after the indenture period. They maintain close contact with relatives in China, quite often have wives there, and sometimes even send for brides from the mainland or Hong Kong. Their adjustment is quite similar to that of the Jamaican Chinese during their period of ethnic consolidation—they are culturally exclusive and socially isolated. These later migrants are among the most urban and the most concentrated in the retail trading business. They are also the most successful in the retail trade. Thus, the same factors account for the ethnic consolidation of this small group of later migrants, who came at a time when economic and social conditions were such that the choice of ethnic consolidation was both possible and economically viable. It is doubtful, however, whether this group will survive. Their children are extremely ambivalent about China and their parents, and the pressure to become absorbed by the T'u-sheng group is strong—indeed, irresistible. Generally, the children of the small China-born population seem to accept this fate with resignation.[45]

In the case of Jamaica, economic conditions were such that the best interests of the group were served by an exclusive concern with retail trade. Success in this venture allowed for and reinforced a choice of ethnic consolidation based on cultural distinctiveness. Later, economic pressures and interests promoted a shift first to segmentary creolization and soon after a further change to a situation in which synthetic creolization was chosen but with a fundamental difference between those who further chose to abandon ethnicity altogether and those who chose to strengthen it by changing the basis of their ethnic identification from cultural to somatic and kinship ties.

In the Guyanese context, economic and social conditions were such that a wider range of occupational choices was in the best interests of the Chinese. In pursuing these occupations, the choice of synthetic creolization and the abandonment of Chinese culture were the most rational courses of action. Ethnic consolidation was never attempted by the Guyanese T'u-sheng Chinese, who are now completely Guyanese except in their physical appearance; and even this is likely to disappear soon, given the high rate of intermarriage. Later arrivals, finding conditions closer to those existing in Jamaica, made much the same choices as the Jamaicans did in terms of ethnic identification based on cultural exclusiveness.

My case studies, I think, fully demonstrate the theoretical feasibility of my hypotheses. More than anything else, I hope I have shown that there is no a priori reason to believe that individuals always choose ethnic identification over other forms of identification. The primacy of economic factors over all others has been demonstrated. I hope that I have at least tentatively demonstrated that people never make economic decisions on the basis of ethnic allegiance, but, on the contrary, that the strength, scope, viability, and bases of ethnic identity are determined by and are used to serve the economic and general class interests of individuals.

The second and final observation is this: The choices I have discussed were genuine choices. What I hope I have shown, also, is that men choose their economic conditions as well, and once having chosen them, tend in the long run to make adjustments to them that are in their own best interests. The Chinese who went to Jamaica and Guyana chose to go there, in this way choosing their contexts, their economic conditions. Once there, they tried estate labor and peasant farming and chose to abandon them. There is no inherent reason whatsoever why they could not have continued in these ventures. Certainly there was no cultural or racial predisposition not to; it is easy to show how, in neighboring Curaçao, peasant farming is exactly what the Chinese chose to remain in, and they have been quite successful at it.[46]

We have seen, too, how the Chinese changed the basis of their ethnic identity from one period to another in Jamaica, in contrast with Guyana, where the choice was never between the bases of ethnic consolidation, but whether there should or should not be an ethnic group. In both situations, individuals were free to depart from the choices being made by the majority of their peers. In Jamaica today, substantial numbers of Chinese are choosing between ethnic identification and national identification and are deciding on the latter at a time when many Chinese have not only chosen ethnicity but have intensified ethnic bonds on more narrow racial lines.

Guiding these choices were peoples' conceptions of what was in their own best economic and social interests. This is not to imply a concurrence with any simplistic economic determinism. We can fully agree with Engels' statement that "the ultimately determining element in history is the production and reproduction of real life" and still accept the integrity, if not autonomy, of human choice. Indeed, as Engels himself goes on to add: "We make our history ourselves, but, in the first place, under very definite assumptions and conditions. Among these, the economic ones are ultimately decisive." [47]

CHAPTER 6

The Modern Revival
of Ethnicity: With Special
Reference to the United States

There can be no doubt that we are living through a period of the most intense ethnic revival. In all the continents of the earth, men and women who for ages related to each other on other terms, or else did not relate at all, now struggle with each other in murderous combat as a result of conflicting ethnic loyalties.[1] The disastrous consequences of this revival should be obvious to anyone who reads the newspapers with any regularity. In black Africa, ethnic and tribal rivalries remain a source of permanent instability and the most unspeakable inhumanities, while in southern Africa a gang of fanatical ethnic thugs murders the minds and bodies of the native peoples with a cold-blooded efficiency that rivals that of Nazi Germany. In the Middle East, Arab fanaticism and Israeli nationalistic extremism remain at daggers drawn, resulting in the brutal displacement of a whole people, the displacement and denaturalization of Jews by Arabs and of Arabs by Jews, and the constant threat to the peace of the world. In Southeast Asia, Chinese, Indian, and other native peoples each day come to loathe each other more and more. In Soviet Central Asia, the one possibly liberal feature of Soviet policy—its attempt to unite the various nationalities into a unified, though not necessarily uniform state sharing a common industrial civilization—has been completely undermined by the revival of conservative chauvinistic forces in the provinces, forces which, in their support of the lowly status of women, to give but one example, cannot be condoned by any civilized man or woman.[2] In Latin America, where official ideology proclaims the existence of racial and ethnic harmony, whole tribes of Indians are still being decimated, while others face the cruel paradox of being romanticized in the abstract by "indianist" poets, novelists, choreographers, and other intellectuals, while treated like brutes in face-to-face contact or simply excluded altogether. In continental Europe, after the stunned, post-Nazi lull, economic forces have led to the creation of yet another dangerous revival of ethnic rivalry. France, Germany, and Switzerland, having invited southern Italians, Turks, Spaniards, and Algerians to migrate into their societies in order to meet critical labor needs and help sustain the "economic miracle" of the postwar years, now find themselves incapable of and unwilling to absorb these alien workers. And even if they were able to do so, it is doubtful whether the impending ethnic tragedy would be averted, for the migrants themselves cling to their national loyalties, wanting it both ways: the rewards of an industrial culture and the preindustrial cradle of their ethnic groups.

But developments in the United States give the greatest cause for concern. For here, at least, was the one part of the world which did seem to offer the best prospect for the universalist ideal. Here, it was hoped, was the one great refuge for all exiles, not only from specific ethnic domination but from all ethnicities. The universalist ideal is, however, now under the most serious attack in the United States, and the tragedy is that the forces combined against it come from both the right and the liberal wings of the American intelligentsia.

How did this extraordinary state of affairs come about? The first disaster that befell the ideal of universalism in America was the poor image used to express it, namely, "the melting pot." Actually, this ugly term was not always used to describe universalism. At the turn of the century, the much better term "Americanization" was in vogue. It was later replaced by misguided liberals who failed to understand what was actually happening in America and who designated an entire, complex process with a term that applied strictly to only one element of it.[3] Americanization meant three kinds of cultural developments. One was the emergence of separate ethnic cultures of the adaptive type or of the more permanent symbiotic type. The second was the synthesis of the separate cultures producing a new mixed culture. This is the now notorious melting pot. I have already argued that this is a poor way for peoples in contact to solve their cultural problems, for there is no guarantee that the product that emerges will be the most satisfactory. But there was a third development, which almost everyone who discusses these issues seems to conspire to neglect: This is a universal culture which is partly a product of the structural imperatives of the new socioeconomic order and, on the symbolic level, draws on the most convenient cultural patterns of the groups which make up the society. These symbolic borrowings are largely matters of convenience and timing. As one would expect, the earliest migrants tend to contribute more to this generalized culture, simply because they were there first. The Anglo-Saxons effectively conquered and settled the United States and, as a result, their language became the national language. It is silly for an Italian or Pole to moan over this. No one is saying that his or her language would not have served just as well in the creation of the generalized symbolic structure of the universal culture.

But there is another reason why it is trivial to complain about the fact that the generalized culture may have borrowed unduly from the symbolic patterns of certain groups. Once an element of culture becomes generalized under the impact of a universal culture, it rapidly loses all specific symbolic value for the group which donated it. It is a foolish Anglo-Saxon who boasts about "his" language today. English is the language which the Anglo-Saxons originated; it is in no sense any longer an Anglo-Saxon language. It is a child that no longer knows its mother, and cares even less to know her. It has been adapted in a thousand ways to meet the special feelings, moods, and experiences of a thousand groups, all alien to the experiences of the culture group that first spoke the language.

What is true of language is also true of the other areas of the universal culture. I will give simply one more example from the field of music. Jazz is now the music of the universal culture of America. It is no longer a black American music, although some blacks have desperately tried to hold some special claim to it. And yet I strongly suspect that most black Americans have resigned themselves to the fact that they have lost all specific ethnic claim to this music, in much the same way that Anglo-Saxon Americans have given up all claim to English. It is most significant that it is not jazz, but the nonuniversalized blues and soul music that ethnic black Americans now choose to identify with.

I think I have said enough to suggest the difference between a melting pot culture and a universal culture. The melting pot is in no way a structural imperative; it is not required by the underlying economic and social demands of the civilization; it is a mere accident of history and the stew that emerges may well be completely inconsistent with the structural demands of the society. In the symbolic areas of culture a melting pot is merely a mosaic: It is the Italian or Chinese or Greek corner restaurant; it is the Polish folk dance here, the Czech folk song there, and the black soul brother strumming his blues guitar down yonder. Some people like to call this colorful, and the description, if it implies a lack of organizational depth, is apt. Others like to call it rich, but it is the richness of a northwest Indian potlatch: At best, it can only result in the purchase of pride and honor; at worst it descends into self-destruction. The universal culture's symbols and patterns, on the other hand, are shed of their ethnic specificities in the process of being universalized. They become the property of everyone. And, as such, they are enriched and developed by all. American English owes as much to Norman Mailer and Saul Bellow as it does to Henry James. And the American music we call jazz owes as much to Benny Goodman and Dave Brubeck as it does to Duke Ellington.

I am in complete agreement with those who reject the melting pot. But by identifying the melting pot with everything that developed in America, the universal culture is also being rejected. And it is this underhanded assault on the universal culture which all humanists who sincerely believe in the unity of mankind and in the possibility of a just and free society must strongly deplore.

The disguised attack on universalism now taking place involves two false identifications. The first is the identification of the melting pot with the universal culture. We are then told by the chauvinists that the melting pot was merely a smokescreen used by the WASPs to ensure the continued domination of their own culture. It is never possible, however, for peoples to meet for any sustained period of time without mutually influencing each other. A good case could be made by those who still believe in the melting-pot creed that the charge of one-way WASP domination is simply not true. But since I too reject the melting pot, it is not for me to make such a defense of it here.

More important is the way in which the chauvinists extend their argument by failing, sometimes deliberately, sometimes out of intellectual confusion, to see that ethnic WASP culture is no longer the culture of the group of Americans we now call WASPs, that with the exception of small pockets such as the New England Brahmin elite, the vast majority of WASPs have abandoned the ethnic specificities of their original culture in favor of the elite version of the American universal culture. The chauvinists insist that every culture must be a specific ethnic culture and that, therefore, whatever the culture the WASPs now share must be their own primordial traditions. Thus by rejecting what they claim to be WASP ethnic culture, they kill, ideologically, two birds with one stone: WASP cultural domination and the universal culture. The latter, of course, is the real enemy. But the enemy cannot be named, for it is still too powerfully sanctioned. Furthermore, the rewards of the universal culture are still being enjoyed even while it is being attacked. Most chauvinist works are composed in suburban homes or elegant apartments.

This rejection, in intellectual absentia, of the universal culture is usually accompanied by another false claim: the view that, as a

sociological fact, most Americans have remained "unmelted." A
vast body of literature has developed in recent years to support
this contention. This literature falls into two categories. The first is
candidly ideological. There is no attempt to hide the author's proethnic biases. Ethnic diversity is asserted as an established fact of
American life and, what is more, this is held to be good for
America. At its worst this category of ethnic writings is nothing
more than the most vulgar chauvinistic polemics in which the
author, while conceding the right of all other ethnic groups to be
equal and separate, is mainly interested in parading the special
virtues of his or her own tribe or in exhibiting its special
grievances. At its best, however, it amounts to a sophisticated
attack on modern industrial civilization and its many problems.
The works of Michael Novak stand as the best example of this
superior class of proethnic discourse. If one substitutes the term
"industrial universal culture" for the expression WASP in Novak's
writings and disregards his special pleading for the Slavic cause,
one ends up with a sensitive, often brilliant, and engagingly
passionate critique of industrial civilization. Novak's works must
be classed as part of the great tradition of Euro-American
romantic thought.[4] We are here in the realm of serious intellectual
discourse and a consideration of the romantic roots of modern
ethnicity must be treated in its own right. The last section of this
work will attempt to do so.

A second category of proethnic writings differs from the first in
its scientific pretentions and in its claim that it is treating the
subject in a detached, objective manner. Often these works are
paraded as scholarly exercises in the social sciences, and the
proethnic bias is given weight by a mass of monographic data,
collected by means of the most advanced statistical and anthropological methods.[5] What most professional social scientists
concerned with the serious study of ethnicity find deplorable
about these works is not their bias—for there is a sense in which all
works in the social science involve some bias—but the attempt to
hide this bias under the banner of "objective science." Invariably,
these works arrive at conclusions that are completely at variance

with the findings of less involved and more theoretically rigorous scholars. The works of Herbert Gans, for example, which constitute a model of the detached, analytic study of ethnicity, point strongly to the conclusions that the vast majority of Americans do share a universal culture; that the basic differences among them are based on class rather than ethnicity; that variations between classes in style of life are reflections of differing living standards and consumption patterns—what Weber called status groups—and that once we control for class, the differences between ethnic groups all but vanish, with only the most vestigial "corner store" kind of peculiarities remaining, along with the remnants of folklore and a few almost "empty" symbols.[6]

Modern American ethnicity is revivalist, then, in the importance it attaches to the value of being different; in the mythology that real differences exist; in the support of these claims by an affirmation of the virtues of segregated living; by the exaggeration and celebration of the social correlates of the urban ghetto; and by the reinvestment of archaic symbols with ideological potency.

The most distressing aspect of this sorry episode in American life, however, is the massive retreat from the universalist ethic by the very group of persons whom one would expect would have been the first to come to its defense: the liberal intelligentsia. How does one explain such intellectual treachery? Where, we want to know, are the humanist thinkers in the realm? What accounts for the present ascendancy of romantic thought and its deformed handmaiden, chauvinism?

In trying to answer the above questions, we must explore two areas of experience. One is the immediate set of social forces which may have induced the proponents of ethnicity to adopt their position. This we may refer to as the sociology of ethnic thought. The second place we must search for an answer is the intellectual tradition that has informed American social thought.

There are four immediate sources of the ethnic revival in

America: the struggle for political rights and equality among the blacks and, other non-white poor; the reaction of the petit bourgeois to the black struggle and to developments in modern American society which seem to be moving against their interests; the alienation of the young, especially the affluent young, joined by the romantic discontent of older, antimodernist intellectuals; and the reaction of the American Jewish community to the threat of assimilation, to the other ethnic groups, and to the state of Israel. Obviously, these four social forces are closely related, each being influenced by and in turn influencing the other three.

The exclusion of black Americans from full participation in American economic and political life was, and still is, the single greatest failure of American civilization. Traditionally, their exclusion was justified on mainly racial terms, so it was inevitable that the blacks, in their struggle for emancipation, would respond on this basis. In addition to the problem of political and economic exclusion, there was the purely internal psychological problem of a negative and demeaning racial and cultural self-image. It was the psychological problem which, more than any other, forced the group to employ the technique of ethnic allegiance.

It seems to be typical of all human groups that psychological compensation can only be achieved by overcompensation. To cure the deep racial hurt and self-contempt it was not enough simply to "prove" by means of black solidarity that blacks were people like everyone else with the same range of beautiful, plain, and ugly or brilliant, average, and dull persons. Sanity and self-respect demanded the celebration of things black, and solidarity demanded the homogenization and loyalty of all. Thus blacks had to believe first that all blacks are beautiful; black culture and "soul" had to be declared superior; and all blacks, no matter what the objective differences, had to become alike, or else be condemned as "Toms."

Black ethnicity was extremely effective in ameliorating the problems of poor self-image as well as certain political and legal disabilities. But in spite of all the rhetoric, it has proven itself to be an almost useless weapon in fighting the major problem of the group: its economic marginality. Indeed, as always, ethnicity has turned out to be a two-edged sword, for one of the major obstacles to black economic progress now is the group's intense ethnicity. Ethnic allegiance works against the interest of the group. First, it has become a form of mystification, diverting attention from the correct kinds of solutions to the terrible economic condition of the group. Many black Americans have failed to see how their fate is inextricably tied up with the structure of the American economy. It is no accident that economics is spurned by almost all Black Studies programs on the campuses, and that black economists and political scientists such as Thomas Sowell and Martin Kilson, who argue strongly for a nonethnic approach to the problem, are dismissed as "Toms."[7] All this, of course, simply plays into the hands of the American establishment, for there is no concerted attack on the economic root cause of the problem—an attack which involves real concessions if it is to be met by means other than repression. Ironically, the cultural and symbolic demands emphasized by most black leaders are all too easily met. It was ridiculously easy for the establishment to respond by changing the color of a few faces in the ads for the "Pepsi generation," by introducing a few network shows in which the traditional role of blacks as clowns and maids was updated (with the added boon that these new "soul" shows have been extremely profitable), by publishing a spate of third-rate books on the greatness of the African tradition, by the glorification of black roots, and, most cruel of all, by introducing into the curriculum of the nation's colleges that strange package of organized self-delusion which goes by the name of Afro-American Studies.

Black American ethnicity has encouraged the intellectual reinforcement of some of the worst sociological problems of the group and an incapacity to distinguish the things that are worthwhile in black life from those that are just plain rotten. The "street culture" of petty crime, drug addiction, paternal irresponsibility, whoring, pimping and super-fly inanity—all of which damage and destroy only fellow blacks—instead of being condemned by black ethnic leaders has, until recently, been hailed as the embodiment of black "soul." Sociologists such as Lee Rainwater and others, who have honestly and sympathetically attempted to analyze the combination of economic and intermediary social forces leading to the massive disintegration of the lower-class urban black family have been condemned as racists, sometimes by the very students they trained.[8] Instead, we find works published proclaiming with pathetic pomposity "the death of white sociology." [9]

As if the ethnic black intellectuals and leaders have not become their own worst enemies, the process of chauvinistic self-delusion has been helped along by a group of white intellectual provocateurs, many of whom like to call themselves "urban anthropologists," who, after a guilt-ridden sojourn in their favorite black ghetto, emerge with the latest "proof" of the argument that the ghetto, but for white exploitation, is a glorious place, rich with vitality, "supportive" black culture, and proletarian romance.[10]

Black ethnicity has prevented the emergence of badly needed leadership both in intellectual and political life. In recent years, the situation has improved considerably in the political arena, and it is no accident that almost all the new faces on the black political scene have quietly dropped ethnic rhetoric. The tradition, however, dies hard among the intellectuals and it is here that we find the greatest failure. The reason is not hard to find. An ethnic ideology has the same effect on the mind as a recently adopted religion. It explains everything (and in so doing explains nothing) by means of a few easily learned, catchy formulas. Its explanations are also easily understood by the masses, so there is a ready audience. Thus ethnicity appeals to both the vanity and the laziness of the intellectual.

Once the right style and the right package of phrases are mastered, the intellectual has no need to think for his living any more. He can throw away his books; indeed, antiintellectualism is part and parcel of the chauvinist intellectual's creed. It is enough to know that all black problems are due to racism; that all whites are untrustworthy; that only blacks can really know and understand the black problem; that white society "owes" it to the blacks to set things right; that black folks must control their own communities and their own schools—to know these thoughts is to know everything.[11]

There is, of course, almost no recognition of the contradictions involved in holding these positions. No one bothers to ask how it is that black self-determination can be reconciled with a conception of black problems which attributes all causes to "white racism"; nor is it ever considered a problem that one should ask for control of one's schools and communities in one breath and attack Irish chauvinists in south Boston for demanding the same thing in the next.[12]

The failure of the black intellectual, (I am thinking here less of the academic and more of the opinion formers) due to the crippling hold of ethnicity, has sadly forced the new black leadership to perform the role which should properly be done by the specialist thinker. Thus it is from the activist leader Jesse Jackson drawing on the humanism of Martin Luther King, that one begins to hear again the call for a reconsideration of the chauvinistic approach. Jackson, a political leader of tremendous skill and effectiveness, should not have been the person to begin such a reconsideration. His time would have been much better spent doing what he knows best. The intellectual poverty of the black intelligentsia, however, has forced him to double as both activist and intellectual. This is most commendable on Jackson's part, but it says little for the condition of black American intellectual life.[13]

Not only has black ethnicity long outlived its usefulness and become a crown of thorns, but it has worked against the interests of blacks in another way, by partly stimulating the emergence of petit bourgeois conservative ethnicity. And this brings us to the second source of the ethnic revival in America. The backlash created by the black ethnic struggle blacks can hardly be held morally responsible for. This backlash, however, has been given support, indirectly, by the very commitment of blacks to their own ethnicity. By continuing to insist on ethnicity as the only path to liberation, blacks have relegitimized ethnicity as a principle of political action. What had become almost prohibited in American political life became respectable once again. For if it was good enough for the blacks, and if the liberals supported it, it surely must be just as good for the lower-middle classes who felt most threatened by the emergence of black demands for greater equality.

Black Americans, then, have found their own weapon used against them. Once the lower-middle-class whites realized that it was now fair play to return to the old technique, the field was wide open for the revival of ethnic politics on a statewide scale. A great deal of white lower-middle-class ethnicity is simply covert antiblack political action, disguised by the use of the famous "code words." It is one of the great ironies of the recent American past that the civil rights movement, which achieved its first major victory with the rejection of segregated education by the Supreme Court, should now have gone full circle with the demand for separate but equal education by white ethnics who use the very arguments they have learned from blacks: ethnic integrity and ethnic control of the neighborhood and its school.

Recently, however, there has been a more sinister development. Certain upper-middle-class forces have joined ranks with the lower-middle class in the call for the preservation of the integrity of the ethnic neighborhood. But they have also taken up and reinforced another favorite theme of the petit bourgeois ethnics: the attack on "big government," on centralization and over-bureaucratization. It is a well-established political fact that the more vulnerable and economically deprived a group, the greater are its chances of improvements from the center and, conversely, the poorer its chances of improvements where power is re-distributed to the periphery. Students of imperial history have long observed this phenomenon. Thus, in Jamaica, the ex-slave population was brutally repressed as long as their former masters remained in control of the internal affairs of the colony. It was not until the imposition of crown colony government and direct rule from the imperial center after the peasant revolt of 1865 that any improvement in the condition of the masses took place.

Black Americans are in much the same situation. Decentralization and the redistribution of power back to the periphery has always meant greater victimization. The attack on big government by both the petit bourgeois ethnic and their upper-middle-class supporters must therefore be viewed as a most dangerous development for black Americans. It is in this aliance that the reactionary nature of white revivalist ethnicity is most evident.

It is therefore tragic that many liberal intellectuals also are calling for an end to "big government." To some extent, this liberal support is due simply to a blind, personal commitment to the virtues of the ethnic neighborhood community. It is also due to a misguided conception of libertarian values. There is no necessary link between the bigness of a state and its threat to basic liberties. Indeed, a big impersonal state may well be a better guardian of libertarian values than a small political unit where ascriptive and familial factors, "cronyism," are more likely to run rampant. There is, however, another reason for the strange liberal support for the white ethnic revival and its attack on "big government." This is the paradoxical attitude of modern American intellectuals to which Edward Shils recently referred:

Most of the dissatisfied intellectuals in the United States are not socialists, whatever may be the hidden and suppressed yearnings deep within their hearts. Many of them, however, believe that only governmental control over resources, governmental allocation, prescription, prohibition and provision can solve irrevocably the problems which face mankind, and can thereby realize the ideals of justice, equality, freedom, material well-being and dignity. They believe this despite their dislike of most American politicians and their abomination of bureaucracy. Therein lies the paradox in the contemporary situation.[14]

There are many other paradoxes in American intellectual life, this being one of the most blatant. They are derived from the propensity of the American intellectual to have his cake and eat it. To Shils's paradox I may, without a moment's thought, add another of equal relevance. While strongly supporting the black struggle for better educational opportunities, white intellectuals have retreated with their families to suburban areas, thereby leaving only the white lower-middle class and proletariat—the least culturally endowed white group—to shoulder the entire burden of integration. Most attempts at incorporating suburban areas into a single school system with the central ghettos are quietly scuttled by these same liberal suburban refugees, with the help of the Supreme Court. With friends like these, any movement must consider itself damned.

The set of personal problems sometimes referred to as the crisis of identity is the third source of ethnicity in modern American life. It is the young, especially the affluent young, who most experience this alienation from self, culture, and tradition, and feel the need to restore it. Erikson has rightly observed that

we cannot separate personal growth and communal change, nor can we separate ... the identity crisis in individual life and contemporary crises in historical development because the two help to define each other and are truly relative to each other.[15]

In the 1960s there developed a special convergence of historical crisis and the crisis of youth which led youth into a desperate search for meaning and roots. There was the coming of what Daniel Bell calls post-industrial society with its superabundance and suburban affluence; and along with it the mindless massacre of the Vietnam War and the profound erosion of faith in the values of industrial civilization among the young and a good many of the not-so-young. There was, in addition, the peculiar demographic development that the sixties coincided with the coming of age of the postwar demographic bulge.[16] Intensifying this quantitative change was another of a more qualitative nature, what Bennett M. Berger, in one of his highly sensitive analyses of today's youths, referred to as the extension of cultural definitions of 'youth' to a period covering at least twenty years and sometimes longer. He adds, "Understandably this may help explain the apparent proliferation of 'new' Zeitgeist and 'new' generation 'movements,' which, if not the creations of precisely 'young' men, are the creations of youthful men with a longer time to be young.[17] Thus, at precisely the time when America was going through its national crisis the population had a larger cohort of young people than at any other period in its history. By weight of sheer numbers, their own personal problems had to be given special attention, as did their views about the state of the society. This identity crisis, which all of us experience in every age, by a fortuitous convergence of events became caught up with the value crisis of the society. The personal crisis of the life process was seen writ large in the collective crisis of a civilization which seemed to have lost its way. The fact that the men who waged the Vietnam war were not racist reactionaries but presumably sane, "liberal" men just like their own fathers, merely reinforced the convergence of the personal and the social among the young.

The first reaction of the younger generation to the crisis of value they faced was to turn to radical politics and the norms of the counterculture. It was a good beginning. The only problem was that America was not really ready for a revolution. The only realistic form of politics available was the black reform movement. There can be no doubt that many of the early victories of the black movement must be attributed to the vigorous support of its young white allies. But it was not long before black ethnicity reacted against this support. Black "pride" and growing separatist sentiment soon created friction and led to the demand for the withdrawal of the young whites.

Cut off from the black movement, the young increasingly diverted their energies to the antiwar movement, along with the escapist resort to drugs. But antiwar escapism was not, and could never have become, a solution to the deep inner problems of alienation. It merely postponed a full confrontation with the problem. As the war waned, the crisis of value reemerged, and the young, or young at heart, reacted in one of several ways: hedonistic escapism, spiritual revivalism, semiapathetic reengagement, and ethnic revivalism.

It is only the last reaction that concerns us here. A growing number of young people have sought refuge in the small face-to-face community. It was a short step from the always fragile and artifical commune to the natural, preexisting ethnic group. Ethnicity seemed the ideal solution to all problems. Above all, it seemed to restore that "lost ... sense of personal sameness and historical continuity," which is typical not only of the personal identity crisis of youth but, as Erikson tells us, of all social crises. The closed, particularistic neighborhood was also the perfect answer to the problems of atomization in modern mass society: It was a place where the individual could feel he belonged and was somehow special. And its certain, traditional values, so familiar, so wonderfully simple yet profound, offered the spiritual support for which drugs, easy sex, and hard rock had simply been temporary palliatives.

The fourth source of the ethnic revival in the United States is the Jewish reaction to recent developments within their own group and in the world outside, one of the most important of these being the creation of the state of Israel, which has become the politico-cultural alter-ego of most Jewish Americans. "After the holocaust," writes Emil L. Fackenheim, "the Israeli nation has become collectively what the survivor is individually." [18] The state of Israel, by its very existence, threatened the moral and psychic foundation of the exilic Jew. His exile, after all, is no longer necessary. Where he lives he lives by choice. Unless he belongs to the Hasidic sect, that special identity which is based on the idea of the eternal return is no longer possible.

The problem has become especially acute for the cosmopolitan, nonreligious Jew who had worked out a rather complex relationship with the more religious and ethnically conscious members of his group. The community of worshippers, from whom he was physically cut off, had become a kind of surrogate home for the liberal cosmopolitan who saw himself as being exiled twice over, from the past and future Israel, and from the more immediate ghetto or synagogue-based community in which he was reared and to which he made his ritual pilgrimages. The creation of Israel was to shatter this tidy compromise between the primordial world of feeling and commitment and the dispassionate world of the liberal intelligentsia or the Gentile marketplace. Israel, for the first time in over two thousand years, made the definition of Jewishness painfully unambiguous.

The cosmopolitan Jew's guilt and pride demanded unswerving support for the state of Israel by every means short of emigration to it. Support for Israel, in short, became the new basis of Jewish identity. In the same way that the traditional community of worshippers had been a surrogate for the unrealized Jewish homeland, so now support for Israel became a surrogate for returning to it.

But the emergence of Israel as the major basis of Jewish identity was to have a paradoxical effect on the more traditional segment of the exilic community. The latter was, ironically, no longer necessary for the nonreligious Jew. One paid one's moral and financial dues to Israel in addition to the ritual trip every now and then, and of course, one rattled the sabre every time the Arab enemy became too restive. To make matters worse, there was the growing embourgeoisment of the Jewish community at exactly the same time that the traditional basis of its identity was shifting.

It is one of the many ironies of Jewish history that too great a success in the host society presents its own special kind of crisis for the traditional exilic community: the crisis of assimilation. It was not just the cosmopolitan intellectuals and upper-middle-class professionals who were now moving out and moving away. A critical mass had joined the outward movement and the signs were there for all to read: startling declines in synagogue attendance; an alarming increase in the rate of intermarriage; a distressing increase in the rejection of traditional Jewish values and community association, especially by the young.

Faced with this growing crisis, the leaders of the traditional Jewish community responded in the only way they knew: by a strong reaffirmation of Jewish ethnicity. In this resurgence of particularism, the Jewish intellectual was put on the spot. As if the pressures were not already great enough, another development complicated matters, something quite new in the experience of the Jewish American, the growing political conservatism of his group.

Jewish political liberalism had many strong roots. "It is true," as Richard J. Israel points out, "that Judaism is not generally interested in democracy, but it is passionately concerned with justice." [19] There was the historical experience of the group itself which would naturally predispose most of its members toward a sympathy with the plight of the oppressed. There was the urban location of the Jewish population, the stronghold of the Democratic party and of the most progressive elements in the Gentile world. As a small minority in a democratic country, it was obviously good politics to ally with those more demographically powerful groups. Traditionally, there was nothing to be gained by an alliance with the politically conservative elements of American society.

All this was to change in recent years. Upper-middle-class status and material affluence naturally breeds complacency and forgetfulness, a forgetfulness reinforced by the declining influence of the traditional religion and its ritualized commemoration of other times, other places, and other statuses. Then there was the growing unpleasantness of black anti-Semitism.[20] In their demand for community control, blacks increasingly turned on the white merchants in their neighborhoods, who, in most cases, happened to be Jewish. Ironically, the black demand for control of local business, so-called black capitalism, was encouraged by none other than Richard Nixon in a stroke of pure malevolent political genius, for it killed several birds with one stone. It won some support from black spokesmen who were foolish enough to believe in such economic idiocy. It intensified black hostility toward the scapegoated local Jewish merchant and diverted attention from the real source of the black economic dilemma, and in turn, alienated Jewish support from the black movement and helped to break the traditional Democratic party alliance between the two groups.

Jewish leaders were now more than ready for the conservatve Republican embrace. The Arab-Israeli war and the sudden realization that the Arab armies were not all incompetent and

Israel not invincible, simply sealed the new conservatism. For Israel's sake the community had to be on good terms with any government, no matter how reactionary, in Washington.

Jewish intellectuals have responded in several ways to this revival of Jewish ethnicity and massive shift to the right by the community. Some have muted their liberalism or have simply taken refuge in silence. Others, a growing number, have given in to the demands of the conservatives and the chauvinists, have returned in sentiment, if not religion, to the Jewish fold, and blindly support the Zionist cause. This group is best represented by the intellectuals centered on *Commentary* magazine, the journal of the American Jewish Committee, which for years was the bastion of all that was finest in Jewish and American liberalism but which, during recent years, has, sadly, retreated to the tribe, taking an uncompromising rightward course.

The net effect of these developments was to intensify what David Riesman once described as the attempt to "erase Jewish marginality wherever found, to normalize the Jewish situation." He wrote further:

Whereas once such efforts were manifested by plastic surgery on "Jewish" noses, they were now manifested by psychic surgery on "Jewish" souls, taking such forms as Zionist nationalism, the religiosity of the self-Judaizing Jews, artificially sustained Jewish and Yiddish usages, and so on. The chauvinistic and normalizing Jews are, in turn quite aggressive against the "homeless cosmopolitan," that is, the margin-hugging Jew who owes his existence to the Enlightenment. . . .[21]

Many, I suspect most, Jewish American intellectuals found it impossible to be silent or to move so overtly to the right. Instead, they responded by taking to its logical conclusion a social philosophy which had been long in the making, especially among such early liberal Jewish theorists as Horace Kallen. It was a social creed whose time had clearly come: what is now called ethnic pluralism.

Ethnic pluralism was the perfect solution for the Jewish

intellectual who wished to maintain the trappings of his liberalism but remain loyal to the group. It served the same function for the formerly liberal members of other ethnic groups who, for other reasons, were also committing themselves to conservative ethnic revivalism. Pluralism fully legitimzes ethnic solidarity. What was formerly a suspect and slightly unpatriotic way of thinking is now being projected as one of the country's major social goals. Pluralism is also, on the surface, a liberal philosophy. It is a creed that is supported, after all, by the most oppressed elements in the society, the blacks and other non-European minorities. Superficially, it could be made to appear the very model of tolerance and the fullest expression of the country's democratic ideals, with each group respecting the values and heritage of all others and their rights to promote and maintain them.

There is, however, nothing in the least bit liberal about the pluralist dogma. It is, in fact, a thinly veiled form of conservatism, and should it become institutionalized as America's new social creed—as it seems on the point of becoming—it would be a disaster not only for the non-white minorities who now misguidedly support it, but for all Americans, and for everything decent and virtuous that this civilization has stood for. What follows is a statement of my main objections to the new dogma.

If our critique of ethnic pluralism is to be fair and persuasive, we must begin by stating the creed in its best form. No one would deny that, of all pluralist thinkers, the most brilliant was the man who was its founder: Horace Meyer Kallen. As Milton R. Konvitz observed in his authoritative review of Kallen's life and works, [22] Kallen embodied all that was best in the Jewish tradition. He was a man of remarkable vitality and presence, a scholar who eschewed the ivory tower of academe for the active life which he informed with a powerful intellect, considerable learning, and humanistic passion. Kallen's philosophy may be seen as a lifelong effort to reconcile the metaphysical pluralism and individualism of Henry James and the other American pragmatists, who were his greatest secular influences, with the secular tradition of Jewish humanism. Kallen was a true intellectual prophet in that although he began writing from before the First World War, his ideas and the problems he sought to overcome are identical with those of present-day secular Jewish and other ethnically involved intellec- tuals, such as Michael Novak. His early life anticipated in an uncanny way the problems of many young people today who, having rejected their ethnic groups for the cosmopolitanism of college life, return to it to find themselves. Kallen, while at Harvard, had abandoned his Jewish identity, but soon he reacted against assimilation. Konvitz writes: "He maintained throughout his life a strong anticlerical suspicion and bias: he rejected Judaism insofar as it is a religion; his anticlericalism and agnosticism became transmuted into Jewish secularism, Jewish culture, Zionism, Hebraism, and cultural pluralism."[23]

Kallen's attempt to reconcile Jamesian metaphysical pluralism with cultural pluralism was a noble effort, but in the end it must be judged a failure. For metaphysical pluralism is strongly rooted in individualism. It refers to the freedom of the individual from the constraints of time and place and culture. It embraces change and eschews traditions. The individual's only loyalties are to his or her own conscience. Indeed, as I shall show shortly, individualism is not only irreconcilable with cultural pluralism, but positively undermines it.

Kallen had too brilliant a mind not to have detected these underlying problems. He remained troubled by the ascriptive nature of membership in the ethnic group. His pluralism was liberal and relativistic in its deep respect for the rights of all other ethnic groups to exist and in its acceptance of the equal worth of other ethnic groups. He also assumed in Konvitz's words, that, "What was true of Jewish difference ... was true as well of all other ethnic-cultural groupings, 'each with its own singularity of form and utterance.' " All these assumptions, however, can be shown to be untenable.

It was Kallen's Hebraic faith that allowed him to live with contradictions. Hebraic faith rejects reason as a basis for under-

standing or of coming to the real truth about man's condition.
Konvitz summarizes Kallen's final acceptance of Hebraic faith as
follows:

> Thus to be a creative American the Jew must be a Jew; and to be a Jew,
> he must be creative both as a Jew and as a human being, one who has
> inherent and inalienable rights, who has freedom and the right to be
> different, and therefore the right to be a Jew: to express the human
> essence as a Jew, to belong to the family of man as one who belongs to
> the family of Jews.[24]

If one replaces the word Jew in the above passage with the
words Polish, Black, Indian, Puerto Rican, etc., one has a perfect
statement of the pluralist ethic, as it is held by all proethnic
Americans who still maintain their liberalism. Later pluralist
thinkers have added little or nothing to Kallen's brilliant exposition of the creed and they have certainly not resolved any of the
problems which, with his far more powerful mind, Kallen left
unsettled. They have, however, popularized the philosophy, given
it a more formal statement, and finally won support and official
approval for it. There is now a National Coalition for Cultural
Pluralism, the official intellectual guardians and promoters of the
new creed and Harry N. Rivlin and Milton J. Gold quote its
official definition of pluralism and comments on it as follows:[25]

> The National Coalition for Cultural Pluralism defined cultural plural-
> ism as:
>
> > a state of equal coexistence in a mutually supportive relationship
> > within the boundaries or framework of one nation of people of diverse
> > cultures with significantly different patterns of belief, behavior, color,
> > and in many cases with different languages. To achieve cultural
> > pluralism, there must be unity with diversity. Each person must be
> > aware of and secure in his own identity, and be willing to extend to
> > others the same respect and rights that he expects to enjoy himself.
>
> Cultural pluralism views the United States as becoming a multicultural
> society in which the different ethnic cultures live in a symbiotic
> relationship which enriches each other.

The authors later added the liberal qualification that: *"Different* means *different,* not *better than* or *worse than."*

I have done, I think, as much justice as I can do to the pluralist creed. Its basic principles are these: First, that America is and should be a society made up of different ethnic groups. Second, that each ethnic group, while different or separate, should be considered equal and treated by the members of different ethnic groups with respect. Third, that this diversity is not only desirable but that it is consistent with individualism; that indeed, American democratic principles are best realized in a respect for such ethnic diversity. It assumes further Kallen's position that what is true of the difference of one ethnic group is true of the difference of other ethnic groups; that is to say, all ethnic groups are capable of living in a symbiotic relationship with each other and, as such, with the totality of ethnic groups which make up the society. Finally, underlying all these assumptions is the relativistic dogma: Others must be judged and understood in terms of their own values and standards if the cultures and traditions of others are to be treated as of equal worth, "not better than or worse than."

I am not for a moment questioning the motives or the honesty of those who hold to the pluralist creed. I do believe that the great majority of Americans who hold this position have come to it in all sincerity.[26] If I argue that the creed is inherently conservative, even reactionary, I do not mean to suggest that many of those who hold it do not believe that it is liberal; what I am stating is that their manifest liberalism is inconsistent with their philosophy. And in emphasizing the dangers of the creed I am not necessarily suggesting that these dangers will be realized by those who hold it under the mistaken belief that they have found support for their liberalism. It will at least be granted, however, that the history of human thought presents innumerable cases of creeds which were promoted in all honesty by men and women of good will and human decency but were taken over and used for evil purposes. There are two reasons why such a distortion of purpose may come about. The creed in question may have been intrinsically good and logically quite consistent, but deliberately distorted by evil persons. Or the creed may have been intrinsically inconsistent and, beneath the surface, potentially dangerous. In the latter case it is the good who hold such creeds who must be judged misguided and guilty of distorting what is intrinsically bad for the purpose of good, whereas the evil users of the creed simply took it to its logical conclusion or exploited its inconsistencies. My argument will be that the creed we call ethnic pluralism falls into the latter category of intellectual malevolence.

Let us begin with the most fundamental philosophical assumption of the pluralist creed, the fact that it is relativistic. The weaknesses and underlying self-contradiction of relativism as the basis of a social and moral philosophy and as a mode of thought have been revealed many times before. Relativism was revived by modern social science, especially by anthropology, as an academic and moral strategy in the study of alien peoples. It asserts that each culture or subculture must be treated on its own terms because of the basic premise that the values, attitudes, and prejudices of each group are determined by that group's own peculiar form of conditioning. Human values, in short, have no absolutes, and those belonging to one group can be taken as no better or worse than those of another.

Now if the values of all men and women are the products and specific attributes of their own groups, and if anthropologists and other relativists are men and women, then anthropologists and other relativists hold values that are the products and specific attributes of their own group. And since relativism is one of the values held by that group who claim to be relativists (there being no absolutes in human values), then relativism is itself the product of a particular group. Thus relativism turns out to be hopelessly self-contradictory, since it asserts the need to view all peoples and their values in their own terms, but in the very act of doing so asserts the need to see other peoples and their values in terms of a specific culture, that of the relativists.

In more precise logical terms, relativism is self-contradictory both in a general categorical sense and in a substantive, specific way. It postulates, on the most general level, a basic negative statement (there is no universal value) that is the implication of its own contradiction (there is at least one universal value, relativism). In more specific, substantive terms, it is also self-contradictory, since it asserts a general value (the values of all peoples are of equal worth), then contradicts it by implying the superiority of the values of the group consisting of relativists (it is good to see other peoples in their own terms), a value clearly not shared by most other peoples, as the researches of the anthropologists themselves have demonstrated.[27]

In an effort to salvage something from the relativistic dogma, a few of its advocates, while conceding its logical contradictions, have argued that as an ideal it is worth pursuing, since it encourages a liberal sense of tolerance toward other peoples. But even on this purely ideological level, relativism turns out to be a risky business. It is often associated with a liberal and tolerant attitude, but it is doubtful whether the association is in any way casual. Tolerance does not require relativism.

Relativism, in fact, can be associated very easily with a reactionary view of the world, and can easily be used to rationalize inaction, complacency, and even the vilest forms of oppression. It is all too easy for the reactionary white South African, or American, to say of the reservation Bantus or Indians, that it is wrong to interfere with their way of life since what might appear to be squalor and backwardness to us may be matters of great virtue to them. Apartheid intellectuals, it should not be forgotten, quite self-consciously rationalize their perverse racial doctrine by appealing to the relativistic dogma. And what is most unnerving is that they do so without the slightest trace of cynicism, a point that Isaac Schapera, the distinguished South African anthropologist, often made in his conversations with me.

Tragically, the relativistic creed, as we have seen, is fast taking root among well-meaning Americans in their efforts to establish a moral basis for interaction in their multiethnic society. The American increasingly uses one of two strategies in his relations with others. One strategy is summed up by the dictum: "Do unto others (belonging to a different ethnic group) as you imagine they would do unto themselves." The other is expressed in the more familiar dictum: "Do unto others as you would wish they would do unto you."

If, however, there are so few shared values between you and all the members of another group that you have to relate to them relativistically, it is hardly likely that what you imagine to be their way of doing unto themselves is going to be right. Only professional anthropologists can pretend to such knowledge and even they have trouble operating with it. In no other area of human relations is the old adage that a little knowledge is dangerous more relevant than in interethnic, especially white-black, relations.

Relativism, further, is often nonreciprocal and easily degenerates into unintended patronage. It is one thing for the white pluralist to attempt to relate relativistically to blacks; how blacks respond to this attempt is quite another matter. As often as not, blacks are not interested in a relative response. Insofar as they become morally involved with whites at all, their main concern is either to judge the white person in much the same way that others are judged, or to judge in the manner that best insures condemnation. The benign relativist, then, is trapped in a patronizing situation, in spite of all his good intentions, for he is implying cultural and moral differences where the other party is refusing to accept the existence of such differences. To his astonishment he will have found that he has exposed himself to the charges of double standards, or moral superiority, or both. What is true of black-white relations stands equally true of black-Puerto Rican, Jewish-Italian, or any other set of relativistic interactions between the members of different ethnic groups.

My next criticisms follow from the above critique of relativism. One of these is the fact that pluralism is socially divisive. No society can survive for long without a common set of values whereby other members can be judged and consensus can be achieved. Intellectual supporters of pluralism strongly deny this, but their arguments are logically unpersuasive or, when empirically grounded, tend to undermine their own position.

From our critique of relativism it should be clear that there is no reason why tolerance should be part of the ethnic tradition of any of the groups that make up the plural society. It is, on the contrary, a well-established fact that many groups define themselves as "chosen peoples," for example, the Jews. Others, such as the blacks, claim that their special manner of behavior among themselves is inaccessible to other people—only black folks are capable of "soul" and whites can never relate successfully or honestly with blacks, because they lack the special mystique which comes only with a black upbringing or, sometimes more crudely, with a black skin. The pluralistis have no response to these claims of "chosenness" or these denials of the possibility of interaction. They are forced to accept as of equal worth, "no better no worse," the very denial of the humanity or nonchosenness of others. Should the pluralist attempt to pass judgment on such denials, the judgment must be based on universal values which transcend all the groups involved, and it is precisely such universal or "mainstream" values which pluralists begin by denouncing. The dilemma I have just described is no mere intellectual critique with little relevance to reality. It is tragically demonstrated in the concessions which otherwise sensible and civilized college presidents have made to chauvinists who have insisted on being quartered separately. Having accepted the pluralist dogma that humanistic values relating to all human beings are no longer possible, such presidents had no choice but to bend their knees and look on helplessly as what they thought were the values of a higher liberalism were taken to their logical conclusion. It would not only be cruel of me to say that it served them right, but also foolish and shortsighted, for any action which denies one segment of humanity, as does segregated living (whether voluntarily or involuntarily), denies the humanity of us all.

Some pluralists simply avoid the illogicality of their position and, instead, point to the fact that Americans, in spite of all their problems, do get along with each other, more or less.[28] But here it can immediately be demonstrated that they get along only where they share a common set of values and pursue goals which are common to the groups involved. In other words, they get along only insofar as they behave in a nonethnic way and relate to each other as individuals who share certain universal values accessible to all. Thus to the extent that the facts of American life show that Americans can and do get along with each other, to that extent do these facts prove that ethnicity is not as important in real life as the pluralists claim it is.

By emphasizing ethnicity, by encouraging its development, pluralist thinkers are emphasizing the very set of developments which will prevent communication between individual members of different groups. In the end—and sadly, we seem already to have reached this point with respect to some groups—the only kind of communication possible will be the formalized interaction of ethnic spokesmen who meet like ambassadors from warring camps during a truce to work out the best ways of living beside each other with the least amount of conflict. Such a state of communal truce is indeed the very most that a society organized on pluralist lines can ever hope for. There can be no such thing as a positive consensus, a search for meaning and purpose that transcends the petty interests of each separate group. This, amazingly, is the position Andrew Greeley, one of the foremost spokesmen for the new pluralism, seems willing to accept. In a recently published dialogue with me, Greeley, after applauding the fact that there has been relatively little ethnic violence in America compared with other ethnically plural societies, adds: "The Southies after all, have not yet invaded Cambridge and tried to massacre the citizenry." [29] It is by means of this incredibly low, one might say base, standard that the pluralists ask us to judge a society which is not only the most powerful and technically advanced in the history of mankind, but one whose leaders also insist on assuming moral leadership in the contemporary world. Pluralism is not only dangerous for Americans; taken to its moral and social conclusions, it is clearly dangerous for the rest of the world.

My third critique of the pluralist creed is that it is politically an inherently conservative doctrine. It can tolerate civil rights, but never any program of action that changes the relative statuses or the absolute position of the various ethnic groups. Thus, at best, it freezes the relative position of the various competing groups: It allows each to veto legislation against its special interests but, by the same token, prevents the deprived groups from making any gains relative to those groups which are better off.[30] And, worse, it encourages unscrupulous political leaders to play off one group against the other, or one collection of groups against another. The vicious and divisive "law and order" rhetoric of the Nixon-Agnew years had nothing to do with law and order, but was an appeal to the worst fears of the white working-class ethnics with respect to blacks and other nonwhite minorities.

The next criticism of the pluralist doctrine I shall call the generosity fallacy. It is the well-intentioned view, held by those pluralists who are most sincerely liberal, that what is true of one ethnic group with respect to its relation with the society at large is true of all other ethnic groups. Yet, ethnic groups are of different types and relate to the wider society in fundamentally different ways. The fact that most symbiotic ethnic groups have been able to achieve enormous success in the wider society while maintaining their ethnic loyalties does not mean that all other types of ethnic groups can do the same.

Indeed, a strong commitment to an ethnic culture, or what is believed to be a coherent ethnic culture, can, as I have argued with respect to black Americans, work against the other, more pressing objectives of the members of the group. I have pointed out earlier that *in the long run,* if ethnicity does not work in the interests of group members, it will either be discarded or a new culture adopted while the group shifts the basis of its ethnicity to other means of support; and that it is only where a group faces grave survival risks on ethnic terms that it will persist with its ethnicity in the face of conflicts with other, especially class interests. Herein lies the tragic failure of leadership among black Americans and several of the other non-European ethnic groups. Their leaders have persuaded them that they continue to face survival and, indeed, genocidal risks in American society. Paranoia has actually become an acceptable style of leadership among many non-European ethnic groups and at least one respectable black psychologist has asserted that paranoia is functional for blacks. Thus the commitment to ethnic separatism is prolonged long after it has not only ceased to serve any purpose but become counterproductive.

In the long run we are certain that most blacks will come to see the dangers of ethnicity and, on so doing, will reject it. There are already signs that a growing minority are coming to just such a conclusion. Reports from many colleges suggest that separatist sentiments are waning. And a small but significant body of popular leaders are moving in an antiethnic direction. The late Martin Luther King and Malcolm X both saw the dangers involved in the years just before their assassinations. More recently, the Reverend Jesse Jackson and the former nationalist poet Leroi Jones have both come out against ethnic chauvinism. The majority of the new generation of black politicians have also steered clear of a too close indentity with ethnic rhetoric. The problem, however, is one of timing. The overwhelming majority of black and other non-European ethnic leaders still remain strongly committed to the principles of ethnic pluralism. And the problem is that ethnic identity is powerful enough to institutional-ize the culture which it uses as the basis of its expression. Thus it may well happen that if blacks are too slow to realize the dangers involved, by the time they do come to such a realization and decide to abandon ethnicity they will have found that their formerly idealized cultural patterns will have become a yoke around their necks.

Middle-class ethnic groups such as the Chinese in the Carib-bean or the Jews in America have far greater flexibility in this regard precisely because they are more educated, often more secular, and because their own ethnic styles promote competence. It becomes a relatively easy matter for them to throw off the vestigial cultural or symbolic trappings of ethnicity should they choose to do so, and to live in what Morris Janowitz has called "the community of limited liability."[31] An educationally deprived ethnic group will find such a feat incomparably more difficult and painful. The problem is similar to that of a developing nation which, having abandoned nationalism and traditional values and fully committed itself to modernization, finds that the traditional values it has revived during its nationalist, decolonization period, become the major obstacle to its development.

It is therefore not true, as liberals believe, that all groups are different in the same way. Such generosity is laudable, but it betrays a sociological naivete that, in the end, can only hurt those ethnic groups for whom ethnicity can only have been of temporary political value and, having served its purpose, has become an obstacle to progress and full participation in their society.

My last critique of pluralism is that of the fallacy of moral diversity. This criticism refers to the claim of many liberals that pluralism is not only consistent with, but promotes, greater individualism through greater diversity. Pluralists defend diversity on two moral grounds. One, the more naive, is that diversity is good as an end in itself. It is better to have a society with a varied population, since this adds to the vitality, interest, and possible range of human interaction. How much better it is, we are told, to live in a city such as Boston in which, within a few blocks, it is possible to move from the lively Mediterranean clutter of the Italian North End to the throbbing vitality of Roxbury and, not much further on, the impish charm of old Southie. The suicidal nature of such a promenade, whatever its sociological delights, should be obvious to anyone who has had anything to do with Boston lately or, for that matter, any of America's pluralist cities. But even if there were no risks to life and limb involved in this naive defense of pluralism, it can be questioned whether diversity of this kind is intrinsically good. The second, more sophisticated, defense of pluralism is the argument that it protects the rights of individuals to be different. A respect for the values and customs of other peoples is certainly more desirable than bigotry and ethnocentrism.

In response to these two moral defenses of pluralism, let me say first that I, too, strongly believe that diversity is good and that tolerance is one, if not the greatest, of all virtues. The problem is this: Diversity of what kind? And tolerance of what?

Once we ask these fundamental questions, we immediately come to the heart of the contradiction in the liberal defense of pluralism. For it turns out that this defense centers wholly on social groups rather than on individuals. When liberals today talk about a diverse society, they mean a diversity of ethnic groups; and when tolerance is mentioned, it refers to tolerance not of other individuals but of the groups to which they belong.

This defense of pluralism not only neglects individuality; much worse, an emphasis on group diversity and group tolerance works against a respect for individuality. The fallacy originates in the failure to recognize a basic paradox in human interaction: The greater the diversity and cohesiveness of groups in a society, the smaller the diversity and personal autonomy of individuals in that society.

This follows logically from certain basic principles of social life. It is a commonplace of sociology that in those groups which are of the informal, communal type (as opposed to formal organizations, such as bureaucracies), group strength is a function of the degree to which individual members perceive themselves to share a common set of values, live by a common set of norms, and aspire to a common set of ideals. People feel "together" because they feel alike, or think they feel alike.[32] Thus South Boston is a strong ethnic community because "we in Southie all think alike; we are one." And every "conscious" black person now believes that the strength of the group requires that all blacks become "brothers" and "sisters." The strength and cohesiveness of an ethnic group, then, is bought at the expense of the individuality of members of that group. It was Georg Simmel who first articulated this principle in his famous proposition:

...other things being equal, there is, as it were, an unalterable ratio between individual and social factors that changes only in forms. The narrower the circle to which we commit ourselves, the less freedom of individuality we possess; however, this narrower circle is itself something individual, and it cuts itself off sharply from all other circles precisely because it is small. Correspondingly, if the circle in which we are active and in which our interests hold sway enlarges there is more room in it for the development of our individuality; but *as parts of this whole* we have less uniqueness: the larger whole is less individual as a social group. Thus the levelling of individual differences corresponds not only to the relative smallness and narrowness of the collectivity, but also—or above all—to its own individualistic coloring.[33]

The greater the number of ethnic groups in a society, the greater the tendency toward cohesiveness within each group. The reasons for this are not hard to find. The legitimation of ethnicity in a society reinforces the tendency for ethnic groups to become interest groups. The more ethnic groups there are, the greater the number of groups competing for the scarce resources of society's power and wealth. It is the strength and cohesiveness of the ethnic group—the degree to which it can act "as one"—which determines its success in the competition for such resources. Therefore, as the competition becomes keener, as more and more ethnic groups enter the system, the tendency will be for greater cohesiveness in each ethnic group.[34] Take, for example, the manifesto of Italian ethnicity published in *The New York Times* by Michael Suozzi, director of community affairs and education of the Italian American Center for Urban Affairs: "Italian-Americans are learning through bitter experience that this is a society that rewards only those who organize themselves into political-economic blocs that exert irresistible pressure in all areas of government and private enterprise." Suozzi later concludes: "We know that America does not give to the weak and disunited. It is our intention to unite every Italian-American community in the United States to reach the final realization of the promise that the newcomers of 1880 had sought."

The depressing conclusion to be derived from these two basic propositions should now be clear. Increasing ethnic cohesiveness implies increasing individual conformity, "groupism," or declining individuality. Increasing ethnic diversity implies increasing group cohesiveness. Therefore, increasing ethnic diversity implies declining individuality. Group diversity, in short, is antagonistic to individual diversity and autonomy.

Several objections have been directed against this last critique of ethnicity. The first is that ethnic groups have been the source of political liberation for many groups and, as such, have worked for the freedom of the individual. I have indicated at many points in this work that during certain periods in the historical development of some groups ethnicity has been of temporary value in achieving the goal of equal political and legal rights. This has been true of almost all adaptive ethnic groups such as those of ancient Rome and, more recently, the European ethnic groups in late nineteenth- and early twentieth-century America, as well as blacks during the late fifties and early sixties of the present century. I have emphasized the temporary and transitional nature of this political and legal function. There is no necessary relationship between politico-legal liberation achieved by means of ethnic mobilization and the liberation of the individual from particularistic group pressures. The right to vote or to equal treatment under the law in no way implies a diminution of the ethnic solidarity which may have made such rights possible. It is, indeed, usually the case, as we have seen with black Americans, that the loss of individual freedom from group pressures, what Riesman once called "groupism," [35] is the price to be paid for legal and political freedom. Such a price, I am arguing, is often too great, and at times can amount to the eventual loss of all rights and freedoms. Thus, those "ethnic" Germans who lived in Austria and Poland before the Nazi occupation were certainly politically and racially "liberated" by their fellow ethnic conquerors. But what a "liberation." And what a price they, not to mention millions of other persons, paid both with their minds and their lives.

My final critique of ethnicity is a moral, not a sociological, one. My basic assumption is that individuality is a more desirable state of being than conformity and that, therefore, anything which tends to reduce individuality even as an ideal is undesirable. To argue, as Roy P. Peterson does, that "ethnic pluralism ... is a fact of life for a substantial number of Americans," and that "individual autonomy in such situations cannot produce substantial changes; cohesive ethnic groups ... should, can and will continue to do so," [36] is moral obtuseness of the worst order—what ethical theorists used to call the naturalist fallacy. Organized crime is an established fact of American life. We do not, on this ground, criticize those who condemn it.

It is most ironical that Ronald McAllister,[37] in criticizing my position, should have appealed to the sociology of George Simmel, for no other sociologist has explored with greater depth the nature and meaning of individuality and has shown how it is constrained by certain kinds of groups. In his famous treatise on *Conflict,* Simmel shows how conflict is itself "a form of "sociation." [38] He distinguishes conflict from mere indifference, arguing that the former is "positive" and can be seen to "cause or modify interest groups, unifications, organizations." Societies, to survive, need both the forces of consensus as well as the motor force of constructive or positive conflict. Simmel continues:

Just as the universe needs "love and hate," that is, attractive and repulsive forces, in order to have any form at all, so society, too, in order to attain a determinate shape, needs some quantitative ratio of harmony and disharmony, of association and competition, of favorable and unfavorable tendencies.[39]

Those who support ethnic differences, however, will find little comfort from Simmel, for he goes on to discuss the limits of conflict as a constructive force, and it is here that his analysis completely refutes ethnicity. For there are "borderline" and extreme cases in which conflict leads to disintegration. One such case is that in which conflict is "exclusively determined by subjective feelings, where there are inner energies which *can* be satisfied only through fight." In such cases, the resolution of conflict through "its substitution by other means is impossible." [40] Ethnic conflicts, by virtue of their emotional intensity, are exactly of such nature, as the seemingly mindless violence in Northern Ireland, Lebanon, and South Boston clearly demonstrate.

A second principle articulated by Simmel also argues strongly against ethnicity. He argues that human beings share two basic kinds of commonality: "common qualities and common membership in larger social structures," and he notes that "a hostility must excite consciousness the more deeply and violently, the greater the parties' similarity against the background of which the hostility rises." [41] When the desire to "get along under all circumstances is lacking . . . people who have many common features often do one another worse or 'wronger' wrong than complete strangers do." [42] Now when we consider the remarkable commonality of class qualities such as economic interests and consumption patterns shared by working-class whites and blacks in the United States, we immediately recognize the truth and implications, in structural terms, of Simmel's remarks. Ethnic differences and the glorification of these differences become that small yet highly explosive difference which intensifies antagonisms and destroys all awareness of common experiences and interests. In the end, of course, only one party—the establishmentarian third—benefits from such irreconcilable antagonisms.

Mark Granovetter, the distinguished network theorist, has attempted to use another, closely related principle of Simmelian sociology in arguing against my position.[43] Simmel, in his piece "Group Expansion and the Development of Individuality," argued that: "Individuality in being and action generally increases to the degree that the social circle encompassing the individual expands." [44] I am in complete agreement with this. Granovetter, somewhat ingenuously, argues that the typical ethnic group in America can be interpreted as a similar kind of group expansion. Ethnic groups, he argues, are really "cliques," and in the relation of members to those of other ethnic groups "there is a sense in which the ethnic sameness is irrelevant, a red herring." In defining the ethnic group in America, Granovetter with uncharacteristic tendentiousness speaks of the widest possible level of ethnic allegiance—that vague statistical abstraction which exists on the total societal level. From this he moves to the polar extreme of the intimate primary group. This will not do, for it neglects that important intermediate level of ethnic allegiance which may be called the functioning ethnic group. By this I mean a regionally demarcated, communally conscious, subsocietal group, membership in which is ascriptively determined by the possession of certain *believed-in* qualities such as race, religion, national provenance, or shared cultural patterns. This I distinguish from the ideally perceived ethnic group, which rarely comes into being and which, when it does, operates only for the attainment of specific objectives. Normally the idealized ethnic group exists only as a figment, but an important and dangerous one, in the minds of alienated intellectuals and opportunistic politicians.

There can be no doubt that there has been an increase in the significance of the functioning ethnic community in America in recent years. I agree with Granovetter that ethnicity is not the primary or ultimate explanation of the busing problems in South Boston, but my major concern is with ethnicity as a thing-in-itself. Ethnicity per se is wrong in what it demands of individuals and in the way it contradicts and undermines many of our most basic moral principles. It is only a certain kind of pseudoscientific arrogance that has led people to think that because something is not causally significant it is not morally important. By the way, most statistically oriented social scientists share this arrogance with all vulgar Marxists and other crude determinists. In ethical terms, it is enough that blacks and the Irish in Boston relate to each other in ethnic terms, explain and understand each other in such terms, and articulate their underlying problems in such a manner for us to condemn their behavior. And, of course, to the extent that each group sees itself in such terms they are even more open to our criticism. A "cognitive map" it should be understood, is first and foremost a moral statement.

The effect of an ethnically induced action, while it may have minor consequences for the actors in question, and as such is not a dominant theme in their lives, may have major consequences for other groups, forcing such outgroup members to respond in a predominantly ethnic manner. This invariably happens where ethnic groups are not competing on equal terms. Thus it takes only a few ethnically motivated acts on the part of that tiny

fraction of the Boston Irish community which dominates the
Boston school committee to perpetuate the miserable school
conditions of black ghetto children in that city. Blacks are thereby
forced to respond in a continuously ethnic manner in order to
redress this grievance. A minor theme in the politically dominant
group generates a dominant theme in the politically subordinate
one.

To be morally consistent, one must deplore such ethnic salience
in the behavior and attitude of blacks. One would hope, too, that
they would explore nonethnic means of reaction, since such
nonethnic responses are not only likely to be morally less
deplorable in their internal consequences but in the long run
educationally more effective. Even so, the extenuating circumstances, in the case of the blacks, must weigh heavily in any
judgment on the group. Quite the opposite is true in our
assessment of the aggressor community which stimulated the
ethnic response in the outgroup by its infrequent but devastating
acts of ethnic viciousness.

While Granovetter and I may strongly disagree on the extent of
the problem, we are both in agreement in our emphasis on the
primacy of structural factors in explaining, ultimately, the origins
and persistence of ethnic problems. Ethnicity cannot, in the final
analysis, be explained in teleological terms. Nor can it explain, in
a primary way, the group tensions often associated with it.

Finally, my last critique can in no way be taken as a criticism of
all forms of group life, as Ronald J. McAllister claims. My
criticism was directed rather at a certain kind of group association: the closed, particularistic group which demands strong
conformity from its members, the kind of ascriptively defined
group which Ferdinand Toennies classified as *gemeinschaft* and
within which members interact on the basis of what Durkheim
called "mechanical solidarity." In contrast with this kind of group
is the open, freely willed *gesellschaft* association, which recruits its
members on the basis of achievable criteria and in which
participation is assumed to be voluntary and complementary.
Such groups assume individual differences, and integration is

achieved not by means of the sameness of members but by means of their complementary differences, what Durkheim called "organic solidarity." The development of what have been called "communities of limited liability" indicates that in the absence of chauvinistic provocation this is the normal thrust of American society.

Autonomy does not imply isolation. But in a free society that places a high value on individuality, a humanistic version of the open, consciously created community must be considered the most desirable form of group life. Liberalism, if it amounts to anything, must mean the freedom of the individual to choose his or her allegiances and to develop to his or her maximum potential with a minimum of economic, cultural, and social constraints. To each according to his or her need; from each according to his or her ability. This implies, politically, an egalitarian society, since only in such a society are the nonhuman constraints of poverty eliminated. And it implies, morally, at least two restraints on my freedom with regard to other individuals: one, that I am not free to participate in groups which impose entry requirements that make it impossible for all individuals to join solely according to their ability; second, that I am not free to participate in groups which demand undue conformity (for example, ethnic groups or political groups, such as some communist parties), which constrain my own individual development in whatever way I choose, since the legitimation of such a development, implied in my consent, allows for the majority of people in my society to accept this as a principle of total social organization.

Defenders of ethnic pluralism like to see signs of progress in the movement from Anglo-Saxon domination to ethnic pluralism. What they forget is that it is an even easier step from ethnic pluralism to conformist totalitarianism. The alternative to ethnic domination is not ethnic pluralism, for the cancer is not healed but simply goes into a dispersed remission. The only meaningful alternative is the universalist culture of a democratic and egalitarian state.

CHAPTER 7

Modernity, Universalism and Development: A Clarification

The problems of modernity and ethnicity are closely related to problems of economic backwardness and development.

In talking about modernity and universal cultures, I am not adopting a neoevolutionary mode of explanation. While I have, for example, learned much from Talcott Parsons [1] and borrowed many of his insights, my position remains far removed from his, as the following remarks should make clear.

I am not suggesting that all areas of the universal culture will be the same for all societies that adopt industrialism. I made a clear distinction between the symbolic area and the underlying structural imperatives of industrial culture. I believe that industrial culture will generate a substratum of social patterns all industrial societies share. To give a few examples, an industrial society cannot work if people do not change from traditional to more regulated rhythms of work; people must learn to get to work on time, whatever sacred views they may hold about the correct relationship between the rising of the sun and the rising of the human spirit; they must acquire greater literacy, however much such literacy undermines traditional cosmologies; they must acquire specialized skills, however satisfying the activities of the materially self-sufficient person; they must recognize the rights of women to greater independence outside the household economy, however dearly held the traditional sexist views on the matter; they must abandon traditional conceptions of ritual purity with respect to other groups if a modern transportation system is to work; they must accept the rules of bureaucratic structures; they must be willing to migrate from the regions of their birth; they must increasingly abandon familial favoritism in favor of generally accepted standards of competence; they must forego the preservation of a large number of extended kin-ties; and they must accept the inevitable drift toward a more secular view of the world. These are only a few of the imperatives which students of industrialization have demonstrated, to my satisfaction, as the inevitable correlates of the choice of industrialism.[2] And it would be both foolish and tragic to deny their necessity or to minimize the numerous social and personal problems they bring in their train.

Even so, the political context within which these basic changes come about, and the distribution of the increased income generated by industrialism are not imperatives, as many of the functionalists and neoevolutionists seem to think. Laissez-faire capitalism is not the only context within which industrialism can develop. Judging from the evidence of the developing world, it would now seem to be the worst possible political context, as the dismal failures in Puerto Rico and several South American and Asian societies clearly indicate. Nor is there anything in the nature of industrialism requiring gross inequalities or dehumanizing conditions of work. So even at the most basic structural level there is room for differences, for varying degrees of humanistic intervention. In the final analysis, it is people who make change and the choice is up to them to select a substructure which while materially successful degrades human beings as in Korea or Brazil or one which serves the interests of the entire population as in Cuba and Tanzania.

With respect to the second major area of the industrial culture, the symbolic, we find that the possibilities of variation are even greater. When I speak of a universal culture, I refer not to a world culture, but to the values that are held to be universal by the members of a particular civilization. Since I am not a relativist, it is obvious that I hold the view that there are values which apply to all human beings. Such values are quite independent of the presence or absence of an industrial base and a start has already been made in identifying them.[3] But it is true that as more and more societies become industrialized, and as the peoples of the earth come closer to each other through better communications and an increased sharing of similar structural problems, the need to recognize and articulate such universal core values in symbolically meaningful ways will become ever greater.

David Riesman has expressed this position more eloquently than I can:

... the most important passion left in the world is not for distinctive practices, cultures and beliefs, but for certain achievements—the technology and organization of the West—whose immediate consequence is the dissolution of all distinctive practices, cultures and beliefs. If this is so, then it is possible that the cast of national characters is finished: men have too many to choose from to be committed to one, and as their circumstances become more similar, so will many attributes held in common, as against those unique to particular countries. Increasingly, the differences among men will operate across and within national boundaries, so that already we can see, in studies of occupational values in industrial societies, that the group characters of managers or doctors— or artists—becomes more salient than the group character of Russians or Americans or Japanese, or indeed the conscious ideologies held in these societies.[4]

However, one may see these basic world-related values as a symbolic base very similar to the imperatives of the structural substratum of industrialism. Between societies, the range of symbolic variation in the expression of these humanistic core values is vast. Thus Japanese, African, or Latin American societies can express these underlying universal values symbolically in different outward forms, creating in this way different "worlds," to use Simmel's phrase, worlds which, however, are united in their commitment to an underlying humanism and its core values or absolutes. It is my belief that to the extent that the symbolic structure of a particular "world" faithfully expresses a humanistic substratum, to that extent will it cease to be nationalistic. Thus my concession that different "worlds" are possible in the symbolic signata of different societies, is in no way a concession to nationalism; it is, rather, on the one hand, a rejection of uniformity, and, on the other hand, a reaffirmation of humanism, for the concession assumes that the different signata signify the same valuational signans or core values.

The situation is somewhat different within state boundaries. Within the state the basic units are not the subcultures of different ethnic or regional groups, but as Simmel would say, the "subjective cultures" of individuals. Within societies it is individuals that are being thrown upon each other, so to speak, and the critical relationship is between the universal culture and the individual culture. There is a need for an outward and an inward movement away from particularistic ethnic and regional cultures. The inward movement will be toward the individuality of freedom based on equality.* Such individuality will allow for the emergence of creative persons who, in their interactions in voluntary groups or even in their struggles with themselves, generate the subjective cultures that will become the new raw material upon which the universal culture will draw.

This brings me to the second critical difference between my conception of a universal culture and that of the neoevolutionists. There is nothing immanent about the emergence of the universal culture as I see it. It is something wrought by men and women in their struggles within themselves and their relationships with each other. To some extent I share George Homans' view that a culture can be seen as a kind of economy. What emerges is the result of the conscious choices of freely acting and interacting individuals. But I immediately depart from Homans in my view that the economy analogy must be specified to mean a planned economy and not a laissez-faire system. Indeed, with this qualification in mind, it can now be argued that the universal culture that has so

* This will be discussed at greater length in Chapter 9.

far emerged in America, though better than nothing, and certainly worth supporting if the alternative is a return to ethnic pluralism, suffered from the laissez-faire manner of its development. To be sure, the consequences of laissez-faire in cultural development are nothing as iniquitous as those in the economic base, for the great difference between symbolic and tangible goods is that tangible goods are unfree and unequally shared, while symbolic goods are free and equally distributed. Nor is my objection to a laissez-faire approach in the development of the universal culture due to any respect for ethnic representation. It is due to my fear, rather, that a universal culture might emerge which distorts the ends of humanity in the same way that the material ends of people have been distorted in its application to the economic sector.

Finally, my position differs from the neoevolutionists in its emphasis on change. Not slow, immanent, blind change, but change that varies in its pace according to human needs. This is already implied in my position that individuals and voluntary groups—and not some mystical "process of selection"—will determine the universal culture. In my "world," as many million symbolic flowers will bloom as there are free, creative individuals. From these millions, some will achieve ascendancy in the "planned economy" of the universal culture with the transience of dress styles, while others will be more lasting, like the plays of a Beckett, the novels of a Bellow, or the melodies of a Coltrane.

One final set of problems needs to be cleared up—the relationship between modernity and development, that is the growth of economic security and independence of a group of persons, an economically deprived minority, class, or an economically backward state.

There is much heated argument about this relationship among social scientists. A good deal of the debate, however, revolves around two fallacies. The first is what I shall call the "cargo-cult" fallacy. The sociologist Everett Hagen [5] and the social psychologist David McClelland [6] are among the most prominent purveyors of this error. Peter Worsley, in his brilliant study of the shock of cultural contact in Melanesia,[7] describes how the tribesmen, amazed by and envious of the incredible standard of living of the colonial administrators, yet totally unable to comprehend much less accept the vast civilizational network that supported the Europeans' way of life, came to the conclusion that there was a simple, magical, causal relationship between certain of the observable behavior patterns and life styles of the colonial administrators and their enormous affluence. Thus the cargo cult leaders believed that by dressing up in the uniform of the administrators and by sitting behind a desk on a verandah scribbling away, even though illiterate, they would find a cargo of goods miraculously appearing from the big silver bird from the sky.

Now one can understand how confused tribesmen, going through the pangs of cultural shock, could come to such a bizarre conclusion, but it says little for the scientific status of social science that some of its practitioners could commit the same intellectual error. Yet this is exactly what Hagen, McClelland, and others in their school have done. They have observed that certain values and life styles are invariably associated with modernity and development and have concluded that in order to promote development these values and styles must first be adopted.

However, their critics, in dismissing their logic, often back themselves into an equally serious error. In rejecting the view that values associated with modernity are preconditions for a modern, developed society, they assert that these values are not necessarily related to economic development;[8] indeed at least one critic has gone so far as to argue that a traditional set of values is the best precondition for development.[9]

Both are wrong. The confusion lies in failure to see that an imperative is not a precondition. The set of values which constitute modernity are imperatives in being required *by* development, but they are not required *for* it. It is quite reasonable to argue that anything which stands in the way of their emergence will also stand in the path of development, not because they are the causes of development but because rejection of them implies a rejection of those underlying factors—whatever they may be—that promote development. A commitment to modernity is, quite possibly, a significant indicator of a commitment to changes that promote development. But it is not necessarily such an indicator; and it is never a cause of development.

There are many reasons why this is so, but perhaps the most important is that modern values can be learned by those who are currently underdeveloped and economically dependent from those groups or societies which are currently developed or independent.[10] This learning process, however, may, and often does, take place within a socioeconomic context which remains constant and which is stacked against any real and meaningful change in the condition of the learners. Herein lies the great difference between Third World countries currently trying to develop and the advanced Western societies during the late seventeenth and eighteenth and nineteenth centuries, when they were going through the process of development. Herein, too, lies the critical difference between the European ethnic groups who developed in the more flexible society that was the United States at the turn of the century and the black and other Third World minorities now attempting to achieve some greater measure of development. Until the underlying, structurally determined state of dependency changes, it is utterly futile to simply transmit the cultural package—the styles and values—of modernity in the hope that this will promote development.[11]

The second of the two fallacies mentioned earlier is the reductionist error. The sociologist Alex Inkeles and his students are most guilty of it. Inkeles does not make the crude error which the cargo-cultists do of assuming that by simply teaching people the values of modernity development and its rewards will miraculously emerge. But the only reason he does not do so is because his objectives are less ambitious. For he is less concerned with the task of promoting development and is more involved with the description of development as a process of change. Even so, his basic assumption remains untenable, for he is clearly of the opinion that a society is modern or even developed to the degree that its members are modernized. This is simply not true. A modern society is not simply a collection of modern individuals. And it is most certainly not necessarily a developed society.[12] Jamaica, Trinidad, Barbados, and Puerto Rico are all societies in which substantial majorities are modern, but they are not modern societies, and in economic terms they remain backward. Indeed the great tragedy of these societies over the past two or so decades has been that as their populations have become increasingly modern their economies have become increasingly dependent and underdeveloped. As Michael Barratt Brown points out: "The problem for the underdeveloped nations is that underdevelopment is not non-development but a distortion of development." [13]

The reasons are the same as those mentioned earlier, namely, that there has not yet been a serious assault on the underlying structural state of economic dependency on the advanced industrial economies. But there is one further point to note. Marxist and other critics are right in emphasizing the economic state of dependency as the crucial factor in explaining poverty and backwardness—for example, the unequal terms of trade between rich and poor countries and the condition of structural unemployment among blacks—but one finds something curiously wanting in these analyses.[14] For after specifying the structural constraints which prolong dependency, they simply call for a change in this state of affairs and let the matter drop.

If the poverty of the oppressed is so much a function of their dependency on the rich, and if the rich so benefit from this state of affairs, how is the situation to be changed? Marxists, when pressed, either remain silent on this issue or call vaguely for some kind of revolution or, worse, resort to the position that real change can only come about by changing the economies of the rich countries. This kind of argument has always struck me as reflecting the worst kind of intellectual arrogance. And it betrays an imperialist mentality to boot! When one reflects on the healthy, powerful, and increasingly conservative state of the advanced industrial societies, it would seem that the wait of the Third World for the world socialist revolution advocated by Immanuel Wallerstein will not only be long but eternal.[15]

It is clear that sooner or later we must go beyond Marxian structuralism. Eventually, human beings must be brought back into the picture. And it is perfectly obvious that these men and women can only come from the underdeveloped world or the underdeveloped minorities. But this is in no way an argument in favor of the view that we must first modernize men and women before we can create a modern and developed society. What we consider critical is not the imitation or learning of the modernity package—that bridge will have to be crossed in due course, and its pangs and its rewards experienced. But, first, a commitment to change, to the idea of change itself;[16] then, second, an understanding of the nature of the change required, namely structural change which, almost by definition, means radical change. "The tradition of all the dead generations weighs like a nightmare on the brain of the living," Marx wrote,[17] but it is clear that he was thinking primarily of European peoples. Ironically, it is perhaps one of the greatest advantages of many Third World peoples that the dislocation of recent centuries has reduced the weight of previous generations. Perhaps that is why a West Indian radical such as the economist Lloyd Best could declare: ". . . development has to be concerned with how man can outwit Fate. That is what it is about." [18]

But the opportunity to defy fate will never be seized if the underdeveloped persist in their ethnic and nationalistic allegiances, for they merely prolong the nightmare of tradition. Ethnicity works against the development of a truly modern and developed society, then, not because it rejects modernity but because its implicit or explicit rejection of modernity is symptomatic of other, more crucial rejections: the rejection of a viable state apparatus; the rejection of a clear understanding of the real structural basis of poverty and backwardness; the rejection of a commitment to change and the future as opposed to tradition and the past; and the rejection of a commitment to struggle along lines that are meaningful and effective in removing dependency rather than along paths that are particularistic, self-deluding, and ultimately counterrevolutionary.[19]

II

DOCTRINE: THE INTELLECTUAL ROOTS OF WESTERN ETHNICITY

Fact influenced and, if one may say so, enriched doctrine, but doctrine also, in its turn, determined the conditions in which fact developed. Both acted and reacted upon each other in such a complex way that it is often impossible to discern which is cause and which is effect, or to perceive whether the facts are expressing doctrine or the doctrine is merely a reflection of facts. We shall therefore have to follow successfully the development of doctrine and that of fact—without however forgetting that the two things cannot be separated.

Maurice Goguel, *The Primitive Church*

Faith cannot debate with faith because they have no ultimate common ground. Faiths can only rail at each other. Yet all are human things and we can analyze them. The acceptance of faith is a free act, and we cannot compel any man to believe one vision rather than another. However, we can show up the inadequacies of some faiths for the human situation. With this done, a given faith loses much of its recruiting power.

Gustave Weigel, *The Modern God*

CHAPTER 8

The Universal and the Particular
in Western Social Thought

Beneath the numerous currents running through the history of Western social thought is one great idea which, however frequently suppressed, distorted, or violated, remains the supreme intellectual achievement of the civilization. This is the tradition of universalism, the idea of the brotherhood of mankind, the psychic unity of the human race, and the equality of man's and woman's worth.

It would be going much too far to claim that the idea is unique to the West. For not only does the experience of Islamic civilization challenge such a claim, but the brief and glorious reign of the idea in Egypt fourteen centuries before Christ under the extraordinary tutelage of Ikhnaton, whom L. A. White has justly called the "first prophet in history," also robs the West of the right to claim that it was the first civilization to have conceived it. But in no other civilization has this noble idea taken root to the same degree; and nowhere else has it received such mutual intellectual support from both the secular and the sacred minds.

It is an idea that the West has found difficult to live with. Its beauty, born in the very germ of Christendom, has been buried in endemic prejudice, religious bigotry, economic iniquity, and political conservatism. Those who have recognized it have found it swept away from their consciousness by the prevailing or reacting wizardry of parochialism. When the princely forces of the Enlightenment finally fitted its truth to the Western ethos the reaction that set in—what, with profound historic irony the West has come to call romanticism—was so brutal and prolonged that the idea had soon to go in hiding, surfacing occasionally over the past two hundred years in various pathetic intellectual disguises, but no sooner recognized than ushered back to obscurity.

After making another brief but promising reappearance in the civilizational promise that was once America, the intellectual forces of parochialism now man the barricades against it. Legions of particularistic minds, in the intellectual cave, victims of what Jefferson once called their "monkish ignorance," now call the faithful to another rally.

In order to understand the origins and development of universalism and particularism, it is necessary to place them within the context of the wider intellectual traditions to which they both belong and which they help to define. To do so, we must contrast two approaches to truth, to the ways of knowing it, and to the nature of that which is known.

Richard Kroner is correct in seeing reason and revelation as belonging to two essentially competing intellectual spheres. Speculation, he argues, is the work of reason and is essentially secular, whereas revelation or faith is believed to be given to man by God and is sacred truth. He argues further:

Speculation is a method by which truth is known. The truth that speculation knows is scientific, i.e. "theoretical," detached, demonstrative, impersonal; it is disengaged from the thinking subject as an individual. The truth mediated by revelation, in contrast, is "practical," "committing," undemonstrable, personal—in short, religious; it is addressed to man as an individual.[1]

This great methodological polarity owes its clarification and articulation as intellectual types to two peoples: the Greeks, who introduced speculative reasoning in its purest form to philosophy in their application, as George Boas has noted, of the "law of contradiction," of logic and consistency as the only arbiter of truth;[2] and the Hebrews, who, while certainly not the first people to think in terms of revealed truth, were the people who have most strongly and persuasively defended it, especially in the Western tradition.

If one were to read traditional Judaic writings, one would search in vain for any articulated defence of the method of faith. For one important way in which revelatory truth differs from speculative truth or the truth derived from reason, is the unselfconscious, experiential nature of the former compared with the self-conscious articulation of the latter. A great deal of critical philosophy is concerned with the problem of defining the nature of reason, and it is usually such philosophers who bring to the surface the nature of faith or revelation. To the person who thinks in the Hebraic tradition, truth is like art: it conceals itself. It is felt truth; not cognized truth. It may even be that to articulate it by means of reason is to begin to destroy it. This clearly presents a problem for anyone, like myself, who tries to talk about it without doing it, without being with it. I can only say that it is a form of truth with which I am not entirely unfamiliar, given my own religious upbringing.

The distinction between universalism and particularism is not methodological but substantive. It refers to profoundly differing and antagonistic views about mankind and the groups that go to make it up. Since particularism is true of all primitive and archaic peoples, this antithesis arose with the development, rather late in human history, of the idea and ethic of universalism. The universalist ethic had a sacred and a secular origin; it evolved independently both by means of the method of reason and the method of faith.

I propose to argue that there are four great traditions in Western social thought and that these traditions are essentially defined by the relationship between the two axial dualisms of method and substance. For clarity of exposition the four traditions may be classified as follows:

Methodological Dualism	Substantive Dualism	
	PARTICULARISM	UNIVERSALISM
Reason	1) Platonism	3) Stoicism
Revelation or Faith	2) Hebraism	4) Pristine Christianity

The Platonic tradition is the configuration of reason and particularism. The connection is not accidental but intrinsic. Another name for Platonism is rationalism, but I will try to avoid this term, since it is often used to refer to all products of speculative reason. Plato was one of the earliest thinkers to articulate this position, and has been the most important. It has had a profound influence on Western thought, especially social thought. One immediately thinks of Whitehead's oft-quoted aphorism that the history of Western philosophy may be read as a long series of footnotes to Plato. Even allowing for the exaggeration inherent in all sweeping statements, I think this is a terrible commentary on the Western intellectual tradition. But it is, sadly, largely true.

The Hebraic tradition is the great tradition of Biblical revealed truths and the method of knowing through faith. It is also a strongly particularistic, although a complex and humanistic method. All traditions in the Western world which combine revealed truth with particularism, whether secular or sacred, trace their intellectual roots back to Hebraism. The secularized version of Hebraism came to be known in the modern world as romanticism.

The Stoic tradition was born within the intellectual climate of the Hellenistic world, but is in many respects thoroughly alien to the Greek view of the world and mankind. It is the intellectual origin of all secular forms of universalism. Its seminal role in the development of Western humanism is still not sufficiently recognized. As late as the mid-fifties Edelstein found it necessary to caution his audience against the vulgar nineteenth century distortion that the Stoic sage was "the stony similitude of a Platonist," and to reaffirm once and for all the truth that "European humanism from Petrarch to Erasmus and to Matthew Arnold is imbued with Stoic thought." [3] The Enlightenment, in particular, was in most respects simply a restatement and development of basically Stoic principles.

Pristine Christianity refers to the teachings of Jesus, the divine Jewish rebel who, through the Hebraic method of faith, came to a universalistic conception of mankind as equal before and in God, a revolution in religious thinking which Judaism found itself on the verge of achieving, especially during the late Hellenistic period, but in the end could not bring itself to consummate. Jesus did and created a new religion. The force of particularism soon began to take its toll during the period of the routinization of his charisma. Pristine Christianity must therefore be carefully separated from other forms of Christianity, especially the form that eventually triumphed in the late Roman World and Middle Ages and which came about under the influence of the intellectual convergence that began with what I shall call the patristic betrayal.

When I attribute the invention of speculative reason to the Greeks I do not mean to suggest that the Greeks were the inventors of logical reasoning. Long before the emergence of Greek philosophers of any note, the Egyptians, to name one example, had developed various forms of abstract mathematical reasoning. The Greeks were unique in the value they placed on reason and in their firm belief that the universe was an ultimately reasonable and understandable entity. To the Greeks everything was accessible eventually to logic. Theirs was also an essentially nonutilitarian view of reason. Reason became an end in itself, an intrinsic good, and not the handmaiden of astrology, religion, or mere practical activities such as the proper construction of irrigation works.

Most prominent Greek thinkers, however, were rationalists in the narrower meaning of that term. They believed in the superiority of deductively derived truths rather than truths which came from the application of reason to the data presented by the senses. A distinction was made between the sensible world and the truly intelligible world. It was generally thought that behind the world presented to us by our perceptions was a really real world which could be penetrated only by means of logic. Greek thought led naturally to what Popper has called "methodological essential-ism"—to the theory of forms or ideals. Behind the specific manifestation of things lies their ideational forms. It is these ideas or forms that are truly real: they are the eternals, the universals, which constitute genuine reality. Particular things are merely approximations of the metaphysical forms.

A theory of universal forms might seem to the superficial interpreter as conducive to a universalist social view of mankind. But there is no reason why this should be so; indeed, as we shall see shortly, the opposite was the case. It is always dangerous to attempt to derive, analogically, substantive conclusions from metaphysical ones. This, as we have seen, was the error that undermined the philosophy of Horace Kallen in his effort to derive, by analogy, a philosophy of social pluralism from the metaphysical pluralism of Jamesian pragmatism.

It was Karl Popper's great contribution to our understanding of Western social thought to show, in the face of the incredible conspiracy of classical scholars and Western philosophers to hold the opposite view, that all forms of idealist or Platonic philosophy lead logically to a particularistic and totalitarian view of the social universe. We can do no better, then, than to begin by following Popper's arguments closely in demonstrating the intrinsic connection between Platonic idealism and totalitarian particularism.[4]

Sociologically, the years immediately before the birth of Plato and those of his early life were ones of tremendous change.

Ironically, these changes were all for the betterment of the Greek people and moved in the direction of greater democratization. Reactionary and conservative elements were naturally appalled. For Heraclitus the whole world was in flux and the consequences could only be disastrous. From this developed the view that what was at rest and unchanging was ideal and good. Reality was conceived of as a constant departure from this ideal state of rest, a state which in political terms was seen to lie in the past.[5] A political conception of reality soon transmuted into a metaphysical statement about the universe.

Plato's great task was to find a way out of this seemingly eternal state of flux. Both his theory of knowledge and his social thought must be seen as a reaction to the dilemma of change posed by his times and so pessimistically articulated by Heraclitus, who greatly influenced him. Plato solved the problem in his political philosophy by returning to an ideal form of the state which was not so much a utopia as a refined reconstruction of the pristine state of the Greeks. He extended this idea to his entire philosophy by developing the theory of forms. Plato's political conservatism and philosophical formalism were one of the same piece. He was being quintessentially Greek, for as Kitto along with many other commentators has pointed out, "a sense of the wholeness of things is perhaps the most typical feature of the Greek mind."[6] Popper has neatly summed up the totalitarian wholeness of Platonic thought:

His fundamental demands can be expressed in either of two formulae, the first corresponding to his idealist theory of change and rest, the second to his rationalism. The idealist formula is: Arrest all political change! Change is evil, rest divine. All change can be arrested if the state is made an exact copy of its original; i.e. of the Form or Idea of the city. Should it be asked how this is practicable, we can reply with the naturalist formula: Back to nature! Back to the original state of our forefathers, the primitive state founded in accordance with human nature, and therefore stable; back to the tribal patriarchy of the time before the Fall, to the natural class rule of the wise few over the ignorant many.[7]

Popper also showed convincingly that the Platonic view of the world was essentially antiindividualistic. On the one hand, it attacks individualism by confusing it with selfishness, completely failing to see how individual interests can be complementary. On the other hand, individualism is discarded because it conflicts with the collectivist harmony of the Platonic state and with the view that the individual existed to further the ends of the group, especially the state, rather than vice versa.

The tragic irony of Plato's view is the fact that reason, in the end, becomes the instrument of the destruction of all reason. Plato, who began his career under the inspired influence of Socrates dying in the name of truth, ended up with a metaphysics and a political philosophy which rationalized the very murder of his teacher. The "holy lies" of an outmoded religion and conservative ideology are not only justified, whether believed in or not, but are required on pain of death, in exactly the same way that the modern ethnic leader demands conformity to the ideals of the group and belief in outmoded cultural symbols which must be reinvested with ideological potency. Plato rationalized such holy lies on the grounds that only some men are capable of reason; the rest, who constitute the masses, are little better than beasts and must be fed with lies that are good for them. The all-consuming love of reason made Plato and all Platonic rationalists blind to all virtues that did not spring from intellectual prowess. A simple man was incapable of goodness; he had to be forced to be good. As George Boas notes: "Contempt for the many became an integral part of classical rationalism. The many were incapable of wisdom and hence it was folly to attempt to impart it to them." [8] If Platonic rationalism could come to such conclusions about the mass of fellow Greeks who at least had a "superior" culture to support them, it is easy to see the contempt in which it held the rest of humanity who were "barbarians." The Greeks did not need Plato to come to a highly particularistic conception of the social universe. What Plato did was to generalize this particularism to the level of metaphysical thought.

Nowhere is this more evident than in Plato's theory of slavery. At about the same time that Popper was preparing his exposition of the intrinsic link between Platonism and totalitarian particularism, two distinguished classicists were examining the role of slavery in Plato's thought: G. R. Morrow [9] and Gregory Vlastos.[10] Vlastos argues persuasively that a basic key to an understanding of Plato's political theory and cosmology was his use of the "slave metaphor." Plato, he argues, "thinks of the slave's condition as a deficiency of reason. He has doxa, but no logo. He can have true belief, but he cannot know the truth of his belief." The master-slave relationship became the paradigm of the relationship between the wise ruler and his reasonless subjects, and "the absence of self-determination, so striking in the case of the slave, is normal in Platonic society."

However, the slave metaphor has deeper roots in Platonic thought, for it is also a key to an understanding of much that is otherwise puzzling in his cosmology. Plato, in rejecting traditional Ionian physics for being too empiricist, assumed that "a scientific explanation of the shape and position of the earth must prove that it has that particular shape and position because these are best for it." The mechanical causes of things are rejected as "slave causes," that is, causes that are "secondary" and are "necessary, irrational, fortuitous and disorderly." The paradox of "disorderly necessity" is explained by the use of terms like "persuading necessity" and "compelling necessity" which, as Vlastos argues, "make sense only if one keeps steadily in mind the slave metaphor." "Persuading the law of gravitation does not make sense. Persuading a slave does." Vlastos concludes his illuminating exposition as follows:

... his views about slavery, state, man and the world, all illustrate a single hierarchic pattern; and that the key to the pattern is his idea of logos with all the implications of a dualist epistemology. The slave lacks logos; so does the multitude of the state, the body in man, and material necessity in the universe. Left to itself each of these would be disorderly and vicious in the sense of that untranslatably Greek word, hybris. Order is imposed upon them by a benevolent superior: master, guardian, mind, demiurge. Each of these rules in his own domain. The common title of authority is the possession of logos. In such an intellectual scheme slavery is "natural": the perfect harmony with one's notion about the nature of the world and of man.[11]

In such an intellectual scheme particularism is equally natural. Plato's world, like that of all his followers, is a pluralist world with the added venom that this "disorderly necessity" is held in check by the rigid hierarchy of an elitist state in which the bigoted wise reign supreme.

There have been many attempts at contrasting the Greek and the Hebrew views of the world. The famous essay of Matthew Arnold immediately comes to mind.[12] The work of Kroner, mentioned earlier, is based on an exploration of these two competing modes of thought and being. And more recently, William Barrett begins his excellent analysis of existentialism by examining the same distinction.[13] Often it is either implied or stated that these two traditions together make up the essential structure of Western thought. Such a synthesis is untenable, however tempting, as it implies a neat but incomplete dialectical progress in the emergence of Western thought: the impassioned Hebraic man of faith forming the antithesis to the detached, intellectual Greek man of reason, both being resolved in the great civilizational synthesis of Christendom. Indeed, Arthur A. Cohen, has gone so far as to dismiss the idea of the Judeo-Christian tradition as a myth.[14]

This is a gross oversimplification of Western thought. It neglects several clearly defined traditions and fails to isolate differences which are sometimes irreconcilable. It fails to see that Hebraism influenced the Western tradition in two ways: directly, as a tradition in its own right, and indirectly, through its influence on the separate tradition of Christianity.[15] Few commentators have explored the peculiar genius of the Hebraic vision with greater penetration than Baron, perhaps the most distinguished contemporary student of Jewish history. Baron begins his epic work, *The Social and Religious History of the Jews,* with just such an analysis. He observes, first, the critical interdependence between Judaism and the Jews, and states categorically that: "To Judaism the existence of the Jewish people is essential and indispensable, not only for its actuality, but for its potentiality. The Jewish religion without the 'chosen people' is unthinkable. Neither could it, like the other religions, be transplanted from the Jewish to another people." [16]

Particularism, then, is the central socioreligious quality of the Hebraic tradition in its pristine, Judaic form. Sociologically Jewish particularism and Greek particularism are the same thing: They involve the division of humanity into at least two basically different groups of people. And yet, in origin and implication, the two particularisms could not be further apart.

Jewish particularism is substantively derived, whereas Platonic particularism is methodological and rooted in its metaphysics. Platonic essentialism implies divisions even within the ethnic group. Hebraic particularism, on the other hand, springs not from its method so much as from its conception of human beings and from its substantive conception of the relationship between persons and their historical-cultural environment. Judaism is essentially a historical creed, the very first such creed, and as such it marked a revolutionary departure from all previous natural religions. Even where specific Judaic rites can be traced back to their prehistoric, natural origins, it is significant that they have been transformed from their original natural settings and meanings and given new historical meaning.[17]

Also, we find in Judaism the supremacy of law. Judaism is an essentially ethical creed and the laws that govern the relations between persons and between persons and God have their origin in the divine covenant. It is God's laws and not the laws of nature that determine the course of history. To the Greeks there is an inner logic in nature and if there is a God, such a divine essence is nothing more than the ultimate logical unity of the universe. Humanity's capacity to find and know this ultimate inner logic is optimistically upheld. To the Hebrew way of thinking this is heretical nonsense. The Hebrew, like the Greek, has a historicist view of the world; and there is a predetermined plan. But the plan is God's vision; and the logic, if it exists, is beyond humanity's comprehension. The plan is revealed and known through faith, through intimate involvement with the divine presence, not through reason.

Ernest Barker makes this point neatly by contrasting the historicism of the second-century Greek historian Polybius and that of the contemporaneous author of the later chapters of the Book of Daniel (c 166 B.C.). Both lived in times of great change, and both had grand, catastrophic conceptions of world history. But here the similarity ends. "The difference," writes Barker, "is that the scheme of Polybius has an inner logic, and his doctrine of succession is based on a principle; the scheme of the writer of the later chapters of the Book of Daniel is *merely temporal and the doctrine of succession . . . is a doctrine stamped on to historical vicissitudes rather than elicited from them.*"[18] (Emphasis mine.) It is an apocalyptic and prophetic vision. History does not proceed through gradual stages but through "miraculous transformations."

Instead of searching by means of reason for the truth of history, the Jewish writer, by means of faith, comes to know the revealed truth of his past and of his future. And the source of this faith, of course, is the one living God. But here we come upon the great paradox of the Hebraic mind: the universalist paradox, if it may be so called. It was the Jews who developed to its purest form, from the henotheistic and monaltristic beginnings of fellow Semitic peoples, the idea of monotheism.[19] A conception of God as one and indivisible implies spiritual universalism. And yet, the very religious genius that made this strong belief in a single God possible also demanded a personal and concrete view of other human beings and of their relation to the world and to God. Humanity occupies a central position in the Judaic cosmology. God is above all a God of justice. The Judaic God is obsessed with humanity. There is no fooling around with logos and nature and whatnot. God's actions direct the course of mankind through the Law. The ultimate purpose of the universe is an essentially human-benefiting purpose. In all these respects Judaism reveals itself as a supremely humanistic creed. But precisely for these reasons the concrete and the particular became important. To the Judaic mind universalism is an intellectual abstraction and for this reason must be dismissed as useless. Only the concrete, individual human being can be known meaningfully and loved. Thus while the extreme monotheism of Judaism implies a radical universalism, this was not an implication that could be meaningfully pursued.

Yet there is no sociological reason why the implication should not be followed through. Both Christianity and Islam did this. Furthermore, while universalism can be an abstraction and, as such, a sterile creed lacking human content, genuine universalism requires individualism. It is possible, indeed it is only possible, to love all humanity through the love we share with and the respect in which we hold all the individuals who come within our compass. So to reject universalism on the grounds that it is a mere abstraction is to reject a straw man. We must therefore ask the critical question: Why did Judaism leave the universalist implication of its monotheism dangling, so to speak, in its cosmology?

The answers are extremely complex. It seems to me that the historical timing of the full flowering of the monotheistic conception of God among the Hebrews is critical. The Jews did not come to a complete conception of monotheism until the Babylonian exile of the sixth century. This, I must add immediately, is a controversial statement. There are many students of Jewish history, including even Baron, who hold to the view that such a development took place from the Mosaic period. The weight of historical evidence is against such an interpretation.[20] The Biblical evidence, while ambiguous, seems on the whole to weigh against this early dating of full monotheism. I simply do not see how the Mosaic command, "Thou shalt have no other *gods before* me," can be taken to mean anything other than that state of deistic development which F. Max Muller calls monaltry, a form of relativistic monotheism. It is a far cry from polytheism and a radical departure from henotheism, the belief in a common essence behind the separate identities of all the gods such as we find in Greek religion, but it is not yet pure monotheism, for it concedes the possibility of the existence of other gods for other peoples. It also assumes that those other gods can be very strong and capable of creating all sorts of supernatural mischief. But it assumes, further, that one's own god is superior and will triumph in the end. In this context Moses' commandment makes perfect sense.

Absolutist monotheism, or monotheism in its pure and extreme form, came only with the Babylonian exile. It was partly a response to the trauma of defeat. We now find Yahweh's wrath being directed not at the Jewish people for their sins but at other peoples and gods for their injustices. The enemy, at last, is believed to be controllable by Yahweh. This is a new and essentially inclusive kind of condemnation. However, the experience of exile itself and the growth of the diaspora community further nourished the idea of pure monotheism, encompassing other peoples within the moral universe of the Hebrews.

However, the very same forces that led to the full flowering of monotheism promoted the development of group solidarity. It was during the Babylonian exile that the foundations of exilic Jewry were laid down. The Jews, now forced upon the world as a people without a state, had to mobilize themselves as a symbiotic ethnic group if they were to survive as a people. Religion once again became the focus of group life, and with it the emergence of the community of worshippers centered on the synagogue. To ensure group cohesiveness and to prevent the disintegrative pull of outgroup pressures toward assimilation, the particularistic and exclusive rules and rites of purity had to be emphasized. Ironically, this particularistic emphasis was intensified by the very tolerance that came with the Persian conquest of Babylon.

What, in essence, the Jews did was to return to the tribal religion of the pastoral period, because, ironically, that earlier and more pristine version of the faith was more congruent with a mobile, stateless condition.[21] Indeed, one may interpret the whole history of the Jews from this point onward as a creative rationalization and adaptation of their pristine nomadic tribalism to the exigencies of exilic life. The messianic hope of the once and future Davidic kingdom replaced the lost state and became an integral part of the exilic experience.

Because pure monotheism developed at precisely the time when the Jews, to survive as a people, had to emphasize ethnic solidarity, the universalism implicit in monotheism could not be taken to its logical conclusion; nor could the emphasis on the concrete and the humanistic be allowed to run its full individualistic course. The individual, to be a whole person, had to be a person committed to the ethnic group and had to bow to the dictates of its elaborate set of laws, which were made especially demanding in order to emphasize, without intermission, the separateness of the Jew and the need to guard against Gentilic encroachment.

When the prophet Jeremiah was inclined to go the whole way to universalism, the exilic Jewish population interpreted this as a recipe for extinction. At the other extreme were the messianic prophets with their highly particularistic hope of an imminent restoration of the past days of Davidic glory. In the end most Jews responded by a subtle reinterpretation of the "chosen people" doctrine. Baron observes that:

Since the universal God is simultaneously the Holy One of Israel, he felt, the unity of mankind and the holiness of the Jewish people are complementary aims. The Jew must live a different life from that of other nations, not so much for his sake as for theirs.[22]

This was as far as the Jews were prepared to go in coming to terms with the awkward implication of their monotheism. It was not a happy compromise. If the Jews really believed it, it is unlikely that their Gentile hosts would take kindly to it. In any event, the tension between the universal and the particular was hardly resolved with this peculiar conception of group mission. For one brief period during the Hellenistic age, the universalist tendencies seemed on the point of triumph. On the religious level there was a massive expansion of Judaism as the poor and dispossessed all over the Mediterranean world converted to the creed with the encouragement of Jewish proselytizers. On the intellectual level, the complex dialectics of Philo struggled with the problem of Jewish religious thought as a vision for all mankind, a problem he eventually solved by Greek analogic reasoning, culminating in his famous and glorious statement that Israel is a state of mind available to everyone.[23]

But this first and last experience with universalism soon came to an end. The existential humanism of the Hebrew could simply not transcend its particularistic anchorage. The price the Jew was asked to pay for the universalization of his faith was a twofold movement which implied the extinction of the group: one, a movement outward toward all humanity encompassed in the brotherhood implied by a single God; the other, a movement inward from the conformist individualism of the tribe toward a radical personal individualism. Humanistic pluralism was about as far as Hebraism could go in coming to terms with the universalistic imperative of ethical monotheism.

The sacred tradition at the heart of pristine Hebraism, plus the fact that the Jews have until very recently been a politically vulnerable group has saved the Jews from the dangers inherent in their particularism and their conception of themselves as a chosen people. Not all those who hold to the Hebraic tradition, however, are Jews or religious. When these two conditions cease to apply, Hebraism as a mode of being becomes, especially in alliance with certain other traditions, the source of the most terrible tragedies.

The tradition of Stoicism, in contrast, is the secular derivation of universalism by means of reason. It developed first from the somewhat isolated political philosophy of Alexander the Great; second in the more strictly defined philosophy founded by Zeno of Citium; and third, after the corruption of the tradition during the period of middle stoa with the infusion of neoPlatonic pollutions. The final repoliticization of the pristine tradition came during the later stoa phase when it became the favored philosophy of the Roman imperial upper class.

In view of the excessive particularism of the Greeks, it may seem highly paradoxical that the secular tradition of universalism should have developed in the Hellenistic world. All the major figures involved in the development of secular universalism were either non-Greeks or Greeks marginal to mainstream Greek culture. It is fashionable among modern classicists to play down this important fact. One would be inclined to applaud such a tendency if it were inspired by a universalist ethos which underplays the nationality origins of human thought. Alas, this is not the case, for modern classicists insist on neglecting the non-Greek origins of the founder of secular universalism and the early Stoics merely as a chauvinistic device to make the tired claim that everything original and secular in Western thought was of Greek origin. Zeno was a Semite, a Phoenecian from Cyprus; Cleanthes, his successor, came from Asia Minor and, although racially Greek, was, as Ernest Barker observes, the most "un-Greek" of Greeks. It cannot be an accident that all the Greeks in the early Stoic phase came from the outer, Asianized regions of the Greek world.

But what about the figure who first developed and articulated the secular version of universalism, Alexander the Great? He was a Macedonian, and the most striking thing about Macedon was its marginality in the Greek world. Most Greeks viewed Macedon with something approaching disdain. The Macedonians were not quite barbarians, but it was greatly to be doubted whether they were quite Greek, an ambiguity exploited by fourth-century Athenian propagandists.[24]

Beneath the surface, one detects in the behavior of Alexander toward his fellow Greeks something not far removed from the underdog or poor cousin who has made good. It is consistent with the neurosis of marginality that Alexander should in the end deliberately and unnecessarily humiliate the Greeks. One can easily imagine the malicious pleasure with which Alexander must have handed out presents to those of his 10,000 soldiers who had taken foreign wives. His reduction of the Greek literary men in his entourage to a state of intellectual fawning must be seen in this light. And it is difficult to explain in any other terms the devastating humiliation he inflicted on Callisthenes when he refused to let the latter kiss him because he had not, like the barbarian guests, first prostrated himself, not to mention the unsavory role he played in the latter's execution.[25]

W. W. Tarn, one of the most authoritative students of Alexander, insists that Alexander was not only the first person to give emphasis to the idea of the unity of mankind but the first thinker to articulate these thoughts in any clear and consistent way.[26]

Egyptologists of the early New Kingdom might strongly contest such a claim, but in defence of Alexander's originality it might be argued that he was certainly the first figure of world importance to hold such extraordinary views, and he was the first person to articulate them in a secular way.[27]

Tarn argues that the radical form of the idea of homonoia (as opposed to the ethnically conservative version of Isocrates) began with the emergence of the idea of the King as the living law who holds the same relationship to his people that God holds to the universe.[28] In the same way that God imposes order on the universe, it was the duty of the good king to impose unity on his subjects. The Macedonian king, however, ruled over an empire of many races and peoples. Hence there came about the radical shift from Isocrates' chauvinistic harmony of all Greeks to the Macedonian idea of a harmony of all races within the state of the dutiful king.

This was the intellectual climate within which Alexander grew up and the political culture he inherited. From this background Tarn thought that it was easy to understand how he could take the radical next step into true universalism: that of propounding the ideas of God as the father of all mankind, the brotherhood of man, and to see his mission, in the words of Plutarch, as a charge "from the deity to harmonize men generally and be the reconciler of the world, mixing men's lives and customs as in a loving cup."

These views of Tarn have not gone unchallenged. Badian, for example, sought to "lay the ghost" of "Alexander the dreamer" by a critical examination of the relevant sources.[29] Badian's critique was not, however, as devastating as he imagined. The most he did was to cast some serious doubts on the view that Alexander actually originated these ideas. The all-important fact remains that Alexander was the first figure of such enormous prominence and influence to hold such views. What is most distressing about the whole debate over Alexander, however, is the fact that it is couched completely within the terms of the great man view of history. It never dawns on any of the classicists that more important than the attribution of originality was the historical content and structural significance of these ideas.

The problems Alexander faced were basically no different from those which confronted all conquerors before and after him: how to deal with the subjected multitudes of peoples and races. The conqueror, no matter how ethnic his background, is forced by his very success into some minimum form of cosmopolitanism. An empire creates a universe. Once the sword is sheathed, the problem of harmonizing immediately begins, for while it is possible to win an empire by the sword, it is impossible to maintain it in this way.

Both temporally and logically there was a symphonic progression in the emergence of the idea and meaning of universalism. The Alexandrian phenomenon represents merely one critical motif in this historical development. The first historical movement was structural universalism, which existed in all empires prior to the Persian. At the very least, it involved the superimposition of certain minimal organizational structures on the wide range of subject peoples. But beyond these structural imperatives of imperial rule we tend to find little in the way of a cultural diffusion of the dominant group. A universal structure exists, but not a universal culture. In this sense Ikhnaton was no more than a prophet. His ideas were at least a millennium before their times.[30] Almost all pre-Alexandrian conquerors found it in their best interests to leave the cultures of their subject peoples alone. Even if they had wished to interfere it is doubtful whether they could have done so, given the poor level of development of communications and the absence of highly sophisticated bureaucratic structures.

The first Persian Empire marked the transition from the age-old tradition of limited, externally imposed structural universalism to the cultural universalism of the Hellenistic world that followed it. Due to their tolerance of and interest in the cultures of the subjected peoples, a positive form of cultural pluralism emerged.[31] Such interest encouraged the preservation and development of the various cultures that made up the empire. But at the same time, by bringing peoples together in a nonthreatening way, and because the Iranian ruling class itself lived for part of the year in one of the conquered provinces, there was a heightened sense of the presence of other cultures and inevitably a cross-fertilization of ideas and cultural patterns. The experience of the Jews neatly illustrates this two-way process of cultural borrowing. They developed rapidly toward a separate ethnic identity during the Persian period, and yet, although the fact tends to be played down in Jewish historiography, it is generally accepted that the Jews borrowed a great deal from the neighboring peoples of the empire. The Judaic tradition of apocalyptic writings was greatly influenced by Zoroastrian theories of history; and the wisdom literature of the Jews was a direct borrowing from an ancient Egyptian tradition.

Even so, while it marked an important departure, the long-term effect of the Persian intermediary empire was toward cultural pluralism reinforced by cultural exchanges. No single culture came to dominate the empire. The historic significance of the Persians is that they paved the way for the second great movement in the historical symphony of universalism. It is this second movement that Alexander initiated. But Alexander's ideas, too, were a little ahead of their times. They were more in the order of a brief thematic anticipation of what was to come later. The new movement which developed immediately after him was external cultural universalism of the Hellenistic era. It was a unique and radical departure from previous traditions. But it still maintained one important link with the older tradition in that the universalism was external and not immanent; it came, rather from without and from above. It was, so to speak, the gift of the conquerors, not the creation of the empire itself. It was culturally elitist and in no way egalitarian. The story of how Greek civilization triumphed over the entire Mediterranean world from the end of the fourth century to the coming of Christ has become common knowledge, especially from the classic works of Rostovtzeff and Tarn. While elitist, it was not politically imposed. The Greeks of the heartland had no policy of assimilation; if anything, they viewed the whole process with some misgivings and the kings were extremely careful to maintain the ethnic identity of the Greeks vis-à-vis the natives.[32]

Secondly, this cultural universalism was not coterminous with a universal structure, for Alexander's empire was divided into three compartments after his death—the empires of the Seleucids and the Ptolemies and the independent western homeland region of the Greeks, which itself continued stubbornly in its political tradition of independent city-states. The dialectical fusion of structural universalism and cultural universalism would be the great civilizational achievement of the Roman Empire. But before this fourth and final movement of the symphony of universalism was to emerge, another critical movement was necessary.

This third movement was the full development of the idea and meaning of the principle of universalism. This great historical movement, which Alexander merely intimated, now developed on two levels: one in the region of the mind; the other, in the region of the soul. The first level, which was secular and intellectual, was the philosophical tradition of Stoicism proper; the second level, which was revelatory and religious, was pristine Christianity.[33]

Early stoa began with Zeno at the beginning of the third century and lasted until about the start of the second century; middle stoa lasted from the early second century until about the middle of the first century B.C.; later stoa dominated the last half of the century before Christ and the first two centuries of our era. All the basic principles of Stoicism were laid down during the early period; an essentially barbarian one. After this, the philosophy was refined, but in the process it was infused with neoPlatonism (middle stoa) and later by the demands of the Roman political genius. We shall follow Rist, then, in concentrating on the early, pure statement of the philosophy.[34]

Early stoa was self-consciously eclectic, drawing upon all the available pools of wisdom in the civilized world. But while catholic in spirit, it was not in substance simply an intellectual melting pot. Unity, a new synthesis, was indeed, its major aim and achievement. The contradictions which Barker detects in the early period—between its materialistic naturalism and ethical naturalism, its theory of free will and determinism, in its astrology and its peculiar conception of marriage—were largely preliminary problems, inevitable at the beginning of any great intellectual tradition, although it is not being suggested that they were all resolved.[35]

As it was for the Platonists, reason was the basic intellectual tool of the Stoics. Logic was to play an even greater role in Stoic thinking, if that was possible, than it did in traditional Greek thought, for the Stoics did not just idealize logic, they made it divine. But where Platonism was essentialist, Stoicism was radically empiricist. Science, physics, was almost sacred to them. Reason was the tool to all knowledge, yet Stoic epistemology was the direct opposite of Platonic formalism.

Plato, like the Stoics, had a conception of the wholeness of things. But the two conceptions could not have been more different. In Platonic epistemology, unity was not "out there"; indeed, if anything, all that existed "out there" was disorder. Plato strongly rejected the mechanistic and causal explanation of what he contemptuously described as the "modern scientists," and in accounting for whatever it was that held things together in the world "out there" presented by the senses, he was forced back on the paradoxical claim that there was merely a "disorderly necessity," held together by "secondary" and "fortuitous" slave causes. Hence Vlastos' argument that the Platonic view of the physical universe only makes sense if we keep in mind the metaphor of the slave in his cosmology. The Stoics rejected such an atomistic view of the physical universe, a rejection which sprang from their empiricist epistemology, true precursors of Lockean epistemology and the empiricism of the Enlightenment.[36]

The unity of the universe on which the Stoics insisted was a causal unity. It was also an immanent unity, inherent in the nature of things as they were, not approximations of Platonic ideational forms. This unity, while it was total, had three dimensions: the physical, the logical, and the moral. The physical dimension of the cosmos, nature, is matter infused with the fiery principle of life. This is the base of the world soul, the divine, rational universe. Human beings are one with this rationally existing cosmos, and it is the dimension of logic, or reason, working in persons, which makes them aware of the preexisting unity of their reason and body with the divine reason of nature. In becoming aware of this unity, goodness or moral action is realized, since the good is the same thing as the truth, and the truth is the awareness of the essential unity of the universe. As Christensen observes, "The Stoic philosopher is a man caught by the quest for unity." [37]

In the vulgar conception of Stoicism, the philosophy stands mainly for dogged fortitude and indifference to suffering. Indeed, there is a quite respectable tradition of classical scholarship which interprets the philosophy mainly as an antithesis to Epicurean dogma. This, as Rist has recently pointed out, is an oversimplification. Certainly, it cannot be denied that the characterologic effect of Stoicism was such as to emphasize courage, fortitude, and self-management: hence its special appeal to both the Roman ruling class and many of the early Christians. But as Rist points out, pleasure to the Stoics was not so much something to be condemned as an experience that was "supervenient," something that was "parasitic on activity ... a concomitant of what is primarily in accordance with nature." This was not an endorsement of indifferentism. As Edelstein reminds us: "The Stoics assert with one voice that although virtue alone is good, other things have value; a term which they invented."

Of more importance was Stoicism's emphasis on self-mastery, for it ties up closely with one of its central philosophical teachings: free will. The Stoics believed that unity always existed and that virtue and goodness lie in recognizing this unity and reconciling oneself with it. In this regard, the philosophy was highly deterministic. But it was a philosophy that also greatly valued personal freedom and autonomy. This is the eternal problem of all moral philosophies. How did the Stoics resolve it? There were several attempts during the long philosophical reign of Stoicism, but according to Rist [38] the most interesting came from Chrysippus, who distinguished between fate and necessity. Fate refers to basic and primary causes. All events are caused and willed by God, by the logic inherent in the universe. But for human beings at any given moment of time, nothing is necessary. Necessity is temporal causation, derived from and consistent with the infinite, transcendental moment which is the basic causal system of the universe. Time and temporal causality present humanity with the freedom-generating possibility of possibility. The wise man with the necessarily good character operating on the principle of temporal causality can always choose. And the Stoics offered a simple proof of this—the possibility of suicide. The fact that one is free to take one's own life at any time is proof that in the final analysis one can always choose one's fate. The fact that one's choice is consistent with that which was causally determined in the basic, cosmic nontemporal sense does not undermine the claim to freedom. For since one is united with the divine reason of the cosmos, one is always a part of the cosmic decision to choose this particular moment to take one's life.

Stoic ethical theory was a direct precursor of Kant's theory of the categorical imperative in moral action.[39] Not actions or their consequences but dispositions are good or bad. There is no such thing to the Stoic as degrees of goodness or badness. One is wholly good or bad in particular actions and in one's total being. This is consistent with the philosophy's unitary conception of human personality. As one would expect, this is a difficult principle with which to live, and it is on this area of Stoic ethical theory which many of its critics concentrate. The Stoics were certainly aware of the difficulties involved and in practical terms they saw the truly moral man as an ideal which did not exist—not even Zeno was felt to be ideal—but to which one should strive. It was certainly unfair of Tarn to argue that in its distinction between the good and the bad person Stoicism undermined its universalism in that it reintroduced another basic division among mankind.[40] In explaining why this criticism is unfair, we come upon other principles of Stoic thought that were precursors of both the Enlightenment and of modern psychology.

In striking contrast with Platonism, Stoicism adopted an environmental conception of human personality. Truth is accessible to all human beings. The potential is there in all persons, and the Stoics believed that the upbringing of the person determines whether he or she will come to see the light of truth and in this way become good. The modern nature of this view of human personality should be obvious. The Stoics proved themselves superior to most modern psychologists in their emphasis on self-mastery. While they recognized the role of socialization, they did not, as so many of our modern determinists do, leave the matter there. Self-mastery implied the possibility, in the final analysis, of self-change, and this in turn upheld their insistence on moral autonomy and responsibility.

The Stoic conception of personality, by its strong emphasis on unity, can be seen as the first statement of what would come to be called gestalt psychology in the modern world. Here Stoicism was ahead even of the Enlightenment psychological thinkers. The human personality was viewed as an integrated whole, and it is for this reason that they felt it necessary, at least as an ideal, to insist on the totality of goodness or badness.[41]

Finally, there was the idea of the brotherhood and essential equality of all human beings. Stoic universalism was not arbitrary. It is implied in its strong insistence on the moral autonomy, worth, and existential freedom of the person, which, in turn, is implied by the unity of man with God or the world soul of the universe. I emphasize this point because the logical connection between moral autonomy and universalism is true of all genuine philosophies of universalism. A social philosophy which emphasizes universal brotherhood and unity without accepting its logically prior principle of moral autonomy and individual worth is an incoherent fraud. It is on this logical rock that all authoritarian regimes which cynically spout notions of human brotherhood fall. But before my liberal friends begin to cheer, let me hasten to add that the relationship obviously works both ways. An ethical system which extols individual worth and autonomy but denies the essential unity and brotherhood of the human race by asserting the false virtue of ethnic separateness (equal or not) is as much of an intellectual imposter as those pseudohumanistic creeds which reverse the equation. Stoic logic, in the final analysis, is the most damning critique of ethnic pluralism.

There was a second level to the movement of which Stoicism

was the intellectual counterpart. Stoicism became the intellectual welding force of the grand synthesis which was the Roman Empire.

The Roman Empire created the two conditions necessary for the final consummation of secular universalism in the ancient world. It made coterminous the structural universalism of pre-Alexandrian empires and the external cultural universalism of the Hellenistic world, but a coexistence is not a fusion. If Rome was to generate not just a melting pot but a genuine universal culture, some welding force, some sociocultural mortar, was necessary to transform the coterminality of structural universalism brought about by the Roman political genius and the cultural universalism inherited from the Hellenes. The two centuries between 100 B.C. and 100 A.D. saw the emergence and intellectual dominance not only of Roman arms but of Roman juridico-political thought. Law and the rule of law, the intellectual underpinnings of Roman structural universalism, replaced the tribal consensus, exclusivistic democracy, and utopian constitutionalism of Greek political thought. For the first time an empire was to move from the tribal definition of citizenship, which made birth a necessary condition of political participation, to the universalist conception in which merit and loyalty, not to native or imperial gods but to certain principles of organization, were the basic requirements of sociopolitical participation.[42]

But laws, however fair, just, and inclusive, represent only one of the two essential conditions for genuine sociocultural unity, what sociologists have come to call the regulatory mechanism. What the Empire needed, if a genuine universal culture was to emerge, was a mind and a soul. Stoicism gave Rome its mind and intellectual purpose. As Barker has written: "With the belief in the world-city of Zeus, and its conception of the unity of the world under a rational government Stoicism served, in its measure, as a basis or cement of the unity of the Roman Empire." [43]

Another catalytic element was still wanting to complete the creation of a universal culture. Stoicism may have filled the spiritual needs of the Roman imperial elite, but it was too advanced and intellectual a creed for the great body of the masses.

Circuses and pagan pageantries served this function for a while, but their limitations were obvious to all. Rome had a body, a structure, represented in its laws; it had the foundations of a universal culture in the inherited Hellenistic traditions; and it had one element necessary for the catalytic process in Stoicism. But it still lacked a soul. The second dimension of the third historical movement of this great historical symphony was the emergence of Christianity, the fourth and last of the great traditions of Western social thought.

Christianity is not, strictly, the religion of Christ, but the religion inspired by Christ. M. I. Finley, in his discussion of Maurice Goguel's *Jésus et les origines du Christianisme,* claims that there is a "single leitmotif" running through all three volumes of Goguel's great work, summarized in the following quotation:

Jesus did not foresee the Church; he did not found it. But from his actions it took its rise.... Without Jesus the Church would not have been born, and yet Jesus did not even foresee the Church. What he desired and proclaimed was not the Church but the Kingdom of God. Without Paul ... it would not have presented the face which it has for us across nineteen centuries of history. And yet Paul had no intention to be a creator or even only an organizer; he did not feel he was so; he only wished to be a witness.... The Christianity of the Church was the extension, stabilization and organization of a religion which had been that of Jesus. Jesus was not the founder and earliest representative of Christianity but its object.[44]

The "religion which had been that of Jesus" is what I am here calling "pristine Christianity," and the above quotation from one of the greatest modern students of early Christianity makes it absolutely clear how this pristine religion differed from the routinized structure that was inspired by it.

Jesus stood in the same relation to the Christian tradition that followed him that Alexander stood in relation to the tradition of secular universalism which he inspired and of which, in the case of his literal hero-worshippers, he was the object. In the same way that Jesus was not only beyond his time but beyond time in the permanence of his teachings, so was Alexander. Finally, it was the timeless quality of the pristine ideas of both men that were to save their great vision from the vulgarizations, distortions, and betrayals of those who immediately followed in their footsteps and routinized their charismas.

The intellectual context in which and against which Plato's thoughts developed bears a striking contrast to the religious context of the development of Jesus' religious ideas. Plato was reacting against change in his intellectual and moral background, Jesus was reacting against religious overstabilization, above all the moral tyranny of Pharisaism. In the same way, finally, that Plato transmuted his conservative personal and political philosophy into his metaphysics, so Jesus, in striking contrast, transmuted his spiritual reaction against law and tradition into a religious gospel that was quintessentially revolutionary.

Almost all students of early Christianity are in agreement on this point. Thus Philip Carrington tells us that Jesus' ethic was in "deadly conflict" with the religious authorities of his time, especially the extremely rigid and traditional Pharisees.[45] And Johannes Weiss writes:

As surely as the Jew must remain under the Law, and at the judgement be judged according to his performance of its demands ... just so certainly the Christian is no longer under the Law ... he has died to the Law ... the Law has been laid aside, both as a document accusing of sin ... and as one making demands; Christ has become the end of the law for the believer ...[46]

Actually, the matter was somewhat more complex than this. Goguel, in his subtle analysis, argues that Jesus was not objecting to the principle of law as such but to legalism and casuistry; that at one and the same time, Jesus' conception of law and obedience was both more rigorous, more demanding, yet more humanistic and liberating. He writes:

Obedience to a Law, however detailed it may be, can never be more than a partial accomplishment of God's will. No system of commandments can embrace all reality and all possibilities. By the side of what it orders and forbids there remains a sphere concerning which it says nothing. It is the domain of action, which being neither ordered nor forbidden may be considered to be permitted and ethically neutral. No legalistic ethic can escape the danger of developing a system of casuistry, in order to extend the field of what is permitted at the expense of what is ordered and forbidden, with the result of restricting obedience to the will of God. The ethic of Jesus was a reaction against the abuses of casuistry and a return to the integrity of the principle of obedience to Law. The accomplishment of God's will is made the first and foremost object of prayer which Jesus taught his disciples ... and the goal of all their efforts. "Be perfect as your Father in heaven is perfect," he said to them ... What is there, in short, which God asks of men except to realize a perfection like his? [47]

Clearly, then, what Jesus' ethic amounted to was a staggeringly new conception of humanity as perfectible, god-like, god-achievable. It demanded of human beings that they behave as active moral agents in their search for god-like perfection. Law exists and is necessary, but it merely provides the framework within which moral choice and development take place.

Change, the possibility of change, and the inevitability of change are the essence of pristine Christianity. Herein lies its uniqueness among all the religions of the world. Herein, too, lies the reason why the Western world has always found it difficult to live with its purity and pristine simplicity.

The destruction of tradition and the proclamation of a new order, then, were the central purpose of Christianity, a new order, however, in which the spirit would be constantly awake. There was no looking back; indeed history, by being realized, was obviated. There was only a looking forward and outward toward a dynamic vision of a new humanity, and a looking inward at a new being in creative congruence with this outward vision. Goguel writes:

The preaching of Jesus, challenged those to whom it was addressed with a personal decision, sometimes at the cost of being separated from the group to which one naturally belonged and being brought into conflict with it. Jesus said, "Think not I come to send peace on earth: I come not to send peace but a sword. For I am come to see a man at variance against his father, and the daughter against her mother, and the daughter-in-law against her mother-in-law. And a man's foes shall be they of his own household." [48]

That the outward vision encompassed all humanity was made perfectly clear by the Messiah. Jesus was "the son of mankind." There were no chosen peoples anymore, only those who chose to see the light and leave the darkness. A radical universalism then was one of the essential teachings of Jesus.

But, as is true of all genuine universalisms, this outward universalism was based on an equally radical individualism. This "unlimited, unqualified individualism," Troeltsch tells us, "transcends all natural barriers and differences, through the ideal of the religious value of the soul." [49] All persons, being the children of God, are obviously equal as brothers and sisters and in worth. The supreme worth of all human beings, as totality and as individual beings, was made manifest by the single divinity and human nature of Jesus. Jesus preached and revealed in his own person the divine grace that is in us all. The divinity of each person makes evident not only his or her worth but makes it necessary to treat each human being as an end in himself or herself. This is no empty, pious creed. Nor is it something inferred from Jesus' teaching. He not only said these things but, more important, *did* them.

Nowhere was this more evident than in Jesus' extraordinary relationship with women and his radical feminism. He revolutionized the human race's conception of marriage by denouncing the pattern of easy divorce then prevalent, which gave women no legal security and placed the married woman at the complete whim and mercy of her husband. He also implicitly condemned polygamy, another correlate of female subjection. He saw marriage as a positive, fulfilling, and lasting experience in which both partners shared equally. Even more important, however, was the fact that he gave women an equal status in his ministry. We have no better proof of Jesus' emphasis on female emancipation—and by implication the emancipation of all subjected groups—than the fact that it was so interpreted by many women in the primitive church. Thus we know that the women of Corinth, drawing directly on his authority, created consternation among their chauvinistic male counterparts by not only insisting on an equal say in church matters but on discarding their veils, the main symbol of female subjection.

Jesus, however, also recognized the fact that human beings are essentially social animals. Thus something was needed to counterbalance the emancipation from tradition and the radical individualism which he preached. Here I must part company with Goguel, who seems to contradict himself when he argues that Jesus' answer was love and discipline within the framework of an organization "which is not made up of individuals placed side by side." How do we reconcile this with his own remarks, quoted earlier in the volume discussed by Finley, that Jesus did not even "foresee the church"? Not discipline (which is not to say that it is not required) but the "communism of love" was, in Jesus' view the supreme social mortar. Abram H. Lewis, in a little-known work published at the turn of the century, has written one of the most elegant statements of this position:

Christ presented love for God, for truth, and for man, as the mainspring of action in all religious living. Under His teachings Christianity arose as a new life, springing from the law of God, written in the hearts of men. New Testament Christianity was a life born of love, and finding expression in loving obedience. It was a system of right living, as in the divine presence, and by the help of the divine spirit. Men were drawn to each other and to Christ by the power of this love. Such was Christianity at its birth.[50]

The radical implications of this view have persisted down the ages, in spite of the opposition and neglect of organized religion. As Troeltsch tells us:

One of the permanent results of the teaching of Jesus . . . was this idea of a Communism of Love . . . free and common to all like light, air, and earth, like the fact that we all come from God and to Him we shall return; earthly possessions should be for the use of all, through the love which shares and keeps nothing back.[51]

As if to leave us in no doubt about the matter, Jesus proclaimed his social ethic in the sublime commandment: "Do unto others as you would wish they do unto you." It is not possible to make a more antirelativistic statement; at the same time it is not possible to make one which is more egalitarian. Absolutist bigotry is denied in the same breath that relativistic self-contradiction is denounced.

It should be noted, further, that Jesus saw love as something inherent in human nature, though reaching its highest point of perfection in the love of God. This point should be emphasized, for one of the greatest betrayals of pristine Christianity has been the Pauline-Augustine denial of this humane conception of love. Instead, we get the view that humanity of itself is incapable of genuine love, that pure, unselfish love is only possible through divine grace. This demeaning conception of humanity is still very much with us, a classic modern statement being Anders Nygren's *Agape and Eros.* George F. Thomas upbraids Nygren for what he rightly refers to as the "dangerous errors" of "Christ mysticism," for, as he notes, such a "statement seems to imply that the Christian is no longer the agent at all, that his will has been replaced by that of God or Christ or the Spirit. It would rob man of the moral responsibility and freedom that are of the essence of personality and make the commandment to love his neighbour meaningless." [52] We are in complete agreement with all this. However, Thomas himself is in error as a result of his too steadfast commitment to the Pauline-Augustine tradition, one that he tries brilliantly, but in the end unsuccessfully, to humanize. Fortunately, the tradition of pristine Christianity is not quite dead among sophisticated theologians, for in two major commentaries on Thomas' work [53] the theologian Peter A. Bertocci has set the record straight. The Pauline-Augustine revisions of Thomas, Bertocci argues, place the Christian conception of love on a moral "promontory" and leave it utterly "stranded" from its human base. Human will is salvaged, but at the expense of human passion and moral context. The love of neighbor and of God, Bertocci contends, cannot be separated from the other forms of human love. The pristine Christian ethic of love "is acceptable, not because it transforms or revises other value systems but because it orchestrates all the values of life in a symphony of values *in which each value lies in creative tension with all others.*" [54] (Emphasis mine.)

Anyone who still entertains any doubt about the radical antiethnicity of Jesus should not only ponder the above commandment but read again the parable of the good Samaritan.

This, in essence, is all that Jesus, as a social thinker, taught; and, if the truth be known, it is all we need to know.

We have now identified, however briefly and inadequately, the origins and purest statements of the four great traditions of Western social thought. My argument from this point on will simply be this: The history of Western social thought can be interpreted as the restatements and convergences of these four great traditions. I shall devote myself to a discussion of only those restatements and convergences which were or are of major significance for the development or repression of universalism and particularism, especially those that paved the way for the modern intellectual roots of ethnicity.

CHAPTER 9

Toward the Fascist Convergence in Modern Western Thought

The basic ideas and systems of meanings of tradition remain the same, but they may be given new intellectual form, and in this way their relevance is renewed. They may, in addition, change from an essentially sacred mode of expression to a secular mode or vice versa. I shall be considering briefly two major restatements in the history of Western thought: one, the restatement of the Stoic tradition in the eighteenth century known as the Enlightenment; the other, the secularized restatement of the Hebraic tradition beginning at the end of the eighteenth century generally referred to as the romantic movement.

All attempts to reconcile the four central traditions of Western thought—Platonism, Hebraism, Stoicism, and pristine Christianity—have necessarily resulted in some violence to one or other of the essential principles of these traditions. Convergences are often made, one should perhaps say forced, by an emphasis on what they may have in common, if anything, and by the neglect of their differences or the suppression of the opposing principles of one tradition by that of the other. The conflicting principles may be forced together and held in their contradiction, or are larded over in a subliminal way under the impact of a powerful dialectician or the moral suasion for good or evil of a major charismatic figure. Such convergences may come about by bringing together not the original statement of the tradition but restatements of the traditions in question. I propose to discuss two major convergences in Western social thought: the Augustinian convergence and the Fascist convergence.

The Augustinian Convergence

The Augustinian convergence is the culmination of the efforts of the patristic thinkers to reconcile the traditions of Platonism and pristine Christianity. St. Augustine, by force of sheer intellectual brilliance, finally made this effort workable in the early fifth century. Seen with the hindsight of history and from the perspective of a committed universalist, this convergence was perhaps the most disastrous development in the history of Western social thought.

The two traditions in question are clearly in violent opposition. That it should have come about, that the very idea was even conceivable, must be viewed as one of the great intellectual betrayals in human history. The betrayal was a long process. It began almost immediately upon the death of Christ with the compromises of St. Paul in his effort to get the young church started and to ensure its survival within the harsh political realities of Augustan Rome. It is perhaps too easy to pass judgement on Paul's work. Compromises of a sort had to be made, as is true of all attempts to put into practice the extremely demanding teachings of a revolutionary thinker, but even allowing for the harshness of the times, it still seems amazing that compromises of such magnitude were made. What is most disturbing is that the thoughts of the early fathers were sometimes not even compromises at all but deliberate violations of the principles laid down by Jesus. Paul and the early fathers saw it necessary to make two basic sets of compromises, social and intellectual. The social compromises were the more understandable, though still inexcusable. The political world of the early Christians was circumscribed by a vast imperial power moving rapidly toward the zenith of its expansion. It was a ruthlessly organized world with an egomaniacal emperor,[1] a world still largely held together by the sword, for the process of sociocultural synthesis was yet to begin in earnest.

Jesus himself had indicated the best strategy in dealing with such a power: Render unto Caesar the things that are Caesar's, render unto God the things that belong to God. This was perfectly good advice, as any revolutionary, sacred or secular, will at once agree. It in no way implied any compromise either with one's religion or *one's social principles*. All it says is: Give the imperial bastards what they want (especially since there was not much to give!) and keep the faith burning. It does not say, "Consort with the imperialists." Nor does it say, "Try to win them over to your side." And it certainly does not say, "Adopt an otherworldly posture." If anything, it implies a certain revolutionary purity, both socially and spiritually.

The attitude of the Roman imperial power to the religions, old and new, of the subject peoples reveals that on the whole it was one of tolerance. Rome, as Finley has observed, "had no mission"[2] and simply did not consider the new creed sufficiently seriously to waste manpower on its suppression. Besides, Rome was tolerant of alien creeds even within Rome itself, where membership in cults was open to both slaves and freemen. The Christian persecutions, which modern scholarship has tended to play down, came long after the early church had found its feet.[3] There was therefore no reason why the early fathers should have had to generalize the saying, to mean "render unto the state." And it was pure neo-Platonic vulgarization to interpret it to mean a withdrawal of the spiritual life from the real world or even the adoption of that "cool indifference" of which Weiss speaks.[4]

If the political compromises of the early church were at least arguable, nothing whatever can be said in support of two other critical compromises which were so extreme as to constitute religious betrayal. These are the early church's teachings on slavery and on the status of women.[5] Jesus' egalitarianism clearly implied a condemnation of slavery. The tired argument that slavery was so much a part of the tradition of the ancient world that good people did not even think of questioning it, will simply not wash.[6] It is an argument we have heard many times from classicists who failed to see that there was something mighty peculiar about the manner in which both Plato and Aristotle went out of their way to bring the subject into their discussions: If it was so natural and undisturbing, why talk about it at all? Until recently, philosophers, for example, never mentioned the status of women, a subject that was truly taken for granted. From what we know about the history of slavery and of thoughts about it at this time, it is simply not true that no one ever questioned it. The Stoics, for one, certainly did, although under the influence of neo-Platonism they recommended patience and concentration on the rewards and equality of the spiritual life.[7]

If the Stoics at least found the problem sufficiently unsettling to come to terms with, why should the bearers of a revolutionary new creed, aimed at these very slaves, not have both considered, and if not condemned openly (since this might have been politically suicidal), at least expressed moral reservations about it? An even more alarming feature of early Christian thought was the use of the slave metaphor in theology. There is an uncanny resemblance between this usage and Plato's. Paul not only justified slavery, as did Plato, but along with the other mystery religions of the time, soon transmuted the master-slave relationship into a paradigm of the relation of believer to his messiah, the "doulos christou of Paul." The idea of redemption is borrowed directly from slave manumission jargon. Thus redemption comes from "redemptio" meaning literally, a "buying back." As Donini has pointed out, in early Christianity "the terminology dealing with all myths of salvation is taken from habits and rules characteristic of slave society," and he notes rightly how "an idea, a myth, once it is born out of a given economic and social background, becomes itself a new material force, capable of influencing, and very much so, the minds and lives of men, without any immediate dependence upon the social and economic world from which it did spring."[8] The real tragedy of the early fathers' attitude toward slavery is that, in addition to condoning the institution at the time in which they lived, they transmuted the very idea of the master-slave relationship into a permanent violation of the egalitarianism of Jesus throughout the ages of organized and establishment Christianity.

The situation was even more deplorable with respect to women, since Jesus went out of his way to demonstrate the virtues of sexual liberation, and there were no powerful vested interests involved in carrying out his clearly implied position on the equality of women. Paul's conception of female status was a deliberate perversion of Jesus' teachings which sprang from what was a highly unusual and questionable attitude toward sex and women. The eagerness and avidity with which the early fathers followed Paul in degrading the status of women and the purity of sex is a mystery I have never seen adequately explained.[9]

Corresponding to these social and political compromises were the intellectual compromises of the fathers. The first question that comes to mind is why did the early fathers find it necessary to justify their creed in intellectual terms? As George Boas has noted, there is considerable irony in the fact that the patristic thinkers should have sought support for their doctrine in, of all thinkers, Plato, "for one might think that the Source of all light would produce His revelations without the help of heathen thinkers." [10] The only explanation is the view that the fathers decided from very early to make Christianity acceptable at all costs to the power elite of the Roman Empire. And since this elite was already enraptured with Greek culture, it was inevitable that they should have rationalized their creed by showing how it converged with the brightest star in the Greek intellectual firmament. The result was what the great nineteenth-century church historian, Harnack, called, "the acute vulgarization of Christianity, or its Hellenization." Significantly, the intellectually more congruent secular tradition of Stoicism was rejected, after an early infusion (though one that had already been influenced by neo-Platonism) for the Platonic tradition. The intellectual genius who brought about this final convergence was St. Augustine.

The first thing that strikes one about St. Augustine is the remarkable similarity in the sociopolitical context of his thoughts and those of Plato's. Like Plato's, Augustine's ideas developed in reaction to times of considerable change. The collapse of the Roman Empire was imminent, the first major sign of which was the sack of Rome by Alaric the Goth in 410. Augustine, like the philosopher that so influenced him, then, was led to reflection out of a deep need for security and stability.

But of the two men, Augustine seemed to have been by far the more complex, sensitive, and humane.[11] Unlike Plato, whom one finds it so easy to despise as a person, it is very nearly impossible to dislike Augustine, even at his most recklessly conservative. For one thing, he was quite a swinger in his salad days. He was the veritable playboy of the eastern and the western Mediterranean, a searching, intense boychild of the North African sun who drove his mother nearly crazy and gave his mistress hell, not to mention an illegitimate baby at the princely age of eighteen. St. Augustine of the *Confessions* still remains "our man"—modern, all too modern, even where we are disagreeing with him. It is with St. Augustine, Bishop of Hippo, that we wish to take issue.

Augustine borrowed, in its entirety, Plato's solution to the problem of flux. As Armstrong has noted, he was "the greatest and certainly the most influential of Christian Platonists." [12] His theology was simply a thinly "Christianized Platonism," although defenders have thought otherwise.

Gordon Leff is correct in asserting that "it provided him with a cosmology, a pattern of the universe by which he was able to judge the relationship of the spiritual and the eternal to the material and the temporal." [13]

Like his predecessors and most of his medieval inheritors, Augustine saw no sharp conflict between the methods of reason and faith. He claimed that the two complemented each other. Faith, however, was given overt priority over reason: "If a man says to one, I would understand that I may believe, I answer, Believe, that you may understand..." [14] But having satisfied Christian scruples, Augustine promptly proceeds to philosophize in a rationalistic manner that leaves us in no doubt concerning the covert priority of reason in his way of understanding.

Not only did he not harmonize faith and reason. He used reason and Platonic epistemology to generate a conservative and ungenerous conception of humanity and a theory of the relationship between God and humanity which left no room for human dignity, departed radically from the highly personal Hebraic conception of God that Jesus preached, and placed between this forbidding abstract deity and man an institution which usurped the early Christian's right to a sense of his own holiness and worth as taught by Jesus and symbolically demonstrated by his incarnation.

In the same way that Platonic conservatism in political and religious matters was derived directly and logically from its methodological essentialism, so was Augustine's conservatism with regard to church and state derived from his own essentialism. To be sure, the matter was made more complex for St. Augustine by the fact that he had to take some account of the idea of a universal church. Augustine's solution was to separate the spiritual from the material, the two cities, with the church being a kind of earthly representation of the City of God. Both state and church were viewed in static and conservative terms. While there is no specially articulated political philosophy, there is a disturbing tendency in his thought to express the relations between man and God in terms of the relationship between subject and emperor. Pelagius, incidentally, was quick to recognize this giveaway in Augustine's language and was rightly scandalized by it.

Augustine's clearest statements on civil authority are all of a highly authoritarian nature. The good Christian should obey the civil authority and is not released from doing so by his faith, but on the contrary is required to do so because of his superior qualities. And yet, Augustine saw civil society as a "compact of wickedness." (This view goes directly back to Plato's "disorderly necessity" and in no way reflects any of Jesus' social views.) How is this to be reconciled with the Christian conscience and with his doctrine of civil obedience? Otherworldliness is Augustine's answer. As Ernest L. Fortin remarked: "It disposed of the problem of the political life not by integrating the Christian fully into it, but by moving beyond it in the direction of a goal which was not only transpolitical but otherworldly." [15]

A related issue concerns what A. Hilary Armstrong calls Augustine's "Churchiness":

St. Augustine can speak magnificently of the beauty and order of the world as a witness to its Creator. But once this thought has served its purpose of leading the mind to the transcendent God, he turns away from the universe to concern himself with God's working in the soul of the Church. And western Christianity has on the whole remained very much too Augustinian in this way. I am inclined to think that the lack of any broad human and humane interest and concern with the world around us, which is so often apparent in Christians and has alienated so many good and intelligent people from the Church and contributed so much to the present general rejection of Christianity, is due not so much to other-worldliness as to churchiness.[16]

Here, from a practicing Catholic Christian, and someone who is considered to be one of the foremost authorities on St. Augustine, is a perfect acknowledgment of what I prefer to call the patristic betrayal. For in its otherworldliness and churchiness as well as its lack of humanity and humaneness the patristic tradition was not just alienating itself from "good and intelligent people" but, as I am sure Armstrong would be the first to admit, from the universalism, humanism, and nonchurchiness, that is to say the individualism, of Jesus' pristine Christianity. But Armstrong is right in emphasizing the social implications of this betrayal, for it is inconsistent with the unselfish individualism and social commitment of pristine Christianity. All anticlerical Christians must view with some outrage "that easy acceptance by Christians of the appalling social inequalities, injustices and cruelties of the late Roman Empire which is one of the worst scandals in the history of Christendom, and *one from the effects of which we are still suffering.*" [17] (Emphasis mine.)

Conservative revolt against change and flux and Platonic essentialism led Augustine to an indifference to the evils of the social world. But there was an even more profound effect of Platonism on his views on free will and determinism. It is in the Pelagian controversy that Augustine most voluminously expressed his ideas on the subject.[18] It is no accident that Pelagius, the great and lonely defender of free will and individualism during the patristic period, should also have been a genuine humanist, universalist, and radical egalitarian. Pelagius stubbornly refused to see the human body as corrupt and dirty or to conceive of humanity as having fallen into sin and Adamic moral squalor. Instead, by recognizing the central element of change in pristine Christianity, he insisted on the perfectibility of mankind and on the existence of free will, claiming these to be God's major gifts to humanity through the love of His Son, Jesus. Mankind is responsible for its own sins and, likewise, for its own redemption and goodness. The very creation of man in this way is an act of divine grace.

Augustine considered Pelagius' views pure heresy. He ended up after volumes of argument with a predestinarian view of humanity, a strong reaffirmation of the essential evil of mankind, a grotesque view of marriage, women, and sexuality, and, as Paul Lehmann puts it, "a wholesale condemnation of the human race for the sake of validating ecclesiastical sacramental theory and practice." [19]

One critical aspect of the controversy points up vividly the impact of Platonic essentialism and totalitarian thinking on Augustine's ideas. Lehmann points out that Augustine and Pelagius were really arguing past each other during much of their controversy, that, indeed, the direction of their logic was the very opposite of each other. Pelagius and the Pelagians had argued from the assumption of the freedom of the will and a humane conception of humanity to the view that the church's doctrine of human baptism needed serious reconsideration. Augustine, however, argued the other way around. Beginning with the assumption of the sacrament of baptism, he moved to the conclusion that humanity's original state must have been corrupt and that therefore this original state was transmitted.[20] Augustine's approach reflected the logic typical of all totalitarian thinkers from Plato through Hegel to Hitler: i.e., one argues from the state or the needs of the group or the ends and rituals of whatever social organism one is defending toward conclusions about the nature of human beings and the ways in which they should behave. Human beings are made to fit the purpose of human organization and not, as is true with all humanists, the other way around.

The Augustinian way of arguing, and more particularly the conclusions of his philosophy, reduced humanity to nothing. This was the intellectual heritage of medieval Christianity, the beginning and the end of the Western view of humanity for the next thousand or more years, and a view which still persists as a dominant theme. The Augustinian convergence led to one of the most extraordinary paradoxes of the medieval world. We have heard often that the medieval world was a highly universalistic one. In one sense, this is true, but only in the negative sense that there were almost no marked ethnic boundaries and that the state was weakly integrated. It is a world which reconciled the unity of the Christian world order with the localized confinement of manorial allegiance. But the universalism of the medieval world was in no way positive. It was nonethnic and nonnational, but it was not cosmopolitan; indeed it was strongly anticosmopolitan and, in keeping with this, was highly suspicious of urban life. It was a religious world with a creed which, in theory, encompassed all humanity, but it was not humane. On the contrary, it was antihumanistic and uncaring in its withdrawal from political realities and in its legitimation of the worst forms of social iniquities even when it had the moral authority to persuade the powers of the world to create a less oppressive and inegalitarian society. It preached a philosophy of divine love, but it was a loveless institution, and its conception of human relationships, especially man-woman relationships, was prurient and disgusting, the very denial of real, actual love. While it encompassed a whole continent, it remained a narrow world, a prejudiced, monkish, ignorant world, cramped, moldy, unliberated, unliberating, and confined. Its universalism, while perhaps significant in narrowly religious terms, had no more real meaning for the human spirit than its political counterpart in the Holy Roman Empire. Furthermore, at the core of the Augustinian convergence was a conception of humanity that was extremely divisive, in that humanity was split into two basic groups which had no possibility of changing their positions: the predestined elect and the predestined damned.

Augustinian predestinarianism, then, may be viewed as a new kind of protoethnicity in the very heart of universalist Christendom. It was an ethnicity of the mind and the spirit. It paved the way for a mode of thought that could easily be transmuted into a conception of humanity that divided human beings into those who are chosen racially and culturally as superior peoples and those who are not. Furthermore, in its otherworldliness and legitimation of social iniquity and in its totalitarian predisposition toward viewing the ends of group action as more important than the individuals involved in such action, it paved the way for the ungodly treatment of alien races and peoples: for the genocidal butchery of the Indians and other native races of conquered lands; for the moral obtuseness of a Bartholomé de Las Casas, who could plead for an end to Indian genocide on the grounds that the large-scale enslavement of Africans was morally better and economically more profitable; for the scandalous casuistry whereby slavery in the Americas and elsewhere was condemned as evil but justified as of such necessity that the church could, in some regions, find itself the major and often most brutal slaveholder, and in others mercilessly hunt down and enslave the bodies of Indians and Africans so that their souls might be saved by means of what the Jesuits liked to call "the rod of iron." [21]

We see immediately the parallels between the Augustinian convergence and its modern intellectual counterpart, fascism. The counterpart is not exact, because the fascist convergence involved the forced intellectual convergence of restated Platonism and restated Hebraism. The latter was an even more lethal convergence, but the two convergences are similar in the dominance of Platonic essentialistic totalitarianism. Fascism, in its intellectual aspect, was, however, a convergence of the *restatements* of two traditions: the *Hegelian* restatement of Platonism and the *Romantic* restatement of Hebraism. Before we come to this final intellectual catastrophe in the Western intellectual tradition, we must first consider three other restatements: the Enlightenment, which was the restatement of Stoicism, and the two restatements which, in historical terms, it stimulated, romanticism and Hegelianism. The last, Hegelianism, is so closely related to Platonism and the manner of its restatement has been so well established that there will be no need to give it any special treatment.

The Restatement of
Stoicism in the Enlightenment

Almost all the major intellectual contributions of the Enlightenment were anticipated by the early Stoics. The eighteenth-century thinkers, however, did not merely rephrase the tradition, but creatively reinterpreted it. Their ideas constituted a positive development of Stoic principles, many of which were merely intimated in early stoa.

With its strong commitment to reason and the rejection of faith, the eighteenth century has justly been called the age of reason. Reason was the supreme human quality through which humanity could best achieve a full understanding of itself and of its world.

But while committed to reason as the sole source of understanding, the Enlightenment thinkers also recognized its limits. This was not a source of pessimism but a basis of strength, especially after the publication of Hume's *Treatise of Human Nature*. True knowledge, the Enlightenment thinkers came to understand, rests as much on an awareness of the vast possibilities of reason as on a

sense of humility in recognizing the limitations of these possibilities and the areas of human experience to which they apply.
And this humility, further, was coupled with what Kant referred
to as the "courage to use one's intelligence without being guided
by another." [22]

At the same time, the Enlightenment thinkers, like the Stoics,
departed radically from Platonic essentialism in their epistemology. The Baconian break with medieval essentialism which
culminated in Locke's epistemology was in most essential respects
a return to and development of the Stoic theory of causation and
the Stoic theory that the physical world—"physis"—was directly
knowable through the application of logic to the ideas received
through, and only through, our senses.

Boas has pointed out that the "self sufficiency which they (the
Platonists) sought was in effect the liberation of eternal man from
temporal entanglements." [23] The Enlightenment thinkers, like the
Stoics, completely rejected this view. They sought not only to
liberate humanity but to understand the underlying nature of
change so as to be able to direct its course for human good.
Natural and human histories were not the approximations of
static, eternal forms, but the workings of empirically discoverable
laws. There was a pattern and a logic to the social and physical
universe, as the Stoics had thought, and these would be discovered
by the application of reason to our observation of their realities.
"All that is required for this enlightenment is freedom," Kant
wrote, "the freedom for man to make public use of his reason in
all matters." [24]

The Enlightenment thinkers went beyond early stoa in their
refusal to simply reconcile themselves to the order of the universe.
Its laws are unchanging, yes; but not the consequences of these
laws. In many respects, several of the early Stoic thinkers had
already moved in this direction in their emphasis on reform, but
the effort had been thwarted through the pollution of early Stoic
principles by Posidonius, whose neo-Platonism dominated middle
stoa, resulting in the dissolution of its conception of unity and a
movement in the direction of otherworldliness. The Enlighten-

ment thinkers returned in intellectual spirit to the pristine Stoicism of Zeno and his immediate successors, thus paving the way for the development of a humane philosophy of change.

The Enlightenment thinkers' return to pristine stoa was most evident in their commitment to the idea of the unity of all knowledge. They were interdisciplinary in their methodology, assuming an underlying unity in the object of their intellectual endeavors. Hence the Encyclopedists and the brilliant attempt to develop a completely "new science" of man.

The humanism of early stoa was also, as a logical necessity, restated. To understand humanity was Enlightenment's central preoccupation. It was "the proper study of mankind," and for Kant the movement's major achievement was the discovery of self-knowledge. The conception of human nature was liberal and humane. The Augustinian and medieval theory of original sin was completely rejected; so too was the predestinarian distinction between the elect and the nonelect. Man, as an end in himself, returns at last to the center of a universe, a "kingdom of ends" to which he belongs as a "sovereign when, while giving laws he is not subject to the will of any other." [25]

Enlightenment took to its logical conclusion the Stoic thinkers' environmental conception of human nature. Implicit in this was the idea of the equality of human beings, the psychic oneness of the human race and its perfectibility. As Helvetius so passionately argued in his *Treatise on Man,* every human being is capable, given the right education, of achieving the vast potential of reason that is humanity's special, almost divine, quality. The Enlightenment's emphasis on reform and its proclamation of the principles of individual freedom and democracy followed from their restatement of these fundamentally Stoic views of mankind.

The social nature of human beings was affirmed by their study of history and society. But not in the simplistic and static manner of Aristotle. The Enlightenment thinkers, because they placed human beings before society, because like all true Stoics, they presented arguments whose course ran from human beings to the ends of human society, realized that to acknowledge the social nature of human beings was not to solve a problem but to pose one: that of reconciling human beings as inherently social and inherently individualistic. Kant saw this as a real conflict in the composition of human beings. But unlike the Platonic or romantic thinker, he was not afraid of conflict. He took the bold intellectual step of arguing that this "asocial sociability" of human beings, this built-in tension, was the very source of all human change and progress.

From this position came the Enlightenment view of politics and society. "The latest problem for mankind," Kant wrote, "the solution of which nature forces him to seek, is the achievement of a civil society, which administers law generally." Kant further argued that "the means which nature employs to accomplish the development of all faculties is the antagonism of men in society, since this antagonism becomes, in the end, the cause of a lawful order in this society." [26]

Through just and equitable laws available to all, the unsocial tendencies of human beings, their extreme individualism, are checked and regulated, but not suppressed. For without this regulated tension there can be no change, and without change there can be no progress. In one sense this view of human beings and society goes beyond Stoicism. It explains change where pristine Stoic thought simply assumed it and took account of it by its theory of infinite causation and implicit unity. But, in another sense, Kant's view is, here, a little disturbing. It is the direct antecedent of Simmel's sociology and the so-called conflict theorists of present-day sociologists and political scientists (although the latter prefer to trace their intellectual ancestry back to Marx), and as an explanation of society it is excellent as far as it goes. What disturbs me about it is what it leaves out. Not only laws, however just, but shared values and sentiments hold society together. This gap in the conflict theory of society and change gives Platonists and romantics their great opportunity to promote their own special solutions. It is easy to see how Plato would have identified such individualism with selfishness, then begin to wax pious about the need for harmony and so on. Hegel and his followers were to do just the same thing soon after Kant. And coming from another angle, but in the end no different in their arguments, the romantics found it easy to parade the virtues of the tribe as a solution to this endemic tension in the human being. Pristine Stoicism avoided this problem altogether in its view that reason prevails, that the good person is he or she who reconciles his or her own individual reason with the reason inherent in the cosmos. This is a morally more admirable position, but it is one which we cannot accept anymore, precisely because of what the Enlightenment restatement has taught us about the limits of pure reason.

It was in this intellectual spirit that the social sciences were born. And what is most remarkable about the Enlightenment thinkers is the fact that both in theory and method, though not in technique (the science of statistics was, happily for them, still in its infancy), their social science was in advance of the nineteenth and most of the twentieth centuries.

In the Stoic tradition of social thought, the Enlightenment thinkers recognized that there could be no artificial separation of history from its sister disciplines of sociology, anthropology, economics, psychology, and linguistics. Furthermore, they saw clearly that there could be only one true method in the social sciences: comparative analysis. Hume, Condorcet, D'Alembert, Voltaire, and in particular Vico in his *New Science* and Montesquieu in his *Persian Letters* and *Spirit of the Laws,* all developed and used the comparative method as the natural and only reasonable way to go about the business of social analysis. What is more, Condorcet, a brilliant mathematician in his own right, indicated clearly the dependence of this method on probability theory in his *History of Human Progress.* But in showing how the mathematics of probability was a necessary tool in comparative analysis, Condorcet never lost sight of the fact that such statistics were mere tools and that to place greater (or even an equal) value on them than on method and theory was as ridiculous as an artist placing greater weight on draftsmanship than on artistic method and vision.

The Enlightenment thinkers, like their Stoic predecessors, also struggled with the problem of free will and determinism and came out in favor of the former. The Enlightenment came to terms with the problem in a more imaginative way. Morality existed beyond the limits of pure reason. We can never derive moral precepts from factual statements, nor can the first principles of an ethical system ever be logically demonstrated as true or false. Practical reason had to come to terms with two basic tensions in human beings: the conflict between the possibility and need for an autonomous ethic demanded by individualism and a world governed by natural social and physical laws; and the inner conflict within practical reason itself between the categorical and the utilitarian. The first, outer conflict, is the ethical analog of the individual-society conflict and is treated in much the same way. Human beings have to live with both. Determinism is required by the laws of nature; autonomy is required by practical reason: Whether true or not, in terms of pure reason, human beings have to behave not simply *as if* autonomy is true but were willed to do so. The second, inner conflict, could be dealt with less arbitrarily, since it is wholly rooted in the moral universe. Kant's emphasis on dispositions, on the rejection of all utilitarian theories of the moral order, was pure Stoicism. So too was his emphasis on the practical necessity for moral autonomy and responsibility. The tension between the determined and the autonomous and between the categorical and the utilitarian is the underlying dynamic of moral action and progress within the individual, in the same way that the conflict between the individual and his social nature underlies all change and progress in the social universe.[27]

The Enlightenment thinkers restored the principle of universalism and the brotherhood of mankind in Western thought. Appalled by Western imperialism and racism, they frequently condemned all forms of chauvinism in their own society, as well. It was because of the unity of mankind that unity in the social sciences was necessary.

There were failures in their philosophy, in their excesses, and in some of the things they failed to think and do. They cannot escape the charge that several of their doctrines, particularly their universalism, even when consciously held, were held without sufficient conviction. Contemporaries who did not share their views were quick to see these faults, and toward the end of the eighteenth century the reaction, beginning with an attack on these largely correctable faults, gathered momentum, culminating in an attack on reason itself, the very foundation of the Enlightenment restatement.

The Romantic Restatement of Hebraism

Lovejoy, one of the leading students of the subject, has argued that there was not one but three romanticisms.[28] This is going too far. If a term has so lost its meaning that it must be understood to apply to three different movements, the time has come to discard it. Lovejoy's problem, it seems to me, springs from his failure to distinguish between the periodicity and the salience of an intellectual movement. Thus the romantic movement began as a reaction against the Enlightenment during the late eighteenth and early nineteenth centuries. Sharing this reaction and period was another movement—the Platonic restatement by Hegel and most of the Jena school. The matter was further complicated because the thinkers of the two contemporaneous schools of reaction knew, read, and borrowed from each other, and indeed in a few cases changed the nature of their reaction from one movement to the other.

Ideas, especially movements of ideas, should obviously not be reified: their historical and social contexts must be clearly understood. Even so, a movement of ideas, if it is to be called a movement, must have some organizing leitmotif. The history of ideas is valuable precisely because such leitmotifs are thereby isolated. But the process of isolation is made easier if, in addition to their periodic and contemporaneous social contexts, movements of ideas are placed within their civilizational contexts. In this regard, romanticism was a new movement, a *weltanschauung*, in the periodic sense that it developed in the late eighteenth century in reaction against an antithetical movement and against certain social developments in continental Europe. But in civilizational terms there was nothing new about it. Indeed, it is one of the oldest traditions in Western civilization, though a tradition which was never dominant. Through its restatement in romanticism, Hebraism, a major configurational force in Western civilization from its very beginnings, now becomes in its own right one of the dominant themes informing its ethos.

The two critical features of romanticism were its reaffirmation of the method of faith, of revelatory truth and its substantive particularism. In these respects, it is pure Hebraism. Its content changed from the pristine Hebraism of the Jews; and its mode of expression, while often still religious, is sometimes not rooted in any particular religion and may even be secular. As it developed, it became increasingly concerned with the numinous, rather than with any particular god, its thought reverential rather than strictly sacred.

John Stuart Mill, in his famous essay on Coleridge, has left us one of the best short statements on the essential features of the romantic movement. He does so by contrasting what he called the "Germano-Coleridge" doctrine with the Enlightenment:

It is ontological, because that was experimental; conservative, because that was innovative; religious, because so much of that was infidel; concrete and historical, because that was abstract and metaphysical; poetical, because that was matter-of-fact and prosaic.[29]

Mill's emphasis on the ontological as the first of the major contrasts between the two movements could not have been more on the mark, for the philosophical point of departure for the romantics was the ontological crisis that the Kantian system laid bare. It is in this sense that Kant, while the greatest of Enlightenment thinkers, was also the transition between that movement and its reaction. Caponigri has given us an excellent account of the way in which this "inner crisis" in the Kantian system paved the way for the romantics. For Kant, as well as all the other

Enlightenment philosophers, the object of sense knowledge was not the thing-in-itself but the phenomenal order. Underlying the phenomenal was the thing-in-itself as object, but it had to remain hypothetical in the synthetic processes of pure reason. At the same time, the *a priori* nature of the synthesis meant that it was carried on in its own formal terms, quite independent of the subject undertaking the synthesis, so it follows that "the subject-in-itself no more than the object-in-itself could appear in the phenomenal order." [30] This, then, was the crisis of Enlightenment philosophy as its critics saw it: There was no room whatever for the thing-in-itself, the ultimate basis of all knowledge, either as object or subject.[31] Caponigri sums up the dilemma:

The phenomenal order thus appears suspended between two invisible poles, the object-in-itself and the subject-in-itself, neither of which could appear in the phenomenal order which they were thought to support. As such, the thing-in-itself under both these aspects constituted a contradiction within the structure of Kantianism itself and demanded to be removed. The first stage of the romantic philosophy, in the period of its maturity, in its development out of the inner crisis and implication of the Kantian philosophy, lay by way of the critical dissolution of the thing-in-itself under both these aspects.[32]

The solution offered by the romantics in coming to terms with the ontological was really no solution at all. They rejected reason altogether or so they thought, and instead returned to the method of faith, of revelation, as the only true means of understanding and knowing the thing-in-itself. Kant anticipated this development in his ironical discussion of what he called "misology,"

... that is, hatred of reason especially in the case of those who are most experienced in the use of it, because after calculating all the advantages they derive, I do not say from the invention of all the arts of common luxury, but even from the sciences (which seem to them to be after all only a luxury of the understanding), they find that they have, in fact, only brought more trouble on their shoulders, rather than gained in happiness; and they end by envying ... the more common stamp of men who keep closer to the guidance of mere instinct. . . .[33]

Few early romantic thinkers restated the commitment to the method of faith more passionately than Jacobi.[34] His was an endless search for "the beautiful soul," the inner transcendental being which was revealed only through faith. In him we find, in its purest form, Hebraic man's insistence on the existential reality and priority of the individual and the concrete. It is not just essence that is discarded in his search, but reason itself. Jacobi was too influenced by the Enlightenment, however, not to have discarded, or attempted to discard, reason without some intellectual and personal trauma. His heart and his head, he constantly confessed, were at war with each other.

Herder, the thinker we most closely associate with early romanticism, had few such problems. The irrational, the immediate, and the concrete revealed through faith alone after the mystical surrender of reason, was the basic theme (it now becomes difficult to speak of ideas or thoughts). The content of that faith could be Judaism or primitive Christianity. For Herder, who remained tolerant and liberal throughout his life, it did not really matter. What mattered was the engagement, the manner of that engagement, and its intensity of passion. Early German romanticism, Lovejoy tells us, was "a rediscovery, for better or worse, of characteristically Christian modes of thought and feeling ... and a sense of the inner moral struggle as the distinctive fact of human experience." [35] It was, however, early Christianity to which they returned. Although they discarded its universalism, they at least maintained its humanism.

Soon, however, the content of faith went beyond all organized religion. Nature rapidly took the place of specific creeds as the basis for revelatory commitment. Hence the pantheism so typical of the movement. Spinoza had partly shown the way with his very special brand of pantheism, but Spinoza, in spite of his Jewish background, was not a thinker in the Hebraic tradition. His rationalism was the very antithesis of that tradition; so much so that he was excommunicated by his Jewish coreligionists. Herder, therefore, was completely mistaken when he claimed that Spinoza was his intellectual father; insofar as he used Spinoza's ideas, he misunderstood and distorted them.

Pantheism was the second stage in the secularization of Hebraism (after the shift from particular creeds to the religious in general). But nature and the natural could be, and were, interpreted in two ways. The state of nature doctrines of earlier thinkers had already anticipated the dualism in the romantic interpretation of nature. There was the Hobbesian state of nature, "nasty, brutish and short," leading to the need for the political leviathan. On the other hand, there was the Lockean state of nature, in which human beings were already social animals with inherent rights. Rousseau, the major eighteenth-century precursor of romanticism, adopted both conceptions at different stages of his philosophical development, and it is for this reason not only that his later writings contradict his earlier ones but that later thinkers of both totalitarian and democratic persuasion were able to trace their major intellectual influence back to him. Rousseau is Herder's real intellectual ancestor, with the important difference that Rousseau was consistent in his conception of the state of nature at given periods of his life, only changing over time while Herder held both views at the same time, with the result that the contradictions in his works are not sequential but simultaneous.

Discussing the conception of nature among romantic thinkers, Lovejoy shows how one subtradition sees it as that which is most instinctive, raw, basic, and irrational. Nature conceived in this way has no order, no laws, no harmony; it is passionate, savage, primitive. Unlike Hobbes, early romantic thinkers adored this noble savagery. One returns to it, celebrates it, and accepts it as the good and the real truth, because it is what is most real, most basic, therefore most authentic; it is soul, true living soul. It is Jacobi's "beautiful soul." The view of the truthful and authentic as the most basic and primitive in one's being has been a dominant theme of most romantic thought up to the present time. For it is the same soul of which the négritude writers talk so ecstatically, only, of course, it is now "l'âme noire" of the Haitian and other Afro-Caribbean poets, the "Africanity" of Léopold Senghor, the "negro soul" of the Harlem renaissance, and the "black soul" of present Afro-American music and poetry. The blacks, of course, think that they are the only group of people to have discovered soul, or at any rate that their soul is better than everybody else's soul. But such particularism is typical of all romantic thinkers. For the German romantics also thought that they were the only ones to have discovered "soul," and when it finally dawned on them that the discovery was as ancient as Hebraism itself, they promptly argued that German soul was better than all other souls. This sinister development was, however, to come later, with the romantic German writers of the nineteenth century. In fairness to Herder and the early German romantics, it must be emphasized once again that they did concede the plurality of the soul discovery, a concession that is disturbingly identical with present-day liberal ethnic pluralists, disturbing because of what history has taught us about the superficiality of this "liberal" concession and the ease with which it reverts to its particularistic statement.

There was, however, the second conception of nature among the romantics. Here nature is the supreme harmony, the unfolding of a perfect logic and design. Nature in this sense is pure reason. This was also the Stoic conception of nature. It came to the romantics, however, primarily through Spinoza, which was most unfortunate. For Spinoza, in spite of his anticlericalism, was a deeply conservative man. Unlike the Stoics, who supplemented the infinite logic and order of the universe with a temporal causality which brought change back into their cosmology, Spinoza completely rejected all temporal causality. This was the weakest part of his system, as all his commentators have pointed out. But Spinozan antitemporality was closely tied up with his conservatism. The truth is that which is most permanent and unchanging in the physical as well as the social universe. Enlightenment thinkers such as Locke avoided this conservatism in their state-of-nature assumptions by defining that which is permanent as something which is identical with basic human rights; hence any present deprivation of rights means a departure from that which is most basic. Kant, as we have seen, went one step further and defined the most basic natural state as one of creative tension and change. There were no such guarantees of freedom in Spinoza's conception of nature. His pantheism, therefore, dovetailed perfectly with the inherent conservatism of romantic thought. Leon Roth has pointed out that, "To Kant morality is struggle—man against Nature; to Spinoza morality is peace and reconciliation—man within Nature." [36]

It was a short step from the idealization of nature and the natural to the idealization of culture and tradition. When this happened, romanticism became fully particularistic. Here Lovejoy's penetrating analysis of Herder is once again most helpful. For he has shown how Herder temporalized Spinoza's cosmological determinism, converting his "fixed chain of being" into "cultural stages." These stages were all necessary and as such right. Herder still tries desperately to hold on to his liberalism even at this point, using the technique which all subsequent pluralists who imagined themselves liberal were to employ: relativism. Lovejoy quotes the following passage from Herder. "Nature has given the whole earth to her human children and has permitted all to germinate upon it that, by virtue of its place and time and potency, could germinate. All that can be, is; all that can come to be, will be; if not today, then tomorrow." [37]

The twin intellectual pillars of relativism and determinism stand together at the font of modern romanticism. As Lovejoy comments: "The rule for the individual is: hold fast to your own place in the Kette der Bildung, be true to your own age, and do not try to imitate or return to any other."

It was another short step from the liberal cultural relativism of Herder to the illiberal cultural particularism that soon set in not only in Germany but all over continental Europe.[38] In France the inherent conservatism of romantic thought soon destroyed the democratic principles for which the French revolution was raised. Indeed, the revolution and its immediate authoritarian and chauvinistic aftermath were an almost uncanny expression, in sociopolitical terms, of the sequential contradictions in the thought of the man who exerted one of the greatest influences on the men and women who made the revolution. Thus in the same way that Rousseau began with a conception of nature which implied a noble, democratic savagery, the early stage of the French revolution was a political expression of noble democratic savagery. In the same way that Rousseau's later romanticism reacted against his earlier version (so lyrically articulated in *Emile* and the *Discourse on the Origin of Inequality)*, condemning it in Hobbesian style as brutal and incompatible with civil society and replacing it in the *Social Contract* with the authoritarianism of the common will, so did the later stages of the French revolution and its Napoleonic aftermath replace the primitive democracy of the early revolution. However, there was continuity in this change. The Rousseau of *Emile* is similar to the Rousseau of the *Social Contract* in its romanticism. Where Hobbes' leviathan was a draconian set of laws aimed at suppressing all resistance to the supreme power, Rousseau's leviathan was the common will of the people. And, as we have argued in a previous chapter, it was this common will of the French people that became the basis for their totalitarian nationalism, their chauvinistic wars of conquest on other continental Europeans, and, as if to leave history in no doubt about the totality of their rejection of their earlier, primitive democracy, their attempt to reimpose slavery on the "primitive" blacks of Haiti.

After the revolution, French social thought was cleansed of all democratic contradictions. Its authoritarianism was as pure as its romanticism. Nowhere is this more evident than in the works of the most brilliant social thinker of the postevolutionary period, Joseph De Maistre. As Becker and Barnes point out, his ideas "would necessarily be anti-progressivist, anti-rationalist, authoritarian, and anti-democratic." [39] At its core was "a deep-seated distrust of reason." Reason is used "only in the end to refute reason." Individualism and personal freedom are rejected by a recourse to an organicist theory of society: "Societies are real organisms; individuals are only parts of these organisms, living in and through them. The demand for individual liberties is 'mad egoism'; it is the part revolting against the whole. The healthy organism demands proper subservience of its parts to the efficient functioning of the whole." [40] And as is true of all organicist theories of society, culture comes to play what functionalist sociologists today calls the "integrative function." For De Maistre, "Societies must be ruled by customs and institutions, the origins of which are lost in the mists of history. Laws must be the edicts of a king which are accepted blindly, not on their merits, but as emanating from a source of authority divinely ordained." [41] In this tradition of romantic authoritarianism the "sovereign," as Richard Nixon recently reminded us, can break the law for the common good, for reasons of "national security" which he alone has the right to determine.

But in spite of these alarming developments in France, it was in Germany that the romantic tradition was to find its most fertile soil. There, as Talmon tells us, Romanticism "had become a religion." Germany was far too weak in the early nineteenth century to create the same kind of social havoc that France did. So the romantic tradition had time to take deeper root, to flourish and grow like the "invisible worm" of William Blake's "sick rose." A century and a half later European thought, casting its bludgeoned mind's eye upon the teutonic core that had so informed its genius, would find Blake's little poem one of the great unwitting and ironical, prophesies of romanticism:

> Oh rose thou are sick;
> The invisible worm
> That flies in the night,
> In the howling storm,
> Hath found out thy bed
> Of crimson joy,
> And her dark secret love
> Does thy life destroy. [42]

Already, by the early nineteenth century, we find in Schelling a casting out of all the remaining vestiges of Enlightenment liberalism. Schopenhauer is both a tragic and pivotal figure in this development. While agreeing with Kant that there is no way in which the thing-in-itself can be known by means of reason, he borrowed from Fichte's absolute idealism the idea that reality is the realization of will. The potential for a disastrous convergence of essentialism and romanticism lurked constantly beneath the surface of Schopenhauer's thought and explains many of his contradictions as well as his notorious propensity to have it both ways. Schopenhauer, however, although he possessed the genius to forge such a convergence, lacked the inclination to do so. His pessimism, his profound loneliness, his personal experience of displacement, all gave him a healthy contempt for power, even while persuading him of the essential evil of willed reality. His later writings reflect a growing pessimism not only about the willed nature of the world, but about the very possibility of knowing the nature of will itself. As Patrick Gardner has pointed out, inner knowledge and perceptual awareness came to be seen by Schopenhauer as offering "no more than expressions of the will experienced at the level of idea." With inner knowledge, "the 'thing in itself has in great measure thrown off its veil' (but) the point remains that it still does not appear 'naked.' " [43]

None of these constraints operated on Schopenhauer's two major successors. In Hartmann's romanticism at the middle of the nineteenth century is a fully developed theory of the unconscious, a theory elaborated into the doctrine of force-as-will, along with a deeply pessimistic view that there is an inherent conflict between the progress of industrial civilization and the happiness of mankind.

It is in Nietzsche, however, that we find the culmination of all that was vile in romantic thought. In him, too, we find the major and most immediate intellectual progenitor in the nineteenth century of European fascism. Within the past two decades or so Nietzsche's ideas have been riding the crest of a new popularity and scores of intellectuals seem to have found it their special mission to restore the good name of this dangerous maniac. It is true that Nietzsche was not superficially a German nationalist.

Throughout his writings he speaks contemptuously of the "damn folk soul" and warns that "we want to be careful about calling something German." But a contempt for the masses is a natural development in all romantic thought that begins with relativistic respect for the concrete and for the humble folk, but moves rapidly toward the view that the true self is best realized in the totality of the state, which now becomes the only really concrete thing and at which stage the only true individual is the great man.[44] Nietzsche stands at this other logical and historical pole (with Herder at the opposing liberal end) of the romantic progression. While he did not celebrate the German state as such, his idea of the state as it should be was German, all too German. In this sense, Nietzsche's rejection of German nationalism runs like a streak of dishonesty throughout his works, a dishonesty betrayed by the fact that although he occasionally liked to consider himself a good European, he nonetheless delighted in making the most asinine and adolescent attacks on the British, who are, after all, both physically and culturally, the most European of peoples.

Nor, secondly, is it necessary to hold that Nietzsche was an anti-Semite to demonstrate his direct influence on Nazism. His frequent references to the Jews are sometimes confused, but on the whole one cannot reasonably maintain that he was an anti-Semite. It would, indeed, be easier to prove just the opposite: that he held a deep respect for the Jewish people. But having said all this, we should not let our emotions influence our judgment here. The fact that Nietzsche was not a Treitschke or an H. S. Chamberlain says nothing, one way or the other, about his contribution to European fascism. For the genocidal anti-Semitism of Nazism was not, in the final analysis, the essential component of that monstrous movement, but its most virulent symptom, its most catastrophic consequence, as the fate of the Slavs and other "inferior races" scapegoated by the Nazis clearly indicate.

In what sense, then, was Nietzsche both the culmination of the nineteenth century romantic sickness and the major intellectual source of Nazism? First of all, it must be noted that Nietzsche was a thoroughly sick man, in every conceivable meaning of that term. His significance lies in the fact that his sickness was the personification of the sick romantic rose. He was terrified of change, and it is no accident that his favorite ancient philosopher was Heraclitus. His madness was truly Heraclitean, and he knew it. Thus he wrote in one of his notes of 1873: "This beautiful world history is, in Heraclitean terms, 'a chaotic pile of rubbish' " [Nietzsche, the perfect romantic, was fully aware of its antagonism to idealism] What is strong wins: that is the simple law. And in *Twilight of the Idols,* he wrote: "Heraclitus will remain eternally right with his assertion that being is an empty fiction. The 'apparent' world is the only one: the 'true' world is merely added by a lie."

The ontological crisis takes a new twist. Being is "an empty fiction"; the "apparent world" is the only one and it is made by will, as he learned from Schopenhauer; only now, it is the will to power. Sado-masochistic authoritarianism and the totalitarian conception of the good as the powerful, especially the totality of the all-powerful state ruled by the superman are the culmination of romantic thought. Nietzsche sums it all up in *The AntiChrist* when he wrote:

What is good? Everything that heightens the feeling of power in man, the will to power, power itself. What is bad? Everything that is born of weakness. What is happiness? The feeling that power is *growing,* that resistance is overcome. Not contentedness but more power; not peace but war; not virtue but fitness . . . The weak and the failures shall perish: first principle of *our* love of man. And they shall even be given every possible assistance. What is more harmful than any vice? Active pity for all the failures and all the weak: Christianity.[45]

I cannot think of a more perfect summary of the Nazi ethos than that quotation. We are left in no doubt about the direct influence of Nietzsche's romanticism on Hitler, for Hitler frequently made this abundantly clear. William L. Shirer pointed out: ". . . Nazi scribblers never tired of extolling him. Hitler often visited the

Nietzsche museum in Weimar and publicized his veneration for the philosopher by posing for photographs of himself staring in rapture at the bust of the great man." [46]

It strikes me as incredible that any sane person would wish, today, to rehabilitate Nietzsche and his pathological rantings. Nothing more tellingly demonstrates the continued hold of the romantic tradition on the Western mind than this attempted rehabilitation. When we learn, further, that those most involved with this perverse task are often so-called humanists and liberals concerned with the human condition and the problem of meaning in modern society, we begin to realize how deep and seemingly incurable was the intellectual cancer that began to spread in the social thought of the Western world at the end of the eighteenth century.

Romanticism also developed a peculiar conception of individuality. No thinker has explored this problem with greater subtlety than Simmel in his essay, "Freedom and the Individual," [47] which, though penetrating, remains incomplete and at times misleading.

Simmel argues that "freedom becomes for the eighteenth century the universal demand which the individual uses to cover his manifold grievances and self-assertions against society." Once the constraints of traditional institutions and the vestiges of feudalism were completely removed, it was assumed that the true person would come to the surface in all its rationality and goodness. This conception of individuality assumes "the natural equality of individuals." Because human beings are perfect in their natural state, the removal of constraint must mean the removal of basic differences, since all persons would emerge as equally perfect. "This is why," Simmel writes, "it is man in general, universal man, who occupies the center of interest for this period instead of historically given, particular and differentiated man. The latter is in principle reduced to the former: in each individual person, man in general lives . . ." Freedom and equality are therefore inextricably linked. "It is for this reason," also, Simmel continues, "that 'natural law' is based on the fiction of isolated and identical individuals." Thus the underlying philosophical rationale for freedom and equality, whether it be reason or nature, amounts to the following. "The worth of each individual's configuration is based, to be sure, on him alone, on his personal responsibility, but along with that it is based on what the individual has in common with all others."

This view of individuality, it is further argued, can in practice lead to a laissez-faire conception of the world. The unseen hand regulating the free play of the competing forces of individual self-interest is the underlying natural rationality of human beings released by the removal of constraints on their ability. This, unfortunately, was the way in which the Enlightenment conception of individuality was interpreted in the nineteenth century following the lead of Adam Smith. Such an interpretation was not only unnecessary but actually involved a distortion of true Enlightenment principles. Laissez-faire individuality opens the door for a new kind of inequality, "a new repression, a repression of dullards by the smart, of the weak by the strong, of the shy by the aggressive." It was to prevent this crudely materialistic and opportunistic distortion of their philosophy that the Enlightenment thinkers strongly emphasized the idea of brotherhood, of fraternity. Simmel tells us: "For it was only through the voluntary act of renunciation as expressed in this concept that it would be possible to prevent liberty from being accompanied by the total opposite of egalité."

Simmel is right in identifying this countervailing intellectual role of fraternity. He should also have noted, however, that it is a purely ad hoc kind of intellectual check. If it is a "voluntary act of renunciation," it is not something intrinsic to the philosophy but something tacked on, just in case. It seems to me that if there is to be an intrinsic check on the inegalitarian thrust of a libertarian ethic, such a check will depend upon the causal direction of the equality-freedom relationship. If freedom is derived from equality, then there is no need for an extraneous voluntary check, for any philosophy of freedom which violates the principle of equality must by definition violate the principle of freedom. If, however, equality is derived from freedom, then the laissez-faire distortion immediately follows and those who are careless enough to have accepted this causal direction but wish to remain true to the idea of equality are therefore forced to patch things up, as it were, by appealing to the extraneous principle of fraternity. It was precisely this carelessness of which many of the Enlightenment thinkers were guilty. Many were in agreement with just such a development, guilty not only of carelessness but of betraying the Stoic tradition.

There was, Simmel argues, another reaction to Enlightenment individuality. This form of individuality requires only freedom. It deliberately excludes equality. Freedom is needed to take away institutional constraints, but once the individual personality is released, it moves naturally toward inequality with respect to other individuals, "but this time an inequality determined only from within . . . the quest for independence continued to the point where individuals who had been rendered independent in this way wanted only to distinguish themselves from one another. What mattered now was no longer that one was a free individual as such, but that one was a particular and irreplaceable individual . . . the quest for the individual is for self, for a fixed and unambiguous point of reference."

Two conceptions of individuality emerged by the early nineteenth century. Simmel calls them "the individualism of uniqueness (Einzigkeit) in contrast to that of singleness (Einzelheit)." The first is the individualism of the romantics, the second the individualism of the Enlightenment. Simmel sums up his analysis:

Incessantly, these great forces of modern culture strain toward accommodation in countless external and internal domains and in countless permutations. One force is the yearning for the autonomous personality that bears the cosmos within itself, whose isolation has the great compensation of being identical to all others at its deepest, natural core. The other is the yearning for the incomparability of being unique and different, which is compensated for its isolation by the fact that each person can exchange with another some good that he alone possesses and whose exchange weaves both of them into the interaction of organic parts of the whole. By and large one can say that the individualism of simply free personalities that are thought of as equal in principle has determined the rationalistic liberalism of France and England, whereas the individualism that is based on qualitative uniqueness and immutability is more a concern of the Germanic mind.[48]

Simmel's analysis is both insightful and profound, yet remains incomplete, and the contrast between the two types of individuality, while suggestive, glosses over important issues and differences. Few persons would deny that it places the individuality of freedom and universalism in an unfavorable light when compared with that of romantic particularism. I will attempt to show how the individualism of uniqueness is not what it is cracked up to be, and indeed, that it *necessarily* develops into something quite loathsome. And I will attempt to rescue the individualism of freedom and universalism from the taint of sterile, rationalistic uniformity with which Simmel, unwittingly, paints it.

Romantic uniqueness begins with the assumption of inherent individual differences. The liberal version of such differences, from such thinkers as Herder, is the old view that individuals, while separate and unique, are and can be equal. But such equality is untenable, as the romantics themselves were quick to discover. No human being can be absolutely unique. If such a person existed, he or she would be some strange mutant. When the claim is made that a person is unique, what is meant is that with respect to a certain set of qualities there is a peculiarity due to the degree to which these differences are possessed and the configuration of these qualities. Since the number of qualities on which human beings are capable of being different are limited, the critical variable in determining the uniqueness of the personality configuration must be the degree to which the qualities in question are possessed. For such degrees are truly infinite. If we compare a Mozart with any number of merely competent composers with similar personality qualities, the uniqueness of Mozart comes only from the greater degree or superiority of his musical talents. The individuality of uniqueness is only possible if it assumes inequality among human beings. Indeed, what it celebrates is precisely the relative superiority/inferiority of human beings, for the existence of a separate individual who is at once unique and equal is a logical impossibility. The romantics, as we have said, recognized and accepted this implication of their conception of individuality.

Flowing logically from the individuality of uniqueness is not only an emphasis on inequality but an aggrandizement of the superior human being. It is a short and logically necessary step from the artificially liberal individuality of Herder to the naturally illiberal individuality of Nietzsche with its celebration of the superman, he who is more human by virtue of the uniqueness of his near divine genius.

But there is an even more disturbing implication of the individuality of uniqueness. In reacting against the generalizing social science of the Enlightenment, historical and cultural uniqueness were emphasized in romantic thought. The individuality of uniqueness is critically related to the historicity of romanticism. The attempt to define the individual as unique is one of a piece with the attempt to define the culture and the past as unique. Individualistic particularism and sociocultural particularism are merely two aspects of the same way of viewing mankind. It is not from culture, as such, that the romantic seeks to liberate humanity, but from what were held to be the unnatural outgrowths of society, from institutions which were held to thwart natural culture. Once these institutions are eliminated, individuals can find their natural anchorage in the natural culture of the folk, hence the enormous emphasis on the unique elements of folk culture among the very thinkers who were developing the concept of the individuality of uniqueness. The folk culture is conceived of as raw, irrational, immediate, spontaneous, specifically historical, authentic and unique; so is the individual.

But if the relationship is not to be purely analogic, how is the uniqueness of the individual to be reconciled with the uniqueness of his or her culture? The answer is to be found in the necessarily

held view of the inequality of the individuality of uniqueness and
its glorification of the man of genius. It is only the genius who, in
the end, is truly unique. He is the superman who, by his genius,
becomes the culture-creating individual. He is the only person
who is creator of culture, rather than a creature of culture. By his
genius he not only stands as creator, but he helps to make, along
with other men of genius a unique culture, and a culture that is
not only unique, but by the same logic as that which applies to
individuals a culture that is superior in its uniqueness. In this way
all members of his society share the limelight of his genius. The
masses of ordinary individuals become superior vis-à-vis the
masses of other societies. Thus those who are not geniuses acquire
a collective individuality, by which is meant a collective superiority, which is the gift of the new gods, the supermen with respect
to whom and only to whom the masses of the particular tribe are
inferior. The reward of individual inferiority is the glory of being
an organic part of a superior collectivity and culture.

In this way romantic individuality rapidly becomes
raciocultural uniqueness, collectivistic, chauvinistic, and racist.
There is no need to illustrate this development as it relates to
continental Europe, especially Germany. There is an intrinsic
logical connection between the individuality of uniqueness and
the twin horrors of rationalized inequality and collectivistic
chauvinism.

The individuality of singleness or freedom is not the unlikeable
personal homogeneity Simmel's analysis suggests. Simmel is
correct in arguing that the Enlightenment thinkers, like all
universalists, emphasized what is common to all human beings.
This is as it should be, at least to any genuine humanist, and there
is no need to apologize for it. Indeed it must be a source of
humanistic pride.

But what does such an emphasis mean? Freedom and equality
yes, and these are good. But do freedom and equality and the
assumption of the inherent unity of mankind imply individual
sameness? The answer is a resounding no! In asserting that human
beings can and should be different as individuals, the humanist

proceeds, not by defining differences as a set of human qualities, but as a set of human actions. It is what we do and not what we are that make us different. Because the qualities that differentiate us as human beings are extremely limited, the romantics were forced to emphasize the degree to which these qualities are held if their individuality was to be meaningful. The humanist has no such problems, for the basis on which human differences rest are, in the first place, almost infinite, subject only to the structural imperatives of the society. There is no theoretical limit on how an individual is capable of doing and only a few on what is possible. Even if he or she restricts the range of activities to a small set of occupations, the possibilities still remain endless. Thus, a woman who restricts herself to the task of being a mother has a wide range of possible ways in which she can achieve perfection, fulfilment, and singleness in practicing motherhood. But the universalist does not stop here. For if there is reason to believe that the range of possibilities for such a woman has been restricted by the constraints imposed by a sexist society, the humanist must and will immediately raise the banner of freedom. The choice of the range within which the individual chooses to act must also be left open to the individual. If a woman chooses motherhood, the possibilities of individuality should be made achievable within this range and cannot be demeaned. But if she also chooses to do something else—to be scientist, lawyer, teacher, anything—the power to expand the range of activities should also be made possible by her society.

By its emphasis on what we do and how we do, humanistic universalism, while maintaining the idea of the unity and equality of mankind—indeed because it remains committed to such ideas— makes possible a near infinite range of truly different and unique individuals. Such differences are as much open to the least as to the most intellectually gifted among us. Because we respect the inherent equality and worth of all individuals, we also respect the inherent equality and worth of the things each person *freely chooses* to do, whether it is the street corner hippie making his or her nail jewelry or the mathematician spinning out his or her latest theorem. This, I submit, is the true and only meaning of the individuality of freedom.

The Fascist Convergence

German philosophical idealism was as faithful a restatement of the Platonic tradition as was possible. From the very beginning the German idealists drew the inevitable particularistic conclusion of their essentialistic epistemology. In the same way that Plato idealized the most totalitarian version of the Greek state, Sparta, as the closest approximation to the really real form or idea of the state, so did the Jena school, especially its most famous spokesman, Hegel, idealize and glorify the German state as the ultimate realization of the spirit of world historical forces. The nationalistic vulgarities of Fichte's *Reden an die deutsche Nation* was no mere accident, no isolated aberration in the total corpus of his philosophy as so many of his apologists have claimed. Rather, it was his occasional expressions of liberal views which were accidental and at variance with the essentialism of his philosophy.

The development of German idealism and its totalitarian implications is well trodden ground and too well known to require much elaboration here.[49] German particularism had a double source: the substantive particularism of its romantic tradition and the essentialistic particularism of its idealistic tradition, the one a restatement of Platonism, the other a restatement of Hebraism. The two traditions ran concurrently throughout the nineteenth century and, of necessity, reinforced the particularism of each other. But the rationalism of the one and the revelatory method of the other made a complete reconciliation difficult, if not impossible. Only a convergence was possible, and what was needed was an intellectual genius of the order of St. Augustine to bring the two together, emphasizing what was common to both traditions and merging, in a subliminal way, their contradictions.

There were many candidates. The one that perhaps came

closest to a successful convergence was Rudolph Hermann Lotze. His bold attempt to stand Hegelian idealism on its head—in his attempt to derive the ideal from the real rather than the opposite, essentialistic route—was ingenious, but in the end unsuccessful. Lotze was no Marx. Schopenhauer, as we hinted earlier, perhaps possessed the genius to forge such a convergence, but lacked the will. Idealism was simply too hostile in its method and epistemology to Romanticism for anything like a persuasive convergence to be made by purely philosophical means.

So in the end it was not the philosophers who made the convergence, but the political ideologists. The philosopher, no matter how totalitarian his propensities, must in the final analysis persuade by reason. The political ideologist has no such constraint; he persuades by means of a mystical appeal to either the passions or to a higher reason. Indeed, since he is under no constraints to appear not to be inconsistent, he can appeal to reason and to faith at one and the same time. The horrible convergence was finally made then by such ideologues and pseudointellectuals as Friedrich List, Gobineau, Heinrich von Treitschke, and Wagner in the nineteenth century, then, more directly, by Houston Stewart Chamberlain, the other ideologists of the Nazi movement, and, of course, by Hitler himself.

This special convergence of the romantic and idealistic gave German fascism its peculiar venom. The other forms of fascism in continental Europe, such as those of Spain and Italy, were mainly political romanticism or nationalism taken to their conservative and totalitarian conclusions. Here we find ourselves in complete agreement with Eugen Weber when, in comparing non-German with German fascism, he writes:

...[The Fascist] rejects theory in favor of practice and relies largely on the attraction of that "fever" to which I have referred. The fascist ethos is emotional and sentimental: at that level the ends of action count less than action itself, and the forces that lead men into the fascist camp can be enlisted on any side whatever, provided they are given an opportunity to indulge themselves—the more violent, the better...[50]

Weber distinguishes this romantically based fascism from Nazi fascism. (Incidentally, he seems to prefer to use the term fascism only for the above type. I prefer to follow convention and use it in the more general sense, seeing Nazism as a specially destructive type coming about as a result of what I call the fascist convergence. The issue, however, is purely semantic.):

The National Socialist, on the other hand, seems much more theoretical. He may use theory merely to rationalize, but he respects it. Whatever he may pretend, words and ideas count for him as much as actions, and sometimes they replace them ... the Nazis of all people were ready to make the most extraordinary sacrifices for the sake of their theories and their twisted ideals.[51]

CHAPTER 10

Ethnicity, the Modern Crisis, and the Possibility of a Secular Reengagement

Was the neoromantic German philosopher Hartmann right in thinking that there is a basic, irresolvable conflict between the progress of industrial culture and the achievement of human happiness? Are we today facing on a mass scale the personal and intellectual crisis that culminated in the profound pessimism of Arthur Schopenhauer? Sometimes it seems to me that the answer to both these questions might be in the affirmative. The modern cry that there is a tension between material progress and moral security has been heard from the very beginning of Western civilization. According to E. R. Dodds, after a brief period of optimism about the beneficial consequences of material and social development in the late fifth century B.C., a pessimistic reaction set in among almost all Greek thinkers: "The tension between belief in scientific or technological progress and belief in moral regress is present in many ancient writers—most acutely in Plato, Posidonius, Lucretius, Seneca."[1] Such pessimism has been endemic in the conservative traditions that have dominated Western thought. The most recent expression of it is Nisbet's view that current demands for equality account for "the twilight of authority" and, of course, the twilight of our happiness. Could so many people be just plain wrong? And yet, I still dare to hope; idly, perhaps even foolishly, I still believe that in reason and modernity lie both the source of our discontent and the solution to our problem. This is not to indulge any naive optimism such as Pope's view that there is in "All chance, Direction which thou canst see." A Humean scepticism is still consistent with a certain Stoic commitment to the virtues of reasonableness, if not reason itself; and it certainly does not imply any extreme pessimism. As Ernest Geller once said of the transition from traditionalism to modernity: "Paradoxically, the only safe base is to be found in doubt rather than dogmatism."

In the course of this short work I have worn two hats. Wearing one, I have explored the problem of ethnicity from a sociohistorical perspective. Wearing the other, I have examined its intellectual and moral roots as a social critic. But the matter does not end here. It cannot. For the stark fact remains that ethnicity persists. Thrives. The fact remains that millions of men and women all over the world are retreating to the embrace of the ethnic group. This is not the work of intellectuals, not just the abstractions of the mind, but a real recommitment of millions of concrete individuals. Ethnicity lives, it grows. Clearly it pretends to meet a deep human need or seems to offer some irresistible solution to the most profound problem of our age.

The object of our inquiry remains elusive. Our analysis of its intellectual roots has given us some hint why this is so. It seems as if ethnicity is impermeable to sociohistorical and intellectual analysis. As Schopenhauer would say: it has "thrown off its veil" but is still not "naked." Ethnicity, as social process, as idea, has been made comprehensible. But as a thing-in-itself it still defies our understanding.

There is only one recourse. The thing is an intellectual guerrilla. So there is only one way to come to grips with it, to form a total understanding of it. We must meet it on its own terms; struggle with it in its own terrain; learn the secret paths of its primordial jungle; find its hidden caves; meet head on the god that nourishes its being. We must, in short, probe the ontological core of ethnicity, the kernel of its source in the human soul.

To do so adequately would require another volume; as things

are I have already gone much beyond the limits of my own discipline, although this is a matter that hardly concerns me, since I refuse to recognize such limits. Here, however, I can only hint at the source of the problem, only intimate an understanding. We have identified the true source of ethnicity in the Western mind in what I have called the Hebraic tradition. We can now disregard Platonic essentialism, for in spite of its lethal association with ethnicity, its role is mainly reinforcive and catalytic.

No, if we are to probe the nature of the thing we call ethnicity, it is to a more profound understanding of Hebraism that we must turn. For Hebraism, like pristine Christianity, differs from the other traditions in one crucial respect: It is not just a tradition but a mode of being. The problem posed by Hebraism is a problem which all human beings face, and the solution offered by it is one which is, if not the best, at least the most workable humanity has come up with so far.

I have indicated this several times before, but must restate it once more: I make a distinction between Hebraism and the group of people who are most closely associated with it—its pristine bearers so to speak—the Jews. I am saying that, as a mode of being, all humanity can and has been Hebraic. The specific content of Gentilic Hebraism may have differed with the creeds of different peoples, but the nature of the problem as it has emerged in the modern world and the manner of its resolution remain essentially the same. The Jews are special among modern human beings in the priority and intensity of their involvement with the Hebraic crisis, in the monumental courage with which they have approached its challenges, and in the existential genius which they have applied in their attempt to resolve and articulate it. This conception of Jewish "specialness"—the word "chosen" is theirs, but from the viewpoint of a sympathetic Gentile it is both too loaded and misleading [3]—is consistent with the views of one of the greatest of modern Jewish philosophers, Martin Buber, who argued that the dialogical relationship between persons, and between persons and God, the "eternal thou," acquired a special intensity and heightened clarity of expression among the Jews.

One may therefore interpret the Jewish experience, or more properly the Jewish expression of their experience—pristine Hebraism—as a kind of mission in communication. The Jewish experience is a larger-than-life expression of an experience all peoples were eventually to face. In this sense their experience is a kind of light, a revelation of what was in store for all humanity. Their experience, to use another related metaphor, is a concrete, collective, living work of art, an image of humanity's fate "at the end of days."

There is a real sense in which "the end of days" has come. It has been brought about by industrial civilization, which marked a radical, qualitative change in the human condition. Industrial modernity, I am saying, has made Jews of us all, has forced upon us the Hebraic crisis with which the Jews, as Benjamin Kahn tells us, have struggled for the millennia of their extraordinary history.[4] How has industrialism done this? And what exactly is the nature of the Hebraic crisis?

The Hebraic crisis is, quite simply, the crisis of alienation; the crisis of being uprooted, of being cut off from time, from self, and from community. And its challenge is the search, the quest, for a restoration of these lost sources of anchorage, the satisfaction of what Simone Weil called "the need for roots."[5] Furthermore humanity's attempts at disalienation and restoration have all been Hebraic. We use the same means, we seek the same solution. Herein lies the true meaning of ethnicity. Herein, too, lies the central tragedy of modern humanity. Before explaining why the Hebraic solution is no longer tenable, hence the tragedy of persisting in the belief that it is, we must first explore more deeply the symbolic and existential structure of Hebraism. Our approach now cannot be that of the sociologist talking about symbols, their functional significance, and what not; nor can it be that of the intellectual historian trying to understand, from the outside, what is going on in there. We must, instead, follow the lead of modern students of symbolism such as Victor Turner,[6] and explore from the inside, the "forest of symbols" that constitutes Hebraism as it is experienced in the Jewish consciousness.

We begin by noting that the central problem of being Jewish is exile. There were two stages in the evolution of exilic Jewry: the formative exile of Egypt, in which the Jewish consciousness was born, and then the exodus and the nomadic wanderings in the desert. It was during the Mosaic period that one of the two major solutions to the crisis of exile was achieved, the strong sense of solidarity of the nomadic group, a solidarity born of the very insecurity engendered by the terrors of the desert. During this period, too, the true faith emerged: the intense, personal involvement with other persons in a collective identity and with God. Martin Buber's I-Thou relationship finds its perfect expression in the concreteness, integrity, and equality of personal relationships in the pastoral group. And Buber's conception of God as the eternal Thou manifesting itself in the everyday relations of concrete individuals with concrete Thous and Its is perfectly realized in the Mosaic view of God as a personal, immediate being, ultimately unknowable, but with whom direct, experiential contact is always possible.

Yet the nomadic solution remains only partial. There is still the continuous yearning for emplacement, for the security of the promised land. The realization of the promised land constitutes the second solution. No longer is there the insecurity from without, the terrors of the desert, the fear of external foes, both man and beast. But the promised land has its costs. For soon the Jews find that the external dangers of the desert which at least had the positive effect of intensifying the communitarian bond and strengthening the faith are replaced by internal dangers, all negative in their implications. The Davidic state soon becomes corrupt. Internal divisions of class and region and sect set in. Worse, the faith itself is corrupted, on the one hand by the rigid formalism of the priests, on the other hand by the lusting after alien gods by the kings and the ruling class. Disaster and the second and final exile are the inevitable consequences.

It is in the Babylonian exile that, as we have seen, diaspora Jewry is formed. And it is at this point that Jewish history, as an image of the Hebraic mode of being meaningful to all mankind, takes its final shape. There is the acceptance of the reality of exile. Only a small proportion of the diaspora Jews take advantage of the opportunity to return to Palestine when it is granted by the Persians. Exile, then, becomes a permanent state, a way of life, an inherent part of the Jewish condition. This is the Hebraic crisis in its pristine form: Exile is real and eternal. The problem now is how to deal with it. On the practical level it involves the development of what a much later generation would call *gegenwartsarbeit,* work in the present diaspora, which in its extreme form would culminate in the hopeless social philosophy of S. Dubnow, whose "autonomism" conceives of a stateless world of ethnic groups living in sublime, pluralistic harmony. Of greater relevance for us is the more profound resolution of the problem on the spiritual and symbolic level.

The Hebraic answer touches on the three sources of alienation—alienation from history, from self, and from emplacement. The solution to the problem of historical alienation is to be found in the relationship between the concept of the promised land and the messianic hope. The future lies in a reclamation of the past. In this way, past, present, and future are symbolically reintegrated. But there is a hidden tension in this integration; it is the Zionic paradox.

There is not one, but two conceptions of Zion. Zion is the communitarian solidarity and religious purity of the desert, Hibbat Zion, the Mizrachi of Alkalai, Kalischer, and the Ezra Society. But Zion is also the restoration of the Davidic state, *Der Judenstaat* of Herzl, the "land without a people" for "a people without a land," and in its most secular form, it is the Zion of Moses Hess. For most, however, there is a yearning for the advantages and the promise of both. But alas, the two are antithetical. The "synthetic zionism" which Chaim Weizmann tried so hard and eloquently to articulate remains, in the final analysis, a spiritual impossibility. It is impossible to be both nomad and citizen, to maintain the personal god of the desert and the stately god of the temple, to enjoy the communistic equality of the tribe and the inegalitarian affluence of the state. But above all else, it is the tension between being and object, between meaning that comes, on the one hand, from the shared isolation, the intense involvement, the indestructible hope, and the primal intimacy of living only for the sake of living, being only for being's sake, of knowing only as subject, of being one with other thous and the eternal thou; and the meaning that comes, on the other hand, from the objects we create and from mastery over the objects outside our being. The first meaning, being-for-itself, obviates loneliness, for its point of departure is loneliness; in denying externalities it denies separation. But its danger is that it makes one terribly vulnerable, for one has no control, one hardly knows what is going on out there. The second meaning enriches, makes us powerful, leads us to create, build, control the elements. But it leads us right down the path to loneliness, for soon we find that the things we have created become objects apart from us, and insofar as our being is invested in these objects we are separated from it. In our effort to control the outer world we lose control of the one within. The tension between these two forms of meaning is the tension between Buber's I-Thou and I-It relationships.

This takes us to the second problem, the search for a solution to the problem of personal alienation. Who am I then, this strange creature staring at myself in the objects of my creation? The Hebraic solution to this second problem is to transform the question into another. To ask "Who am I?" is meaningless; rather one asks "What am I?" "What" must precede "who," since to be in a situation where it is necessary to ask "Who am I" is to be in a situation where there can have been no "who." This is the tragedy of exile. And the response to the question, "What am I?" is unambiguous. I am a member of a community, a very special community, one held together by a "shared memory" and a shared hope. In this way the resolution of the problem of all three forms of alienation become united into a single problem and a single solution. "Who am I?" becomes "To which group do I belong?" And the last question is answered in the solution to the final question: "Where am I coming from and where am I going?" The solution is, of course, the divinely ordained destiny of the group: the reclamation of Zion. So we are led back to where we began, to the idea of Zion. But the Zionic paradox still remains unresolved. By solving it then, all the other problems of alienation will have been solved.

The Hebraic solution to this paradox has always been the same, from Moses to Martin Buber and, however reluctantly, Simone Weil: faith. All tensions between the I-Thou and the I-It are resolved through faith in the one indivisible God. We do not know how, for such knowledge is beyond us and it is vain to search after it. But we can believe and experience this unity. For Buber, drawing on his Hasidic faith, the Eternal Thou is revealed in all finite relationships, all the finite concrete Thous of our life. It is the ultimate statement of the Hebraic solution to the exilic crisis of mankind.

Unfortunately, this solution is no longer acceptable to or possible for a large and growing segment of mankind. We no longer find it possible to believe, or if and when we do, not with the "ardour" required to solve in a lasting and meaningful way the crisis of the modern world. Our tragedy then is that industrial civilization has made Jews of us all, has forced upon us the necessity to face the Hebraic crisis, but in the process of so doing it has robbed us of the one solution which, in the course of human history, has proven itself to be the foolproof solution of the crisis.

Faith is no longer foolproof. For some still, to be sure. But not for me and not for millions of other persons now confronting the Hebraic crisis of modernity. Furthermore, I submit that it is not workable for most of those who are still desperately holding on to it. Ethnicity and all the other exclusive, communitarian forms of recommitment are bound to fail as solutions to the problems of existence in the modern world for the simple reason that, in the final analysis, there can be no such thing as a truly secular, faithless ethnicity. Because they lack the capacity to sustain faith, it seems inevitable that many of those now recommitting themselves to the ethnic group are bound to come to grief. Fathers

Andrew Greeley and Geno Baroni and their numerous colleagues who now applaud the revival of ethnicity should heed the warning of the distinguished theologian Father Gustave Weigel:

Nationalism is a faith but it is a brittle faith. The national gods are always so small and they have not the greatness to make men great. As a result, a thoroughgoing nationalism can at most produce spurts of action and feeling. In the long run, it loses its power to direct the efforts of men. Nationalism is prevalent in our world, but we can consider it only as a sign of little faith.[7]

Industrialism is the most jealous of gods. Yes, even more uncompromising in its exclusivism than Yahweh himself. Industrialism is the one god that undermines all other gods. It is anti-faith and anti-god. It is the final triumph of reason over faith. It demands of its knowers that they do not believe, and it mocks other gods by making of their most sophisticated believers wise fools who would seek to believe by knowing: "Go, go, go said the bird . . ." There is, indeed, a close resemblance between modern ethnic reconversion and what E. W. F. Tomlin scathingly referred to as "the comedy of a modern intellectual conversion, with its three acts of timid interest, assent not unmixed with exhibitionism, and scurrying retraction."[8] We live in a "post-Christian era," as Gabriel Vahanian calls it,[9] and the ethnic revival is as much a "misbegotten revival" as the recent Christian revival. Beginning with Barth, most modern death-of-God theologians have struggled with the simple religious faithlessness of modern life and have arrived at some strange conclusions. Thus Barth tells us that:

Faith is its own initiation, its own presupposition. Upon whatever rung of the ladder of human life men may happen to be standing—whether they be Jew or Greek, old or young, educated or uneducated, complex or simple—in tribulation or in repose they are capable of faith. . . . For all faith is both simple and difficult; for all alike it is a scandal, a hazard a "Nevertheless"; to all it presents the same embarrassment and the same promise; for all it is a leap into the void. And it is possible for all only because for all it is equally impossible.[10]

Paul Tillich goes even further in his celebrated method of "justification by doubt." "The situation of doubt, even of doubt about God, need not separate us from God," he assures himself.

> There is faith in every serious doubt, namely, the faith in the truth as such, even if the only truth we can express is our lack of truth. But if this is experienced in its depth and as an ultimate concern, the divine is present; and he who doubts in such an attitude is "justified" in his thinking. So the paradox got hold of me that he who seriously denies God, affirms him.[11]

This is not, as some have claimed, the voice of modern religious optimism. It is, rather, the theology of desperation. But in its desperation it is at least more honest than the fraudulent religious revival which Vahanian rightly condemns. As fraudulent and inauthentic as the religious revival is the ethnic revival. Our times are as post-ethnic as they are post-Christian. The gap between authentic ethnicity and what passes for ethnicity today, especially in Western societies, is as great as "the gap between the Gospel and 'the power of positive thinking' " which Vahanian deplores. By extending the analogy between religion and ethnicity we arrive at a vital clue to the true nature and meaning of the ethnic revival. In a brilliant passage Vahanian tells us that "the idea of faith has triumphed over the content of faith. Religiosity has triumphed over Christianity because Christianity has lost its original value." [12] Almost exactly the same thing can be said of the ethnic revival, especially in America. The idea of ethnic commitment has triumphed over the content of such commitment. Ethnicity has triumphed over the functioning ethnic group, because such groups have lost their original value.

We can, of course, still choose. We can reject modernity altogether, including its rewards, and return to the preindustrial culture that is more favorable to faith. For those for whom this is still possible and so choose, I have no complaint. Unfortunately, in the perverse manner of human beings, most of us want it both ways. We demand the rewards of industrial civilization but we are not prepared to worship at its shrine. We still want the solace of the old gods and the old faith. This, apart from being totally unworkable, is simply asking for more trouble. It is simply to intensify that "ontological insecurity" of which R. D. Laing speaks in *The Divided Self.*

We see the results of such contradictory demands all over the Third World, where the attempt to pursue faith and the particularistic allegiance and to promote industrialism has simply resulted in the failure to develop and tragic confusion about the old faiths. We see it in the tragedies of those "underdeveloped minorities" of the advanced industrial cultures who have demanded inclusion into the civilization and its material and social rewards while insisting on remaining faithful to their particular creeds, ideologies and styles of living. And we see it in the personal tragedies of formerly cosmopolitan modernists who have tried to return to the ethnic group or the church only to discover that they no longer possess the capacity or even the will to believe in them.

But perhaps the greatest tragedy of all is the exploitation of this confusion and vain search by unscrupulous leaders who will stop at nothing, including the exploitation of modern humanity's greatest crisis, in attaining power. As none other than Robert Nisbet has written: "All too often power comes to resemble community, especially in times of compulsive social change and of widespread preoccupation with personal identity, moral certainty and social meaning. That is ... the essential tragedy of modern man's quest for community." [13] It is ironical that Nisbet, in his most recent works, has joined the bandwagon of praise for the ethnic revival. Ethnicity, we have just seen, is an empty faith; it is a commitment to nothing more than the idea of itself. Nothing is more dangerous than such empty commitment. "Commitment," Kenneth Keniston wrote in *The Uncommitted,* "is worthy only as its object is worthy." The fanatical believer of something is a menace because he can be manipulated; but there are limits even here: He can only be manipulated by someone who genuinely believes in the same thing. Because he believes so strongly he can easily detect fraud and deception, especially in those who choose to lead him. Far more dangerous than the fanatical believer is the person who merely believes in the idea of believing something. Because there is nothing, no content of belief, there are no limits; there is no way of recognizing fraudulence; there are no canons of authenticity. Here, surely, is the perfect breeding ground for the demagogic and the ruthless. As we have observed before, it is no accident that the ethnic revival in America coincided with the revival of Richard Nixon. But, alas, it has not departed with him.

Assuming that we do not choose to reject modernity, how do we come to terms with our exilic crisis? What solutions are there other than the impossible head-in-the-sand atavism of the preindustrial Hebraic solution? How do we replace faith? I am not so bold as to think that I know the answer to these questions. It is tempting indeed to simply pass the buck to the existential philosophers and say, "There, you take over." To do this, however, would not only be dishonest but would completely misunderstand what existentialism is all about. These philosophers have done humanity a great service by focusing our attention on the problem and by clarifying it. To define the central problem of our times has always been one of the major roles of the philosophers. Where existentialism differs from all previous philosophies is in its refusal to offer any systematic solution. The solution, it says, if it exists at all, is in each one of us. Everyman and everywoman must now become his and her own philosopher, must face the crisis in all its crushing loneliness, and must explore the whole person and bring the whole being into play in the endless struggle with it. The solution is the struggle.

This I am prepared to accept. This we must all accept sooner or later. We have no choice. What I find wholly unacceptable in the reflections of many existentialist thinkers, especially Americans, is the tendency toward a certain implicit, and often explicit, antimodernity, a certain "fear and trembling" in the face of industrial civilization, and a neoromantic (and dangerous!) pessimism about the nature of our civilization. A good example of this tendency is to be found in the work of William Barrett. I choose

Barrett because I consider his work to be one of the finest and most persuasive commentaries and explorations in English on existentialism, both externally, as critic and commentator on the movement as a whole, and internally, as a brilliant, concerned, and involved modern human being.[14]

Barrett argues that industrialism is "the incarnation of rationalism" (I would have preferred the term rationality) both in the central role of science and technology, and in the bureaucratization of social life. This truth, of course, has been one of the central findings and subject matters of sociology, first fully expressed in the classic works of Max Weber and later elaborated in modern French and American sociology in the writings of such thinkers as Raymond Aron, Talcott Parsons, and Daniel Bell. Barrett is right in arguing that the antiintellectual innocence of traditional American thought is irrelevant in the face of this embodiment of rationality in the very structure of the civilization. He fails to observe, however, the growing Platonic rationalism in American social thought, and his own neoromanticism blinds him to the dangers of romanticism inherent in the nonacademic areas of modern American thought. More distressing, he fails to see the greater configurational danger of the potential convergence of romantic antiintellectual "innocence" once this innocence is lost (rapidly becoming the case) with the creeping Platonism of the academic theorists.[15] Even so, Barrett, through his existentialism, has a finely developed sense of the modern crisis, and I am wholly in agreement with him when he writes that "despite the increase in the rational ordering of life in modern times, men have not become the least bit more reasonable in the human sense of the word."[16]

This is the core of the problem. How to become more reasonable in human terms. I agree with Barrett that we simply make matters worse by denying the problem, but I totally disagree with his way of dealing with it. To recognize the existence of what he calls "the furies" in our being, the irrational part of us, is not to throw in the towel to them, and is not to be seduced by them. As Kant once observed, "Innocence is indeed a glorious thing, only, on the other hand, it is very sad that it cannot well maintain itself, and is easily seduced.[17] In being seduced by "the furies," Barrett, like all his fellow American irrationalists—Pound, Hemingway, Aiken, Stein, Sherwood Anderson, to list only a few of the better known—betrays in himself the very innocence which, in his more sober moments, he deplores. Our neuroses, our irrational propensities, and our primeval yearning to be seduced by our prerational lusts are real enough, but this does not make them good, nor is it to imply that they are not thoroughly controllable. You don't deny the problem, but neither do you return to the mid-nineteenth-century romanticism of Hartmann in celebrating the unconscious. And you certainly do not return to late eighteenth-century romanticism in claiming that if it's there and it's real it must be authentic and the ultimate good. For such seductions are precisely what led, as we have seen, to the worst tragedies of modern society. The genocidal monstrosities of fascism, we cannot repeat too often for misguided souls such as Barrett and other pessimistic neoromantics, is nothing more than a gross indulgence of the very "furies" they celebrate.

Ironically, indeed tragically, Barrett, in spite of his extraneously imposed liberalism (so typically American), fails to see that his fanatical attack on the Enlightenment is identical with the culmination of the attack on it in fascist ideology. In all this Barrett epitomizes the philosophical weakness of American liberalism, a weakness which springs from the aversion of Anglo-American thinkers to think through to first principles the essential elements of their social thought. If this is done, it will immediately be found that liberalism requires a return to the principles of Enlightenment thought, that the task ahead involves not an attack on the Enlightenment but a correction, elaboration, and development of its precepts, in the same way that the Enlightenment was a development of the tradition that began with early stoa. In this sympathetic and creative restatement of the Stoic tradition, we must first of all recognize where the Enlightenment went wrong.

I think the Enlightenment went astray in four crucial areas. First, there was the neo-Platonic ghost, which managed to work its way into the thought of Kant, who, to some extent, was to the Enlightenment what Posidonius was to early stoa. Kant strongly denied this, of course, but we must agree with the judgment of those who have clearly identified certain elements of essentialism in his thought, although I think Barrett gloats excessively with talk about "the ungentle hand of history" finally labeling him an idealist. I know of no responsible student of intellectual history who has conspired to do any such thing. It is, as Julius Ebbinghaus has pointed out, a gross intellectual libel to assert, as Dewey did in his *German Philosophy and Politics,* that Kant's ethical theory was in any way related to those currents in German thought that culminated in the Nazi terror.[18] Far more balanced is the judgment that Kant's ideas, because of certain ambiguities created by his rationalism, were easily misrepresented by the idealists. To reject elements of rationalism in Enlightenment thought, however, is not to reject reason, as Barrett does. It is a mistake to identify the two, for reasons that we have already made clear.[19] Reason per se presents its own problems, to be sure. But, as I shall argue shortly, it also offers the solution to its own problems.

A second problem of Enlightenment thought was the somewhat naive commitment to the idea of progress.[20] One must be fair and recognize their enthusiasm as the innocent overzealousness of the innovator. The eighteenth century stood on the frontier of modern industrial civilization. Its thinkers saw and hailed the radical new development in human culture unfolding under their eyes, and they welcomed the elimination of the old constraints on human freedom. They can hardly be blamed for that. Even so, their enthusiasm blinded them to the new dangers that industrialism could and would create, although this is a criticism which we could more realistically make of the nineteenth century. They are to be blamed, however, for their identification of progress with the unchecked forces of the free marketplace and the unrestrained growth of the industrial economy. A careless derivation of equality from freedom rather than vice versa led to a conception of individuality which was not only sterile but paved the way for the reintroduction of gross inequalities. The "unseen hand" of Adam Smith's marketplace is either pure Platonic rationalism or romantic mysticism. In either case it is damnable.

This takes me to the third problem of Enlightenment thought, the Marxist critique that it was, in spirit, a bourgeois movement. It is no accident that so many lost their heads on the guillotine of the early revolution before that movement revealed its true bourgeois colors. The Enlightenment thinkers were reformists in an age that demanded revolution. They were appalled by the iniquities and unfreedoms of the ancient regimes of Europe, but they could see little beyond their own noses. They extolled freedom, but they were republicans, not genuine democrats. Indeed, they feared the masses and were unduly terrified by what they liked to call the "tyranny of the majority," and their lack of compassion distorted their intellect, preventing them from following through to its logical conclusion the implications of their own strong defence of freedom. It was their style of life which mainly accounts for their partial betrayal of their Stoic principles. They were too smug, too rooted. There were not enough exiles among them; their thoughts lacked the driving force which comes only from the anguish of the stranger. They should have read more about the thoroughly hip way in which Zeno and his disciples lived; and they should have read less about, while traveling more among, the humanity they so exalted.

Freedom for too many of them came to mean simply the removal of constraints. They failed to see what St. Augustine had seen (but then only as a weapon to score an important debating point against the Pelagians): that there was a basic difference between the capacity to be free and the power to be free. They failed, that is, to see that it was a cruel hoax to acknowledge a person's capacity for freedom or negative rights, while withholding that person's power to exercise his or her freedom. They failed to see that transcending all particular rights was the greatest freedom of all, the right to enjoy one's particular freedoms. And not seeing this, they failed further to see how freedom is dependent on equality.[21]

Finally, the Enlightenment failed in the abuse of its empiricist epistemology. I have argued that many modern criticisms of the Enlightenment miss the mark by attacking the movement for what it was not, for what, indeed, it was reacting against, namely, Platonic rationalism or essentialism. But now it must be admitted that empiricism also has the potential for abuse. This is the danger that comes from a too great concentration on the generalizations from the particular at the expense of too little concern with the particulars from which the generalizations are drawn. The dangers of abstraction in Lockean empiricism are in no way logically determined, as they are in Platonic essentialism, rather they are habitual and substantive. They come from the careless tendency of human beings to slip into a reification of generalizations. The evil is correctible, but if it becomes a habit it can be just as damaging as Platonic essentialism. It is too easy for liberty to become an end in itself rather than a means of liberating real people, for freedom to mean more than free human beings. For the Enlightenment thinkers, one suspects that cosmopolitanism had become a kind of darling concept to be passed around the genteel drawing room of the ennobled man of the world, and occasionally a chic intellectual device with which the eighteenth century savant could score in smart fictional letters the hypocrisies and conceits of less sophisticated Europeans. It had precious little to do with the real live human beings of other lands and other cultures, with red, black, or yellow men and women in their unique expressions of the underlying psychic unity of mankind. Removed from real people and real problems, their ideas too often lacked compassion.

One sad example of this may be taken from the early nineteenth century. Hubert Cole, in his sensitive study of Henri Christophe,[22] the Haitian slave revolutionary, points out that after the latter's suicide his wife and family fled to England to seek help from Wilberforce, who, from his enlightened European drawing room, had given them the most fervent intellectual support in England over the long years of their struggle. When, however, the black queen and princesses turned up on the steps of Wilberforce's elegant quarters, the saintly Enlightenment hero panicked. In a state of utter embarrassment and perplexity, he refused even to receive the family of the man he had been so stoically defending over the years. It was left to the more genuinely humane Clarkson to make the great intellectual leap from generalized humanity to concrete humanism.

It should be clear that none of the major faults of the Enlightenment were intrinsic. They came mainly from carelessness, bourgeois selfishness, and the overenthusiasm of the intellectual frontiersman. They can all be easily corrected. The manner in which they are to be corrected in any new Enlightenment has been made clear by the nature of my criticisms. There was, however, one additional problem which Enlightenment thought did not come to terms with, partly because the times were not ripe for it. It is the crisis of modernity in its philosophical aspects, the ontological crisis. We owe it a debt for bringing the problem to the surface of advanced thought. But for Kant it was a purely philosophical crisis, one as we have seen that formed the point of departure for the romantic philosophers. Goethe fully recognized this limitation in Enlightenment thought, although his humanistic genius also rejected the romantic solution. As Goldmann points out: "Though Faust leaves the ideal of the Enlightenment behind him, he does not become a Christian. But he does recover the capacity to understand the content of religion and its meaning for men; he perceives the need for an answer to the religious questions to which the Enlightenment completely closed its eyes." [23] Romanticism since it coincided with the rapid rise of industrial civilization, could interpret the problem as one which went beyond the ivory towers of philosophical speculation. But even the early romantics could not have anticipated the degree to which the ontological crisis would become something all human beings would have to come to terms with in a self-conscious way. It would perhaps have come as something of a shock to Heine, who thought of himself as the first man of the nineteenth century, to learn that less than a century after he died his famous description of himself would be true of the majority of modern human beings: "I am a Jew, I am a Christian; I am tragedy, I am comedy; a Greek, a Hebrew; an adorer of despotism in Napoleon, an admirer of communism in Proudhon; a Latin, a Teuton; a beast, a devil, a god." Nor could Heine, so committed to the method of faith, have seen how industrial civilization as it presently exists could offer any hope of a solution to the problems it creates. With his piercing, sardonic irony, the very entertainment of such a hope would be taken as the clearest demonstration of the ultimate absurdity of our existence. One Heine would seem to be enough for any civilization. Several million Heines differing only in the absence of the poetic genius of the prototype must certainly be seen as the surest sign of the end of days.

At the risk of absurdity, however, I will persist in my conviction that modern civilization, while it robs us of the solution offered by faith, makes possible another solution. But this will only be possible if we move, in principle, to a society based on the social ethic of a new, corrected, and developed Enlightenment to a humanistic socialism, that is, to a truly egalitarian social order with a consciously encouraged universal culture. Such a society maximizes the potential of industrialism for good. It will not directly solve the problem it creates, but modern humanistic socialism lays the foundation for each and every one of us to solve it, or at least to creatively struggle with it, in our own individual ways.

In other words, a modern humanistic socialism has the power to release us from the constraints of poverty, ignorance, and oppression. A humanized, universalistic industrialism infinitely increases the range of our choices. And it is in the exercise of choice that we begin to find our salvation. But first, it is necessary that we lose our fear of choosing. It is this fear of choice which, I think, mainly terrifies those of our bourgeois intellectuals who, having benefited from industrialism in all possible respects, still run from the presumed terrors of modernity back to the glorified ethnic group.

God, St. Augustine had argued—perhaps realistically, given his times—is the only one who can give us the power to choose. Poor

Pelagius had no answer to this piece of dialectic from the astute
Bishop of Hippo. How could he? He was 1500 years ahead of his
time. Now we can answer Augustine for Pelagius. Humanistic
socialism gives us just such a power. Yes, the Bishop of Hippo will
no doubt reply, but to choose what? This is the ultimate question.
God, through grace, not only gave us the power to choose, but
also the object of our choice. But as we prepare to answer St.
Augustine, we can see old Pelagius smiling in his grave. For the
answer, of course, was already given in pristine Christianity by
Christ himself: We can choose love, the socialism of love, which is
a concrete and "unchurchy" way of choosing God. Not the
dreadful, miserable, abstract, essentialistic, and ultimately meaningless love of organized Christianity; not the given love which we
passively receive from a jealous unlovable god; but real, concrete
love of other people, of things that are beautiful, of artifacts which
we can now create, and especially of those intangible creations
which we call communities.

Yes, communities, or more properly, communitas, as Victor
Turner defines it. I have made clear that it was not my objective to
attack the idea of community; what I have criticized is a certain
kind of community and a certain kind of commitment. But the
capacity and power to choose allows us to love and relate to others
not only outside of but within communities of our choice,
communities ranging from the dyadic love relationship to the
widest international body, communities which we make and
which we leave open to others, subject only to a commonality of
interest and to a sharing of attributes that are both complementary and achievable. For it is in such communities that those "holy
sparks" inherent in things of which Hasidism speaks so eloquently
are released by our deeds.

Humanistic socialism by releasing, through choice, our capacity
for love also obviates our need to hate. Hate is the product of fear
and constraint. We hate when we feel that something threatens
our freedom to choose. It is because we want ultimately to love
and are afraid of the constraints on our power to love that we
resort to hate. And hate feeds on the "furies" of our irrationality,

those very same furies which our liberal romantics now so pathetically ask us to indulge. And because hate feeds on the irrational, we are blind to the real objects of our constraints, we lash out at the immediate obstacles and the imagined foes. We attack the vulnerable, instead of the powerful, who, by preserving industrialism in its inhumane form, really constrain us. And when misguided liberals join ranks with ruthless demagogues in making a virtue of our irrationalities and in promoting empty but divisive social philosophies and solutions to our ontological insecurities that are as unworkable as they are atavistic, the hate which is already born from our fear of those whom we feel are reducing our power to choose and to love is intensified and makes beasts of us, fascists, murderers.

The sublime and beautiful irony of a humanized, egalitarian, modern civilization is that it denies all previous philosophies and in this sense joins hands with the purpose which faith once served. Forged by reason, it is a world in which there can no longer be grand dogmas and creeds which solve our problems and hand them to us on a platter. As Ernest Gellner has written:

There are no cosy conceptual cocoons into which we can crawl back, even were we so inclined.... There is no "home," no *status quo ante,* to which we could return. The intellectual advances of recent centuries have corroded the inherited belief-systems beyond recovery: the widening of horizons, the flowing together of so many "forms of life" into one Babel-like and rapidly evolving civilization, have also made inacceptable the old local, particularistic, asymmetrical faiths (except as sentimental links with the past).[24]

By throwing us back upon ourselves, by the loneliness it threatens, it forces us to see what is most human in us and how that humanity is also identical with all others. Stripped naked of our creeds, we see the oneness and equality of our composition. With our primordial communities demolishing, we see how it is possible to make new and freer ones. And by giving us the power to choose, it enables us to experience in a nonrevelatory way the eternal Thou, which is the love we exhibit in our free, concrete interactions and in our creations. And, lastly modern, humanistic socialism can perform for the secular, though spiritually engaged modernist, something akin to the Hasidic idea of the "descent in behalf of the ascent." It forces us in our relations with others to what Victor Turner calls the liminal "interstices of structure," and it plunges us into the deep, terrible core of our being, where we can see with Blake, if we have the eyes and the courage to look, the "fearsome symmetry" of the beast lurking in "the forest of (our) night," struggle with it, control it, transcend it, and from which we can emerge again, transforming in the process, the material into the good.

NOTES

Chapter 1
The Tradition of the Sorcerer

1. Immanuel Kant, "Idea for a Universal History With Cosmopolitan Intent" (1784), from *The Philosophy of Kant: Immanuel Kant's Moral and Political Writings,* Edited and translated by Carl J. Friedrich, The Modern Library, 1949, p. 120.

2. Lucien Lévy-Bruhl, *The Soul of Primitive Man,* Allen & Unwin, 1928, p. 68. We do not concur with Lévy-Bruhl's assumption that the cognitive processes of primitives are prelogical, paralleling those of the civilized child. On this see Margaret Mead, "An Investigation of the Thought of Primitive Children," in Robert Hunt (ed.), *Personalities and Cultures,* The National History Press, 1967, pp. 213–237. It is typical of Robert Redfield that in his discussion of the intellectual in primitive society he only recognizes what we here call the conforming individualist, and then only with considerable qualification. See his "Thinker and Intellectual in Primitive Society," in S. Diamond (ed.), *Primitive Views of the World,* Columbia University Press, 1964, pp. 33–47.

3. E. E. Evans-Pritchard, *Witchcraft, Oracles and Magic Among the Azande,* Oxford, 1937. In this work Evans-Pritchard introduced the famous distinction between witchcraft and sorcery: the former referring to a belief in the psychic powers of some persons to harm others by purely spiritual means quite independent of their motivation, the latter referring to the deliberate, conscious practice of using magical techniques to attain specific ends. Not all anthropologists have followed this

usage, partly because among many peoples the distinction is often blurred. On this see John Middleton and E. H. Winter (eds.), *Witchcraft and Sorcery in East Africa,* Routledge & Kegan Paul, 1963, pp. 1–7.

4. P. Huvelin, "Magie et Droit Individuel," in *Année Sociologie,* Vol. X, 1907.

5. R. R. Marret, "Magic," in *The Encyclopedia of Religion and Ethics,* Vol. 8, p. 251.

6. Claude Lévi-Strauss, *The Savage Mind,* University of Chicago Press, 1966, pp. 13–14.

7. Claude Lévi-Strauss, *Structural Anthropology,* Doubleday Anchor, 1967, pp. 160–180. David Riesman also has drawn our attention to the parallels between the sorcerer and the modern rebel. See *The Lonely Crowd,* Yale University Press, 1962, p. 12.

8. Georg Simmel, *On Individuality and Social Forms,* Edited by D. N. Levin, University of Chicago Press, 1971.

9. Harold A. Durfee, "Albert Camus and the Ethics of Rebellion," *Journal of Religion,* Vol. XXXVIII, 1958, No. 1, p. 35.

10. E. R. Dodds, *The Ancient Concept of Progress,* Oxford University Press, 1973, p. 13.

11. We refer here to Robert Nisbet's *Twilight of Authority,* Oxford University Press, 1975. In this amazingly reactionary work Nisbet launches an all-out attack on centralized, welfare government, and on the principles of equality and individualism, claiming that they constitute a "new despotism" and are the sources of all our modern ills. He calls for a return to the "social bond," with its implicit inequality and a renewed respect for tradition and particularism. The "ethnic revival" in America is hailed as a welcome revolt against egalitarianism and the so-called "new despotism." See the excellent review of the work by Gertrud Lenzer in *The New York Times Book Review,* October 5, 1975.

12. F. M. Cornford, *Principium Sapientiae: The Origins of Greek Philosophical Thought,* Cambridge University Press, 1952, p. 95.

13. F. M. Cornford, *Principium Sapientiae,* p. 90. See also Thalia Phillies

Howe, "The Primitive Presence in Pre-Classical Greece," in Stanley Diamond (ed.), *Primitive Views of the World*, pp. 155-169.

14. For a more detailed treatment of the theme of the eternal return in traditional cultures, see Mircea Eliade, *The Myth of the Eternal Return*, Pantheon Books, 1954.

15. These and other fragments, except where stated otherwise, are taken from the complete translation of the fragments by Philip Wheelwright, in his *Heraclitus*, Princeton University Press, 1959.

16. Victorino Jefera, *Modes of Greek Thought*, Appleton-Century-Crofts, 1971, p. 67.

17. F. M. Cornford, *Principium Sapientiae*, p. 89.

18. Walter Burkert, *Lore and Science in Ancient Pythagoreanism*, Harvard University Press, 1972, p. 482.

19. Samuel C. Florman, *The Existential Pleasures of Engineering*, St. Martins Press, 1976, p. 72.

20. S. M. Lipset & R. B. Dobson, "The Intellectual as Critic and Rebel," in S. N. Eisenstadt & S. R. Graubard (eds.), *Intellectuals and Tradition*, Daedalus, spring, 1972, p. 137.

21. Arthur Power, "Conversations with James Joyce," *The James Joyce Quarterly*, Vol. 3, No. 1, Fall, 1965, p. 45.

22. Harry Levin, *James Joyce: A Critical Introduction*, New Directions, 1941, p. 84.

23. James Joyce, *A Portrait of the Artist as a Young Man*, Viking-Compass, 1971, p. 203.

Chapter 2
The Origins and Nature of Ethnicity

1. This thesis is fully developed in his *Elementary Structures of Kinship*, Beacon Press, 1969. See also his "Language and the Analysis of Social Laws," *Structural Anthropology*, pp. 54-65.

2. R. H. Lowie, *Origin of the State,* Harcourt, Brace & Co., 1927, p. 73 and chapter 4, passim.

3. Anthony Leeds, "Ecological Determinants of Chieftainship Among the Yaruro Indians of Venezuela," in Andrew P. Vayda (ed.), *Environment and Cultural Behavior,* Natural History Press, 1969.

4. Cited in Marshall Sahlins, *Social Stratification in Polynesia,* University of Washington Press, 1958, p. 3.

5. For a suggestive discussion of the relationship between hoarding and exploitativeness in a traditional setting, see Eric Fromm and Michael Macoby, *Social Character in a Mexican Village,* Prentice-Hall, 1970, Ch. 5, passim. Clearly, all attempts to interpret the evolution of social class and the state must be conjectural. Modern anthropological studies, however, have elevated such speculations beyond the status of crude guesswork. For a recent review of the literature, see Elman R. Service, *Origins of the State and Civilization,* W. W. Norton and Co., 1975, Chs. 2 and 16. See also Morton Fried, *The Evolution of Political Society,* Random House, 1967. Lowie's classic work, *Origin of the State,* is still valuable. The real breakthrough in this field came with the publication of Marshall Sahlins' *Social Stratification in Polynesia.* A critical paper in this area was published in 1960 by H. A. Powell, "Competitive Leadership in Trobiand Political Organization," *Journal of the Royal Anthropological Institute,* Vol. 90, No. 1, pp. 118–145. Marvin Harris' discussion of the origin of inequality, although modestly buried in a general textbook, is a significant contribution, building on Sahlins. See his *Culture, Man and Nature,* Thomas Crowell, 1971. Service's recently published "theory" is largely a restatement of Sahlins' and Harris' insights with a somewhat anti-Marxist flavor.

6. We have drawn, for this paragraph, mainly from M. I. Finley, *The World of Odysseus,* Pelican, 1956. Following recent criticisms of Finley's chronology by archeologists, however, we will place the world described by Finley somewhat later than he did, that is, no earlier than late ninth-century Greece. See A. M. Snodgrass, *The Dark Age of Greece,* University of Edinburgh Press, 1971; also, V. R. d'A. Desborough, *The Greek Dark Ages,* St. Martin's Press, 1972.

7. Mason Hammond and Lester Batson, *The City in the Ancient World,* Harvard University Press, 1972, p. 164.

8. I am grateful to Nerys Patterson, a Harvard student of early Celtic society, for bringing this fact to my attention.

9. This, of course, nicely complements the segmentary nature of such systems. For the classic analysis of this subject, see E. E. Evans-Pritchard, *Neur Religion,* Oxford, The Clarendon Press, 1956. See also Marshall Sahlins' discussion in his *Tribesmen,* Prentice-Hall, Ch. 6.

10. For the classic analysis of this development, see Max Weber, *The Sociology of Religion,* translated by Ephraim Fischoff, Beacon Press, 1964, especially Chs. 1, 6, and 14.

11. It is not being suggested, however, that the growth in significance of the tribal gods is always or even usually accompanied by a shift to monotheism. The important point is the new conception of them as vital, forceful, and immediate. On this see Mircea Eliade, "Structures and Changes in the History of Religion," in Carl H. Kraeling and Robert Adams (eds.), *City Invincible,* University of Chicago Press, 1960, pp. 351–366.

12. For an excellent discussion of this process in the light of the available ethnographic literature, see R. McC. Netting, "Sacred Power and Centralization," in Brian Spooner (ed.), *Population Growth,* M.I.T. Press, 1972, pp. 121–162.

13. Mircea Eliade, *The Sacred and the Profane,* Harvest Books, 1959, pp. 29–31.

14. Robert M. Adams, "Early Civilizations: Subsistence and Environment," in Carl H. Kraeling, *City Invincible,* p. 280.

15. Kent V. Flannery, "The Ecology of Early Food Production in Mesopotamia," in Andrew P. Vayda (ed.), *Environment and Cultural Behavior.* For a useful classification of the different stages of this development, see Robert M. Adams, "Developmental Stages in Ancient Mesopotamia," in Pan American Union, *Irrigation Civilizations: A Comparative Study,* 1955.

16. Kent V. Flannery, *op. cit.,* p. 304.

17. Marshall Sahlins, *Social Stratification in Polynesia,* p. 167.

18. Mason Hammond, *The City in the Ancient World,* op. cit., p. 46.

19. S. Scott Littleton, *The New Comparative Mythology,* University of California Press, 1973. A thorough and generally critical assessment of Dumezil's work.

20. For an authoritative discussion of this, see T. Jacobsen, "The Assumed Conflict Between the Sumerians and Semites in Early Meso-potamia," *Journal of the American Oriental Society,* LIX, 1939, pp. 485–495. In an early work, Ignace J. Gelb suggests that there might have been short-run ethnic tensions, although he agrees that the long-run trend was toward complete ethnic absorption. See his, "The Function of Language in the Cultural Process of Expansion of Mesopotamian Society," in Kraeling and Adams, op. cit., pp. 315–328. However, in a more recent work, Gelb's own findings on the fate of prisoners of war contradicts his earlier reservations on the Jacobsen thesis (see note 22).

21. I. J. Mendelsohn, *Slavery in the Ancient Near East,* Oxford University Press, 1949.

22. I. J. Gelb, "Prisoners of War in Early Mesopotamia," *Journal of Near Eastern Studies,* Vol. 32, 1973, pp. 70–98.

23. A. M. Duff, *Freedmen in the Early Roman Empire,* Oxford University Press, 1928, p. 50.

24. See, in particular, J. Vogt, *Struktur der antiken Slavenkriege,* Wiesbaden, 1957. On the problem of the differential rates of absorption of ethnic groups in Greece and Rome, see the following: Mary L. Gordon, "The Nationality of Slaves Under the Early Roman Empire," in M. I. Finley (ed.), *Slavery in Classical Antiquity,* Heffer & Sons, 1960, pp. 171–189; Tenney Frank, "Race Mixture in the Roman Empire," *American Historical Review,* XXI, 1916; A. Diller, *Race Mixture Among the Greeks Before Alexander,* University of Illinois Press, 1937.

25. On religion and assimilation in Greece and Rome I have drawn mainly from Franz Bomer, *Untersuchungen über die Religion der Sklaven in Griechenland und Rom,* Akademie der Wissenschaften und der Literatur, 1957. See also A. Toynbee, *A Study of History,* Vol. 2.

26. See, in particular, Alison Burford, *Craftsmen in Greek and Roman Society,* University of Cornell Press, 1972.

27. B. Lewis, *The Arabs in History*, Hutchinsons, 1964, pp. 99–111.

28. A. Popovic, *Ali b. Muhammad et la révolte des esclaves à Basra*, Ph.D. dissertation, University of Paris, 1954.

29. O. Patterson, "Slavery and Slave Revolts," in Richard Price (ed.), *Maroon Societies*, Doubleday, 1973.

30. For an excellent discussion of Welsh ethnicity and its vain, tension-ridden attempt to revive outmoded symbols, see Goronwy Rees, "Have the Welsh a Future," *Encounter*, March, 1964. On Scottish nationalism, see H. J. Hanham, *Scottish Nationalism*, Harvard University Press, 1969. There have been many significant developments since the publication of this work.

31. A. T. Olmstead, *History of the Persian Empire*, University of Chicago Press, 1948.

32. P. A. Brunt, *Italian Manpower*, Oxford, Clarendon Press, 1971.

33. J. H. W. Liebeschuetz, *Antioch, City and Imperial Administration*, Clarendon Press, 1972, p. 62.

34. Quoted in D. K. Fieldhouse, *The Colonial Empires*, Delta Books, 1971, p. 273.

35. J. S. Furnival, *Colonial Policy and Practice*, Cambridge University Press, 1948. Furnival's ideas have been taken over and applied to the Caribbean with limited success by the anthropologist M. G. Smith. See, in particular, his "Ethnic and Cultural Pluralism in the British Carib-bean," in his *The Plural Society in the British Caribbean*, California University Press, 1965.

36. A. T. Olmstead, *History of the Persian Empire*, p. 192.

37. Salo W. Baron, *A Social and Religious History of the Jews*, Columbia University Press, Vol. 1, p. 24.

38. M. Radin, *The Jews Among the Greeks and Romans*, Jewish Publication Society of America, 1915, p. 365; see also pp. 255–256.

Chapter 3
The Nation-State

1. The literature on this subject is enormous. (See A. D. Smith, *Nationalism: A Trend Report,* Mouton, 1975.) The confusion concerning the meaning of the terms is as great as the output on the subject. Benjamin Akzin in his *State and Nation,* Hutchinsons, 1964, speaks of a "terminological jungle" (Chap. 1), and Boyd C. Shafer in his *Nationalism: Myth or Reality,* Harcourt, Brace, 1955, claims that there is "no precise and acceptable definition of nationalism" (pp. 3–6). Hans Kohn, though one of the leading students of the subject, nonetheless makes the fatal error of identifying the growth of the nation-state with the growth of the centralized, absolutist state. See his *Idea of Nationalism,* Macmillan, 1944. Part of the problem lies in the fact that there is confusion not only about the term "nation" but the term "state" as well, as David Easton has pointed out in *The Political System,* Knopf, 1953, pp. 106–115. For what is still one of the best attempts to clarify the terminological mess, see the report of E. H. Carr and his associates in the Royal Institute of International Affairs, *Nationalism,* Oxford University Press, 1939, pp. xvi–xx and the concluding chapter. The following works were of special value in the definition and clarification of terms: E. K. Francis, "The Nature of the Ethnic Group," *The American Journal of Sociology,* LII, 1947, pp. 393–400; B. Akzin, *op. cit;* J. D. Mabbott, *The State and the Citizen,* Arrow Books, 1958; Ernest Gellner, *Thought and Change,* Weidenfeld & Nicolson, 1964. For this chapter we have drawn, in addition to works cited later, on the following: Annals of the American Academy of Political and Social Science, *The World Trend Toward Nationalism,* Vol. 174, 1934; E. Kedourie, *Nationalism,* Hutchinsons, 1960; Hans Kohn, *Prophets and Peoples,* Macmillan, 1952; Hans Kohn, *Nationalism,* Anvil, 1955; E. M. Earle (ed.), *Nationalism and Internationalism,* Columbia University Press, 1950. See also the works cited in note 1, Chapter 6.

2. Victor Ehrenberg, *Man, State and Deity,* Methuen and Company, 1974, p. 22.

3. Jon Manchip White, *Everyday Life in Ancient Egypt,* Capricorn Books, 1967, p. 18.

4. David Riesman, "National Purpose," in his *Abundance for What?*, Doubleday Anchor, 1965, p. 18.

5. William Carroll Bark, *Origins of the Medieval World,* Stanford University Press, 1958, p. 65.

6. Marc Bloch, *Feudal Society,* Routledge & Kegan Paul, 1965, Vol. 1, p. 145.

7. Ehrenberg, *Man, State and Deity,* p. 23. Many liberals, lacking Ehrenberg's profound insight, have for this reason been led to support the nation-state, the classic case being J. S. Mill, on which, see H. Kohn, *Prophets and Peoples,* pp. 12–42.

8. Lord Acton, "Nationality," in Talcott Parsons (ed.), *Theories of Society,* Free Press, 1961.

9. Howard Becker and Harry E. Barnes, *Social Thought from Lore to Science,* Dover Books, 1961, Vol. 1, p. 283.

10. Norman F. Cantor, *Medieval History,* The Macmillan Company, 1971, p. 505.

11. E. M. W. Tillyard, *Myth and the English Mind,* Collier Books, 1962, pp. 43–48. There was another source of Tudor antinationalism. This was their dread of popular government, "the fourth government of men which do not rule." For a penetrating discussion of the Henrician "profound distrust of all forms of popular government," see Franklin Le Von Baumer, *The Early Tudor Theory of Kingship,* Yale University Press, 1940, especially pp. 85–108.

12. Cited in the introduction by J. H. M. Salmon (ed.) to Francis Hotman's *Francogallia,* Cambridge University Press, 1972.

13. John Locke, *Two Treatises of Civil Government,* Everyman Library, J. M. Dent & Sons, 1960, p. 183.

14. Francis Hotman, *Francogallia* (1573). See also William Farr Church, *Constitutional Thought in Sixteenth Century France,* Harvard University Press, 1941, p. 87; and F. Baumer, *The Early Tudor Theory of Kingship,* op. cit., p. 112.

15. Max Weber, "On Ethnic Groups," in T. Parsons (ed.), *Theories of Society*, pp. 305–309.

16. Raymond Firth, *Symbols: Public and Private*, Cornell University Press, 1975, p. 155.

17. Peter Viereck, *Metapolitics: the Roots of the Nazi Mind*, Capricorn, 1961, p. 8. The literature on fascism is vast. For an extremely useful selection of some of the leading views on the subject, see Gilbert Allardyce (ed.), *The Place of Fascism in European History*, Prentice-Hall, 1971.

18. Brian Wilson, *Magic and the Millennium*, Harper and Row, 1973, Chapter 14.

19. Wilson, ibid., p. 463.

20. The ensuing critique of nationalism and the idea of the nation-state uses as its point of departure the works of both Mabbott and Kedourie. While I share fully the general thrust of Kedourie's critique, I am in disagreement on many specific issues; I think, for example, that his discussion of Kant's role is somewhat far-fetched, and I think he neglects some crucial sociological arguments against the idea of the nation-state. Even so, I find Anthony Smith's critique of Kedourie (and, by implication, all those who adopt his ethical stance) both unpersuasive and confused. (See his *Theories of Nationalism*, Duckworth, 1971.) Smith's confusion springs from the fact that he uses an extremely inclusive definition of nationalism and the nation-state, with the result that his work ends up as an analysis of all forms of chauvinistic, collective behavior rather than of one of its subtypes. Thus, his critique is really a heavy-handed attack on a straw man, since Kedourie was being blamed for not taking account of issues in which he had no interest, and was not required to discuss, given his precise definition of his subject. Smith, on the other hand, speaks of the "tantalizing amorphousness" of his subject and his intellectual "ambivalence" in coming to terms with it, all of which is quite understandable in view of the breadth of his definition of what he is about. His confusion is revealed most tellingly toward the end of his work when he speaks of "ethnic nationalism" (see Chs. 9 and 10), a redundant expression if ever there was one.

There is also a certain distressing sociologistic arrogance running through Smith's work. That is, he fails to take people's ideas seriously, and indeed, accuses Kedourie of taking "assertions of nationalists seriously, perhaps too seriously" (p. 14). Opinions such as these give social science a bad name among humanists and social philosophers. Such views are not only patronizing, but make for bad sociology. Throughout this work we have clearly emphasized the importance of structural explanations; but these do not and can never exhaust the explanation of human conduct, and least so when we are dealing with a subject that is essentially moral in nature. Ethnicity, especially nationalism, is, above all, a conscious act of will. In trying to understand it, it is the sociologist who is the interloper rather than the ethical theorist (on this, see Gellner, *Thought and Change,* Chs. 4 and 7).

21. Mabbott, *The State and the Citizen,* p. 166.

22. Mabbott, *ibid.,* pp. 71-94.

23. Firth, *Symbols,* op. cit., pp. 83-85.

24. Victor Turner, "Symbolic Studies," *Annual Review of Anthropology,* Vol. 4, 1975, pp. 145-161. This is the source of the "extremism," the "tension and mutual hatred," of which Kedourie speaks. See his, *Nationalism,* p. 115.

25. Turner, "Symbolic Studies," op. cit. For a further discussion of these kinds of symbols, see Victor Turner, *The Forest of Symbols,* 1967, Cornell University Press, pp. 27-47.

26. Turner, "Symbolic Studies," op. cit.

27. David Riesman has reminded me that the House is in fact a "multivocal and even mystical symbol." Thus the rejection of the party of the House may have been of even greater significance than I suggest. It was not just a vote for one kind of sign, but a vote for signification as opposed to mysticism.

28. Harold Rosen, review of *The Statue of Liberty* by Marvin Trachtenberg, *The New York Times Book Review,* March 28, 1976, p. 3.

Chapter 4
The Nature and Classification of Ethnic Groups

1. R. Dahrendorf, *Class and Class Conflict in Industrial Society,* Routledge & Kegan Paul, 1959, p. 151.

2. See the papers by G. T. Griffith, S. Perlman, H. B. Dunkel, and U. Wilcken in S. Perlman (ed.), *Philip and Athens,* Heffer, 1973.

3. Lord Acton, "Nationality," in T. Parsons (ed.), *Theories of Society,* Free Press, 1961, p. 395.

4. Max Weber, "Ethnic Groups," in T. Parsons (ed.), *op. cit.,* p. 308.

Chapter 5

Context and Choice in Ethnic Allegiance: The Chinese in the Caribbean

1. Harold Isaacs, "Basic Group Identity," in N. Glazer and D. P. Moynihan (eds.), *Ethnicity,* Harvard University Press, 1975, pp. 29–52.

2. For a useful introductory overview, see S. W. Mintz, "The Caribbean as a Socio-Cultural Area," *Journal of World History,* Vol. IX, No. 4, 1966. See also D. Lowenthal, "The Range and Variation of Caribbean Societies," *Annals of the New York Academy of Sciences,* Vol. 83, Art. 5, 1960, pp. 786–795.

3. For an excellent analysis of this period, see R. Sheridan, *The Development of the Plantations,* Caribbean Universities Press, 1970.

4. On the growth of the slave population in the Caribbean, see O. Patterson, *The Sociology of Slavery,* Fairleigh Dickinson University Press, Ch. 4, and E. Goveia, *Slave Society in the British Leeward Islands,* Yale University Press, 1965, especially Ch. 2.

5. E. Goveia, *op. cit.,* pp. 215–229.

6. On their fight for civil rights up to 1830, see S. D. Dunker's unpublished M. A. thesis, *The Free Coloureds and their Fight for Civil Rights in Jamaica, 1800–1830,* London University, 1960. A more substantial work that not only carries the analysis through to 1865 but explores, in part, their fascinating relationship with the Sephardic Jewish community during and after slavery is M. C. Campbell's *Edward Jordan and the Free Coloureds, Jamaica 1800–1865,* unpublished thesis submitted for the degree of Ph.D., University of London, 1968.

7. R. T. Smith, *British Guiana,* Oxford University Press, 1962, Chs. 2–3.

8. P. Newman, *British Guiana*, Oxford University Press, 1964, Ch. 2.

9. On the decline of the plantation system and postemancipation economic developments, see L. Ragatz, *The Fall of the Planter Class in the British Caribbean, 1763–1833*, Octagon, 1963. See also, D. Hall, *Free Jamaica, 1838–1854,* Yale University Press, 1959.

10. On the development of the two segmentary creoles, see P. Curtin, *Two Jamaicas*, Harvard University Press, pp. 23–60. My own work, *The Sociology of Slavery*, discusses the foundations of these segmentary creoles in the slave society. More recently, E. Brathwaite's, *The Development of Creole Society in Jamaica, 1770–1820*, while not in basic disagreement with my own interpretation of the data, suggests that the process of creolization was far more developed during the period of slavery than either Curtin or myself would allow.

11. The term has acquired this special technical meaning among Caribbeanists and linguists concerned with the study of creole languages. It is not to be confused with the rather vague usage found in Louisiana, where it refers to whites of French ancestry. On attempts to sharpen the meaning of the term, see M. G. Smith, *The Plural Society*, pp. 5–9, 307–308, who, however, restricts the use of the term to Euro-West Indian segmentary creoles only; S. Mintz, "Comments on the Socio-historical Background to Pidginization and Creolization," in D. Hymes (ed.), *Pidginization and Creolization of Languages,* Cambridge University Press, 1970. Also see Andre Negre, "Origines et Signification du mot 'Creole,'" *Bulletin de la Societe d'Histoire de la Guadaloupe,* Nos. 5–6, 1966; D. Lowenthal, *West Indian Societies,* Oxford University Press, pp. 32–33; and P. Singer and E. Araneta, "Hinduization and Creolization in Guyana," *Social and Economic Studies,* Vol. 16, No. 3, 1967, pp. 221–236, who emphasize the psychological aspects of the creole process, but their analysis is rather idiosyncratic.

12. On this, see O. Patterson, "The Ritual of Cricket in the West Indies," *New Society,* No. 352, 1969.

13. F. Henriques, *Family and Color in Jamaica,* Macgibbon and Kee, 1968, pp. 52, 57–59.

14. M. Campbell, *op. cit.,* pp. 35–42.

15. H. Paget, "The Free Village System in Jamaica," *Caribbean Quarterly,* Vol. I, No. 4, 1954, pp. 7–19.

16. R. Farley, "The Rise of the Peasantry in British Guiana," *Social and Economic Studies,* Vol. 2, No. 4, 1954, pp. 76-103.

17. For a very sensitive discussion of this development by a West Indian intellectual who is actively involved with creating such a synthesis, see R. Nettleford, "The Melody of Europe, The Rhythm of Africa," in his *Mirror, Mirror: Identity, Race and Protest in Jamaica,* Collins and Sangster, 1970, pp. 173-211.

18. R. Nettleford, *op. cit.* See also, D. Lowenthal, *op. cit.,* pp. 250-292.

19. On the recent army mutiny and riots in Trinidad, see I. Oxaal, *Race and Revolutionary Consciousness,* Schenkman Publishing Company, Inc., 1970. See also, on Jamaica, N. Girvan, "October Counter-Revolution in Jamaica," *New World Quarterly,* High Season, 1968, pp. 59-68.

20. G. Merrill, "The Role of the Sephardic Jews in the British Caribbean Area During the Seventeenth Century," *Caribbean Studies,* Vol. 4, No. 3, 1964, pp. 32-49.

21. See B. Schlesinger, "The Jews of Jamaica: A Historical View," *Caribbean Quarterly,* **13,** 1, 1967, pp. 46-53. On the history of the Jews in Jamaica, see S. J. and E. Hurwitz, "The New World Sets an Example for the Old," *American Jewish Historical Quarterly,* **55,** 37-56; M. Campbell, *op. cit.,* Chs. 5-7 passim; S. J. and E. Hurwitz, "A Beacon for Judaism," *American Jewish Historical Quarterly,* **56,** 3-76.

22. For a general review of the origins and conditions of East Indians in Jamaica and other West Indian societies, see David Lowenthal, *West Indian Societies,* Oxford University Press, Ch. IV.

23. The ensuing discussion of the Chinese in Jamaica is based, in addition to the author's own experience, mainly on the following: R. A. Silin, *A Survey of Selected Aspects of the Chinese in Jamaica,* Unpublished Honors Thesis, Anthropology Department, Harvard University, 1962; P. Morrow, *Chinese Adaptation in Two Jamaican Cities,* Unpublished Honors Thesis, Anthropology Department, Harvard University, 1972. Of special value were A. W. Lind, "Adjustment Patterns Among the Jamaican Chinese," *Social and Economic Studies,* Vol. 7, No. 2, 1958, pp. 144-164; I. Broom, "The Social Differentiation of Jamaica," *American Sociological Review,* Vol. 19, 1954, pp. 121-125.

24. D. Hall, *Free Jamaica, 1838-1865,* Yale University Press, 1959, Ch. 5 and 7.

25. "In fact," Henriques writes, "black women frequently express their liking for Chinese as their 'Sweet man,' and for the care they lavish on their concubines." Fernando Henriques, *Family and Color in Jamaica,* Humanities Press, p. 98.

26. F. X. Delany, S.J., *A History of the Catholic Church in Jamaica,* Jesuit Missions Press, 1930, p. 271.

27. On the decolonization and the role of the middle class in Jamaica, see T. Monroe, *The Politics of Constitutional Decolonization,* Institute of Social and Economic Research, 1972, especially Chs. 2-3.

28. *Spotlight* magazine, May, 1949 and October, 1952, Kingston, Jamaica.

29. Colin Clarke, "Population Pressure in Kingston, Jamaica: A Study of Unemployment and Overcrowding," *Transactions and Papers,* The Institute of British Geographers, No. 38, 1966, pp. 174-175.

30. The theoretical basis of this development has been well-established. See W. J. Goode, "The Role of the Family in Industrialization" and R. F. Winch and R. L. Blumberg, "Societal Complexity and Familial Organization," both in R. F. Winch and L. W. Goodman (eds.), *Selected Studies in Marriage and the Family,* Holt, Rinehart and Winston, 1968, pp. 64-92.

31. R. A. Silin, *A Survey of Selected Aspects of the Chinese in Jamaica, op. cit.,* pp. 45, 59; and P. Morrow, *Chinese Adaptation, op. cit.,* pp. 50-54.

32. R. A. Silin, *op. cit.,* p. 7. Our discussion of the Chinese in Guyana will be based primarily on two published papers by Morton H. Fried, the only modern scholar to have researched the group and an early twentieth-century work by Clementi. See M. H. Fried, "Some Observations on the Chinese of British Guiana," *Social and Economic Studies,* Vol. 5, No. 1, 1956; "The Chinese in the British Caribbean," in M. H. Fried (ed.), *Colloquium on Overseas Chinese,* December 29, 1957; and C. Clementi, *The Chinese in Guiana,* The Argosy Company, 1915.

33. L. Despres, *Cultural Pluralism and Nationalist Politics in Guiana,* Rand McNally, 1967, p. 65.

34. Clementi, *op. cit.,* p. 359.

35. Fried, *op. cit.,* 1956, p. 69.

36. M. C. Campbell, *Edward Jordan and the Free Coloureds, op. cit., passim.* On the changes in Jamaica before and after the upheaval of 1865, see P. Curtin, *op. cit.;* G. Eisner, *op. cit.;* D. Hall, *op. cit.;* H. P. Jacobs, *Sixty Years of Change, 1806-1866,* Institute of Jamaica, 1973; A. Hart, *The Life of George William Jordan,* Institute of Jamaica, 1972; V. J. Marsala, *Sir John Peter Grant,* Institute of Jamaica, 1972.

37. For an excellent account of the sugar crisis in the late nineteenth century, see R. W. Beachey, *The British West Indies Sugar Industry in the Late Nineteenth Century,* Oxford, 1957.

38. K. O. Lawrence, "The Development of the Portuguese Community in British Guiana," *Jamaica Historical Review,* Vol. V, No. 2, 1965.

39. D. Lowenthal, *West Indian Societies, op. cit.,* p. 200.

40. For a general discussion of the reasons trading is the ideal occupation of the stranger, see G. Simmel's "The Stranger," in his *On Individuality and Social Forms,* University of Chicago Press, 1971.

41. Clementi, *op. cit.,* pp. 359-360.

42. Fried, *op. cit.,* 1957, p. 56.

43. The Chinese are cast in the same role of conciliators between the conflicting Indian and Black groups in Trinidad, and there, too, a Chinese was appointed the first Governor General. See D. Lowenthal's remarks on the potential risks to the Chinese of overplaying this role in the East Caribbean in his *West Indian Societies, op. cit.,* pp. 207-208.

44. Fried, *op. cit.,* 1956, p. 67.

45. *Ibid.,* p. 58.

46. P. H. Hiss, *Netherlands America,* Duell, Sloan & Pearce, Inc., 1943, p. 4.

47. Frederick Engels, "Letter to J. Block in Koningsberg," London 21 (-22), in K. Marx and F. Engels, *Selected Works,* Moscow, Progress Publishers, 1970, III, 487.

Chapter 6

The Modern Revival of Ethnicity:
With Special Reference to the United States

1. There is a vast and growing literature on ethnicity. Among the more general modern surveys and collections are: N. Glazer and D. P. Moynihan (eds.), *Ethnicity: Theory and Experience,* Harvard University Press, 1975; Tomatsu Shibutani, *Ethnic Stratification: A Comparative Approach,* Macmillan & Company, 1965; Cynthia H. Enloe, *Ethnic Conflict and Political Development,* Little Brown, 1973; Pierre L. van den Berghe, *Race and Ethnicity,* Basic Books, 1970, and his *Race and Racism,* Wiley, 1967; Victor A. Olorunsola (ed.), *The Politics of Cultural Sub-Nationalism in Africa,* Anchor, 1972; Guy Heraud, *L'Europe des Ethnies,* Presses d'Europe, 1963; and Peter Kunstadter (ed.), *Southeast Asian Tribes, Minorities and Nations,* Princeton University Press, 2 vols., 1967; M. Novak, A. Greeley, et al. "An Exchange on Ethnicity," *Commentary,* 54, 4, 1972. Other references, especially on the U. S. are cited below.

2. This, let me hasten to add, is a controversial statement, especially for those committed to the ideal of ethnic and/or national self-determination. The most objective treatment of the subject, however, suggests that apart from the period immediately after the revolution and the three years of the Great Purge (1935–1937) Soviet rule in Central Asia has considerably improved the material condition of these peoples and has had a liberating effect in many aspects of social life, especially with respect to the status of women. See Geoffrey Wheeler, *The Peoples of Soviet Central Asia,* Bodley Head, 1966, especially Chs. 6 and 7. The same point is made by another Soviet scholar who, like Wheeler, is openly hostile to the political aspects of Soviet rule: see A. Benningsen, "Post-War Migration in the U.S.S.R.," in W. H. McNeill (ed.), *Human Migration* (provisional title), University of Indiana Press, forthcoming.

3. A considerable number of studies were devoted to the problem of Americanization during the early decades of this century. See, in particular Isaac Berkson, *Theories of Americanization,* Teachers College Publications, Columbia University, 1920; Emory S. Bogardus *Essentials of Americanization,* University of California Press, 1919.

4. For example, Michael Novak, *The Rise of the Unmeltable Ethnics,* Macmillan, 1971. Novak's writings on sports, religion, the family, and other aspects of American culture all reflect the essentially antimodernist and antirationalist thrusts of traditional Euro-American romanticism.

5. Typical of this genre is Andrew Greeley's most recent work, *Ethnicity in the United States,* John Wiley & Sons, 1974.

6. See, in particular, *The Urban Villagers,* Free Press, 1969, especially Ch. 11. In view of his earlier position, Gans' more recent works, especially on popular culture, are a little perplexing, for while not proethnic they are certainly romantic and excessively relativistic. As we shall see romanticism and relativism are the philosophical foundations of modern ethnicity.

7. See Thomas Sowell, *Black Education: Myths and Tragedies,* McKay, 1972; and his *Race and Economics,* McKay, 1975. I do not, however, share Sowell's extremely neoclassical economic views. Martin Kilson, "Black Power: Anatomy of a Paradox," *Harvard Journal of Negro Affairs,* 1968, Vol. 2, No. 1, pp. 30–34; "Anatomy of the Black Studies Movement," *The Massachusetts Review,* Autumn, 1969, pp. 718–725; "Dynamics of Nationalism and Political Militancy Among Negro Americans," in Ernest Q. Campbell (ed.), *Racial Tensions and National Identity,* Vanderbilt University Press, 1972, pp. 97–114; "Blacks and Neo-Ethnicity in American Political Life," in N. Glazer and D. P. Moynihan, eds. *Ethnicity: Theory and Experience,* Harvard University Press.

8. Lee Rainwater's *Behind Ghetto Walls,* Aldine, 1970, is still one of the best studies on the urban black lower class.

9. There are, happily, several notable exceptions, among them, William Wilson, *Power, Racism, and Privilege,* Free Press, 1973; Kenneth B. Clark, *Dark Ghetto,* Harper & Row, 1965; and Harold Cruse, *The Crisis of the Negro Intellectual,* Morrow, 1967. It should be understood that our criticism refers mainly to the younger generation of chauvinistic sociologists. We in no way refer to the capable group of prechauvinistic sociologists such as DuBois, Frazier, Cox, Davis, St. Clair Drake and Hylan Lewis.

10. This is not the place to get involved with the thorny debate as to whether or not there exists a distinctive black urban culture and if so, (1)

whether this culture is largely the result of present socioeconomic conditions or is culturally determined, and (2) assuming the existence of this distinctive black urban culture, whether or not it is adaptive or obstructive for black socioeconomic mobility. For an assessment of these problems, see Orlando Patterson, "Toward a Future that Has No Past," *The Public Interest,* No. 27, Spring, 1972; Orlando Patterson, "The Black Micropolis," in Nathan B. Talbot (ed.), *Raising Children in Modern America,* Little, Brown, 1976, pp. 216–236; Ulf Hannerz, "Another Look at Lower Class Black Culture," in Lee Rainwater (ed.), *Black Experience: Soul,* Transaction Books, 1973; Robert Blaumer, "Black Culture: Lower Class Result or Ethnic Behavior?," in Rainwater, *Soul;* Bennett Berger, "Black Culture or Lower Class Culture?," in Rainwater, *Soul;* Rhoda L. Goldstein, *Black Life and Culture in the United States,* Thomas Crowell, 1971; William McCord, et al., *Life Styles in the Black Ghetto,* Norton, 1969; Charles A. Valentine, *Culture and Poverty: Critique and Counter Proposals,* University of Chicago Press, 1968; E. B. Leacock (ed.), *The Culture of Poverty: A Critique,* Simon and Schuster, 1971.

11. For three excellent analyses of such intellectual rhetoric, see Martin Kilson, "The New Black Intellectuals," *Dissent,* July–August, 1969, pp. 304–310; and his, "The 'Put-On' of Black Panther Rhetoric," *Encounter,* April 1971. See also his "Reflections on Structure and Content in Black Studies," in *Journal of Black Studies,* March 1973, pp. 297–314. For a general exploration and critique of such subjectivism, see Robert K. Merton, *The Sociology of Science,* The University of Chicago Press, 1973, Ch. 5.

12. On which, see Orlando Patterson, "The Moral Crisis of the Black American," *The Public Interest,* No. 32, Summer, 1973.

13. Harold Cruse, *The Crisis of the Negro Intellectual,* Morrow, 1967, pp. 420–475; pp. 544–565.

14. Edward Shils, "Intellectuals and Their Discontents," *The American Scholar,* Spring, 1976, p. 182. See also, *Commentary,* Vol. 62, Sept. 1976, the entire issue of which was devoted to this and related problems.

15. Erik Erikson, *Identity, Youth and Crisis,* W.W. Norton, 1968, p. 23.

16. On the sources of the alienation of the young see K. Keniston, *The Uncommitted: Alienated Youth in American Society,* Harcourt, Brace & World, 1965. On the relationship between alienation and political

dissent, see K. Keniston, *Youth and Dissent,* Harcourt Brace Jovanovich, 1971, pp. 270–281; 304–317. For a radical view see R. Flack, *Youth and Social Change,* Markham Publishing Co., 1971. On the demography of youth, see E. H. Bernert, "Demographic Trends and Implications," in E. Ginzberg (ed.), *The Nation's Children,* Columbia University Press, 1960, Vol. 1, pp. 24–49. For a suggestive analysis of the relationship between the demographic bulge and youthful dissent, see D. P. Moynihan, "Peace: Some Thoughts on the 1960's and 1970's," *The Public Interest,* 32, Summer 1973, pp. 3–12.

17. Bennet M. Berger, *Looking for America,* Prentice-Hall, 1971, p. 25. On this, see also Flacks, *op. cit.,* pp. 9–19.

18. Emil L. Fackenheim, *Encounters Between Judaism and Modern Philosophy,* Basic Books, 1973, p. 167.

19. R. J. Israel, "Jewish Tradition and Political Action," in A. Jospe (ed.), *Tradition and Contemporary Experience: Essays on Jewish Thought and Life,* Schocken Books, 1970, p. 200. See also W. Laqueur and N. Glazer, "Revolutionism and the Jews," *Commentary,* 51, 2, Feb. 1971, pp. 38–46; 55–61.

20. For an analysis of what he calls the "head-on collision" between Jews and Blacks, see Murray Friedman, "The Jews," in P. I. Rose et al. (eds.), *Through Different Eyes,* Oxford University Press, 1973, pp. 148–165. For a disturbing commentary by an otherwise thoughtful and decent scholar, see Nathan Glazer, *Affirmative Discrimination,* Basic Books, 1975. See also, M. Sklare, "Jews, Ethnics and the American City," *Commentary,* 53, 4, April, 1972, pp. 70–77.

21. David Riesman, "Some Observations Concerning Marginality," in his *Individualism Reconsidered,* Free Press, 1954, pp. 159–160.

22. Milton R. Konvitz, "Horace Meyer Kallen: Philosopher of the Hebraic-American Idea," *American Jewish Year Book, 1974–1975,* pp. 55–80.

23. Konvitz, p. 58.

24. Konvitz, p. 80.

25. Harry N. Rivlin and Milton J. Gold, *Teachers for Multicultural Education,* Fordham University Teachers Corps, 1975, p. 5.

26. For a spirited though unpersuasive defence of ethnic pluralism by someone whom I am convinced genuinely believes himself to be a liberal in spite of the nakedly conservative implications of his social philosophy, see Michael Novak, "How American Are You if Your Grandparents Came from Serbia in 1888?," in Sallie Te Selle (ed.), *The Rediscovery of Ethnicity*, Colophon Books, 1974, pp. 1–20. For a good critique of the new pluralists, see, H. Isaacs, "The New Pluralists," *Commentary*, 53, 3, March 1972, pp. 75–79.

27. For a more searching critique of relativism, see David Bidney, "The Philosophical Presuppositions of Cultural Relativism and Cultural Absolutism," in Leo R. Ward (ed.), *Ethics and the Social Sciences*, University of Notre Dame Press, 1959, pp. 51–76. One of the best known defenses of liberal relativism is Charles Frankel's, *The Case For Modern Man*, Harper and Brothers, 1955, pp. 45–73. Frankel's attempts to answer Jacques Maritain's charges are lame, wishy-washy and unpersuasive.

28. See, for example, the first chapter of A. Greeley's *Ethnicity in the United States*.

29. See the response of A. Greeley in *Change*, Summer, 1975, p. 4.

30. See the discussion of veto groups and its effects on American leadership in David Riesman, *The Lonely Crowd*, pp. 213–217. "Running fast to stand still" is how Tom Kahn describes, aptly, the dilemma of an oppressed group trying to improve its lot within this political framework. See his "Problems of the Negro Movement," *Dissent*, Winter, 1964.

31. Morris Janowitz, *The Community Press in an Urban Setting*, University of Chicago Press, 1952. See, more recently, Gerald D. Suttles, *The Social Construction of Communities*, University of Chicago Press, 1972, especially pp. 44–81.

32. The important point here is the perception of symbolic reality, "the cognitive map," rather than the reality itself, whatever that might be. As Suttles points out, the major characteristics of "defended neighborhoods" are "structural rather than sentimental or associational": *The Social Construction of Communities*, p. 35. See also Albert Hunter's discussion of the symbolic dimension of communities in his *Symbolic Communities*, University of Chicago Press, 1974, pp. 95–142.

33. Georg Simmel, *On Individuality and Social Forms,* University of Chicago Press, 1971, p. 254.

34. Thus, a recent study concludes that of the three major determinants of community solidarity—economic status, family status and racial-ethnic status—the first has remained constant in significance in recent years, the second has declined and the third has grown tremendously in importance. Hunter, *Symbolic Communities,* Ch. 6.

35. David Riesman, *"Individualism Reconsidered,* Doubleday Anchor, p. 12.

36. Roy Peterson, "Response to Orlando Patterson," *Change,* Summer, 1975, p. 6.

37. Ronald McAllister, "Response to Orlando Patterson," *Change,* Summer, 1975, p. 5.

38. Simmel, *On Individuality and Social Forms,* 1971, University of Chicago Press, p. 70.

39. Simmel, *ibid.,* p. 72.

40. Simmel, *ibid.,* p. 83.

41. Simmel, *ibid.,* pp. 90–91.

42. Simmel, *ibid.,* p. 91.

43. Mark Granovetter, "Response to Orlando Patterson," *Change,* Summer, 1975, pp. 5–6.

44. Simmel, *On Individuality and Social Forms,* 1971, p. 252.

Chapter 7
Modernity, Universalism, and Development: A Clarification

1. See, in particular, T. Parsons, *Societies; Evolutionary and Comparative Perspective,* Prentice-Hall, 1966, and *The System of Modern Societies,* Prentice-Hall, 1971.

2. See, for example, W. Moore, "Industrialization and Social Change," in B. F. Hoselitz and W. E. Moore, *Industrialization and Society*, UNESCO, 1963; T. Parsons, *The System of Modern Societies*, Prentice-Hall, 1971; C. Kerr, J. T. Dunlop, and F. H. Myers, *Industrialism and Industrial Man*, Oxford University Press, 1960; and A. Inkeles, *Becoming Modern*, Harvard University Press, 1974.

3. See Ralph Linton, "Universal Ethical Principles: An Anthropological View," in R. N. Anshen (ed.), *Moral Principles of Action*, Harper and Row, 1952, pp. 654–660; David Bidney, "The Philosophical Presuppositions of Cultural Relativism and Cultural Absolutism," in L. R. Ward (ed.), *Ethics and the Social Sciences*, University of Notre Dame Press, 1959, pp. 51–76.

4. David Riesman, *The Lonely Crowd*, Yale University Press, 1962, XXVIII.

5. E. E. Hagen, *On the Theory of Social Change*, Dorsey Press, 1962. For a shorter statement, see his article, "How Economic Growth Begins: A Theory of Social Change," *Journal of Social Issues*, Vol. 19, 1, 1963, pp. 20–34.

6. David C. McClelland, *The Achieving Society*, Van Nostrand, 1961.

7. Peter Worsley, *The Trumpet Shall Sound: A Study of "Cargo" Cults in Melanesia*, Schocken, 1968.

8. See, in particular, Susanne J. Bodenheimer, "The Ideology of Developmentalism: The American Paradigm-Surrogate for Latin American Studies," Sage Professional Papers, Comparative Politics Series, Vol. 2, 1971; Alan Smith, "The Integration Model of Development: A Critique," in Ken Mortimer (ed.), *Showcase State*, Angus and Robertson, 1973. For two excellent critiques of sociological abuses of the "modernization" concept, see Dean C. Tipps, "Modernization Theory and the Comparative Study of Societies: A Critical Perspective," *Comparative Studies of Society and History*, Vol. 15, No. 2, 1973, pp. 199–228; and R. Bendix, "Tradition and Modernity Reconsidered," in *Comparative Studies in Society and History*, Vol. 9 (1967), pp. 246–292.

9. Alejandro Portes, "Modernity and Development: A Critique," *Studies in Comparative International Development*, Vol. VIII, No. 3, 1973, pp. 247–279.

10. For a thorough assessment of works on this subject, see John W. Meyer, John Boli-Bennett, and Christopher Chase-Dunn, "Convergence and Divergence in Development," *Annual Review of Sociology*, Vol. 1, 1975, pp. 223–246.

11. This is the main thrust of Marxist criticisms of all equilibrium theorists. See note 14 below.

12. See Terence K. Hopkins, "Third World Modernization in Transnational Perspective," *Annals of the American Academy of Political and Social Science*, Vol. 386, Nov. 1969, pp. 126–136; and A. Portes, *op. cit.*

13. M. B. Brown, "A Critique of Marxist Theories of Imperialism," in R. Owen and B. Sutcliffe (eds.), *Studies in the Theory of Imperialism*, Longman's, 1972, p. 64.

14. There is a large and lively literature on so-called dependency theory. See I. Oxaal, T. Barnett, D. Booth (eds.), 1975, *Beyond the Sociology of Development*, Routledge & Kegan Paul; A. G. Frank, *Development and Underdevelopment in Latin America*, Monthly Review Press, 1968; Samir Amin, "Accumulation and Development: A Theoretical Model," *Review of African Political Economy*, 1974, pp. 9–26; Theotonio Dos Santos, "The Structure of Dependence," *American Economic Review*, Vol. LX, No. 2, May 1970, pp. 231–236; F. H. Cardoso, "Dependency and Development in Latin America," *New Left Review*, No. 74, 1972, pp. 83–95; C. Chase-Dunn, "The Effects of International Economic Dependence on Development and Inequality: A Cross National Study," *American Sociological Review*, 1975, Vol. 40, pp. 720–738. For an excellent critique, see Bill Warren, "Imperialism and Capitalist Industrialization," *New Left Review*, 1973, No. 81, pp. 3–44 and the response of Arghiri Immanuel, "Myths of Development vs. Myths of Underdevelopment," *New Left Review*, No. 85. See also P. J. O'Brien, "A Critique of Latin American Theories of Dependency," in I. Oxaal, T. Barnett, D. Booth (eds.), *Beyond the Sociology of Development, op. cit.*, pp. 7–27.

15. Immanuel Wallerstein, "Dependence in an Interdependent World: The Possibilities of Transformation Within the Capitalist World-Economy." Paper prepared for Concluding Plenary Session of "Conference on Dependence and Development in Africa," Feb. 16–18, 1973.

16. On which, see E. Black, "Change as a Condition of Modern Life," in

M. Weiner (ed.), *Modernization: The Dynamics of Growth,* Basic Books, 1966.

17. K. Marx, "The Eighteenth Brumaire of Louis Napoleon," in *Selected Works,* Progress Publishers, Vol. 1, 1969, p. 398.

18. Cited by T. K. Hopkins, "Third World Modernization in Transnational Perspective," p. 130. The present author, who knows Best well, fully shares his conviction, as do most Caribbean and Latin American sociologists. In the realities of the periphery itself there can be no room for Wallersteinian pessimism.

19. It is amazing how many Marxists fail to distinguish between the modern state and the nation-state and to see the reactionary role of nationalism in the nation-states of the Third World. It is the failure to make this distinction that leads Paul Baran in *The Political Economy of Growth* (Monthly Review Press, 1957) to the questionable conclusion that the nationalist bourgeoisie in the Third World states are historically progressive.

Chapter 8
The Universal and the Particular in Western Social Thought

1. Richard Kroner, *Speculation in Pre-Christian Philosophy,* Longmans, 1957, p. 18.

2. George Boas, *Rationalism in Greek Philosophy,* Johns Hopkins Press, 1961. Introduction; see also p. 133.

3. L. Edelstein, *The Meaning of Stoicism,* Harvard University Press, 1966, pp. ix–x.

4. Karl Popper, *The Open Society and Its Enemies,* Routledge & Kegan Paul, 1962. Vol. 1. While Popper's attack on Plato is perhaps the best known, there is a considerable body of literature which takes this critical perspective. See, for example, W. Fite, *The Platonic Legend,* Charles Scribner's Sons, 1934; and R. H. S. Crossman, *Plato Today,* Allen and Unwin, 1937. Plato, however, has not gone undefended, especially by conservative thinkers. See R. B. Levinson, *In Defense of Plato,* Harvard University Press, 1953.

5. Popper's interpretation of Heraclitus might be open to the charge of oversimplification, although that hardly affects the argument. As we indicated in the first chapter, the most likely explanation of Heraclitus is that he both accepted and rejected change and in the process was torn apart emotionally and intellectually.

6. H. D. F. Kitto, *The Greeks,* Pelican, 1962, p. 169.

7. Popper, *op. cit.,* Vol. 1, p. 86.

8. Boas, *op. cit.,* p. 170.

9. G. R. Morrow, "Plato and Greek Slavery," *Mind,* April, 1939.

10. Gregory Vlastos, "Slavery in Plato's Thought," in M. I. Finley, (ed.), *Slavery in Classical Antiquity,* W. Heffer & Sons, 1960, pp. 133–149.

11. Vlastos, *op. cit.,* p. 147.

12. Matthew Arnold, *Culture and Anarchy,* Dover Wilson (ed.), Cambridge University Press, 1946.

13. William Barrett, *Irrational Man,* Doubleday Anchor, 1962, Ch. 4.

14. Arthur A. Cohen, *The Myth of the Judeo-Christian Tradition,* Harper & Row, 1970. We sympathize with Cohen's annoyance, but we think he goes too far in suggesting that this intellectual construct has been motivated by what Solomon Schechter called "the higher anti-semitism."

15. It has also had both a direct and, via Christianity, indirect influence on Western literature, especially its apocalyptic writings. On this see Kaufmann Kohler, *Heaven and Hell in Comparative Religion,* Macmillan & Company, 1923, especially his discussion of Dante.

16. S. Baron, *The Social and Religious History of the Jews,* Columbia University Press, Vol. 1, p. 3.

17. Baron, *op. cit.,* Vol. 1, p. 7.

18. Ernest Barker, *From Alexander to Constantine,* Oxford, Clarendon Press, 1956, p. 104.

19. On which, see S. H. Langdon, "The Mesopotamian Origins of Monotheism," in D. Kagan (ed.), *Problems in Ancient History,* Cornell University Press, Vol. 1, pp. 69–98. See also, S. Moscati, *Ancient Semitic Civilizations,* Capricorn, 1960, Chs. 3 & 6. For a more complete discussion of Jewish monotheism, see Charles F. Whatney, *The Exilic Age,* Longmans, Ch. 6. Also R. de Vaux, *Histoire Ancienne D'Israël,* 1971, Librairie Le Coffre, J. Gabala, pp. 420–440, Schocken, 1970. On the ethical implications of monotheism, see Maurice L. Zigmond, "Judaism as a Source of Personal Values," in A. Jospe (ed.), *Tradition and Contemporary Experience,* pp. 151–175.

20. See Peter R. Ackroyd, *Exile and Restoration: A Study of Hebrew Thought of the 6th Century B.C.,* S. C. M. Press, 1968, p. 42; and Whatney, *The Exilic Age,* Ch. 6. See also, Adolphe Lods' classic study, *Israel, from the Beginnings to the Middle of the Eighth Century,* Knopf, 1962, pp. 311–315; and R. de Vause, *op. cit.,* pp. 431–433.

21. Ackroyd, *op. cit.,* pp. 40–41.

22. Baron, *op. cit.,* Vol. 1, p. 157.

23. See Max Radin's account of the Jewish expansion in his *Jews Among the Greeks and Romans.* Jewish Publication Society of America, 1915, Chapter 11. On the reaction to Hellenization and the growth of separation, see L. Bronner, *Sects and Separatism During the Second Jewish Commonwealth,* Bloch, 1967.

24. Stanley Casson, *Macedonia, Thrace and Illyria,* Oxford University Press, 1926, pp. 157–162.

25. Truesdell B. Brown, "Callisthenes and Alexander," in G. T. Griffith (ed.), *Alexander the Great: The Main Problems,* Heffer, 1966, pp. 29–52.

26. W. W. Tarn, "Alexander the Great and the Unity of Mankind," in Griffith (ed.), *op. cit.* In the same volume, see also C. A. Robinson, "The Extraordinary Ideas of Alexander the Great," pp. 53–72.

27. L. A. White, "Ikhnaton: The Great Man vs. the Cultural Process," in D. Kagan (ed.), *Problems in Ancient History,* Cornell University Press, Vol. 1, pp. 36–68.

28. Tarn, *op. cit.* Incidentally, there is now some doubt as to whether

Isocrates could even be called "the political leader of Panhellenism." See S. Perlman, "Isocrates' 'Phillipus'—A Reinterpretation," in S. Perlman (ed.), *Philip and Athens*, pp. 104–317.

29. E. Badian, "Alexander the Great and the Unity of Mankind," in Griffith (ed.), *op. cit.*, pp. 287–306.

30. White, *op. cit.*

31. See A. T. Olmstead, *History of the Persian Empire*, University of Chicago Press, 1948, pp. 304–307; Whatney, *The Exilic Age*, p. 81, and Ch. 4; M. N. Dhalla, *Zoroastrian Civilization*, Oxford University Press, 1922, pp. 210–211.

32. M. Rostovzeff, *The Social and Economic History of the Hellenistic World*, Clarendon Press, 1967, Vol. 2, pp. 1057–1070.

33. For the classic analysis of the parallels between Stoicism and Christianity, see Ernst Troeltsch, *The Social Teachings of the Christian Churches*, Macmillan, 1931, Vol. 1, pp. 64–69.

34. J. M. Rist, *Stoic Philosophy*, Cambridge University Press, 1969. We have drawn heavily on this work, as well as the following: A.A. Long (ed.), *Problems of Stoicism*, Athlone Press, 1971; L. Edelstein, *The Meaning of Stoicism*, Harvard University Press, 1966; André-Jean Voelke, *L'Idée de Volonté dans le Stoïcisme*, Presses Universitaires de France, 1973; and the article on "Stoicism" in *The Dictionary of the History of Ideas*.

35. E. Barker, op. cit., pp. 38–48.

36. For one of the best treatments of Stoic continuum theory, see S. Sambursky, *Physics of the Stoics*, Greenwood Press, 1959. Sambursky argues that the similarity between Greek atomic theory, intuitively developed and modern physical theory accounts for the neglect of Stoic physics by modern historians. If this is really the case it suggests a remarkable superficiality on the part of such historians, for as the work of Sambursky and others demonstrate, while Stoic physics did not anticipate the content of modern atomic physics, it contributed to such developments in a more meaningful way by laying the epistemological foundations of modern science and, by its very emphasis on continuum theory anticipated at least two key tools of modern mathematics, the

concepts of function and of limits. Furthermore, as Edelstein observed: "the Stoic interpretation of phenomena as events approximates the modern interpretation of physical phenomena more closely than does any other ancient physical theory," *op. cit.*, p. 95.

37. J. Christensen, *An Essay on the Unity of Stoic Philosophy,* Munksgaard, 1962, Scandinavian University Books, p. 11.

38. See the chapter on "Fate and Necessity" in J. M. Rist, *op. cit.* For a more recent and in some respects more profound discussion of the problem of the will in Stoicism, see A-J. Voelke, *op. cit.,* especially part 1.

39. For a discussion of the similarities and differences between Kantian and Stoic thought see Voelke, *op. cit.,* pp. 192–201. The major difference, in his view, lies in the treatment of the relationship between the empirical and the rational.

40. W. Tarn, "Alexander the Great," in G.T. Griffith, *op. cit.* More balanced is his treatment of the subject in his, *Hellenistic Civilization,* Edward Arnold, 1930, p. 73; 295–300.

41. On the psychology of the leading Stoic thinkers, see Voelke, *op. cit.,* pp. 115–130. For a succinct general discussion of Stoic psychology, see Christensen, *op. cit.,* pp. 62–73. And for an interesting, if somewhat popularized discussion of Stoic psychology and its bearing on modern education and democracy, see R. R. Sherman, *Democracy, Stoicism, and Education,* University of Florida Press, 1973.

42. See C. Morris, *Western Political Thought,* Basic Books, 1967, p. 143.

43. E. Barker, *op. cit.,* p. 48.

44. M. I. Finley, *Aspects of Antiquity,* Viking Press, 1968, p. 187.

45. Philip Carrington, *The Early Christian Church,* Cambridge University Press, 1957, Vol. 1, p. 32.

46. Johannes Weiss, *A History of Primitive Christianity,* Wilson-Erickson, 1937, p. 546.

47. Maurice Goguel, *The Primitive Church* (trans. by H. C. Snape), Allen and Unwin, 1964, pp. 417–418. Closely related to Goguel's interpretation

is that of George F. Thomas, *Christian Ethics and Moral Philosophy*, Charles Scribner's Sons, 1955, pp. 37–41.

48. Goguel, *op. cit.*, p. 525.

49. Ernst Troeltsch, *The Social Teachings of the Christian Churches*, Macmillan, 1931, Vol. 1, p. 55.

50. Abram H. Lewis, *Paganism Surviving in Christianity*, G. P. Putnam, 1892, p. 32.

51. Troeltsch, *op. cit.*, Vol. 1, p. 63.

52. George Thomas, *op. cit.*, p. 54.

53. Peter A. Bertocci, "Does the Concept of Christian Love Add Anything to Moral Philosophy?" *Journal of Religion*, Vol. 38, No. 1, 1958, pp. 1–11; and, "Toward a Clarification of the Christian Doctrine of Grace and the Moral Life," *Journal of Religion*, Vol. 38, No. 2, 1958, pp. 85–94.

54. Bertocci, "Does the Concept of Christian Love Add Anything to Moral Philosophy?," p. 10.

Chapter 9

Toward the Fascist Convergence in Modern Western Thought

1. For a succinct discussion of the relationship between the early church and the state, see Louis Duchesne, *The Early History of the Christian Church*, John Murray, 1957, Ch. 3. See also George F. Thomas, *Christian Ethics and Moral Philosophy*, G. Scribner's Sons, 1955, Ch. 12.

2. M. I. Finley, "The Year One," in his *Aspects of Antiquity*, Viking Press, 1969, p. 200.

3. See Duchesne, *op. cit.*, pp. 78–84; J. Weiss, *History of Primitive Christianity*, Wilson-Erikson, 1937, Vol. 2. Bk. 5, especially Ch. 27.

4. Weiss, *op. cit.*, p. 590.

5. See Goguel, *The Primitive Church*, pp. 549–557; Weiss, *op. cit.*, pp.

585–590; E. Troeltsch, *The Social Teachings of the Christian Churches,* Allen and Unwin, 1931, Vol. 1, pp. 129–138.

6. Thus the Sophists and the Cynics opposed both slavery and Hellenistic chauvinism, on which see Robert Schlaifer, "Greek Theories of Slavery from Homer to Aristotle," in M. I. Finley (ed.), *Slavery in Classical Antiquity,* pp. 93–102. The emphasis, however, was more on the fallacy of the theory of innate slavishness than on slavery itself. See also the title essay in J. Vogt, *Sklaverei und Humanität,* Wiesbaden, 1965.

7. See A. J. Raymer, "Slavery: The Graeco Roman Defence," in *Greece and Rome,* 2nd Series, Vol. 10, No. 28, Oct. 1940, pp. 20–21.

8. Ambrogio Donini, "The Myth of Salvation in Ancient Slave Society," *Science and Society,* Vol. 15, No. 1, pp. 57–60.

9. For what is without doubt the best and most balanced assessment of Paul's ethical dualism, see Goguel, *The Primitive Church,* pp. 425–455.

10. George Boas, *Rationalism in Greek Philosophy,* Johns Hopkins University Press, 1961, p. 130. For one of the most thorough discussions of the Platonic influence, see H. A. Wolfson, *The Philosophy of the Church Fathers,* Harvard University Press, 1970, Part 2, especially pp. 257–286.

11. See the account of his life in R. W. Battenhouse (ed.), *A Companion to the Study of St. Augustine,* Oxford University Press, 1955, pp. 15–56.

12. A. Hillary Armstrong, *St. Augustine and Christian Platonism,* Villanova University Press, 1967.

13. Gordon Leff, *Medieval Thought,* Pelican, 1965, p. 35.

14. St. Augustine, Serm. XLIII, iii, 4; vii, 9, in *An Augustine Synthesis,* arranged by Erich Przywara, Harper Torchbooks, 1958, pp. 53–54.

15. E. L. Fortin, *Political Idealism and Christianity in the Thought of St. Augustine,* Villanova University Press, 1972, pp. 35–36. See also J. N. Figgs, *The Political Aspects of St. Augustine's 'City of God,'* Longmans, 1921, pp. 51–67.

16. Armstrong, *op. cit.,* pp. 17–18.

17. *Ibid.*, pp. 29-30.

18. On which, see Paul Lehmann, "The Anti-Pelagian Writings," in R. W. Bathenhouse, op. cit., pp. 203-234.

19. *Ibid.*, p. 215.

20. *Ibid.*, pp. 215-216.

21. See C. R. Boxer, *Four Centuries of Portuguese Expansion*, Witwatersrand University Press, 1963, Ch. 3.

22. Immanuel Kant, ' What is Enlightenment?" (1784), in C. J. Friedrick, *The Philosophy of Kant: Moral and Political Writings*, p. 132.

23. George Boas, *Rationalism in Greek Philosophy*, p. 113.

24. Kant, "What is Enlightenment?" p. 134.

25. Immanuel Kant, *Fundamental Principles of the Metaphysics of Ethics* (Translated by K. Abbott), Longmans, 1959, p. 62.

26. Immanuel Kant, *Idea for a Universal History With Cosmopolitan Intent*, pp. 120-121.

27. See the essays of Ebbinghaus, Harrison, and Kemp in Robert Paul Wolff (ed.), *Kant: A Collection of Essays*, University of Notre Dame Press, 1968 for summaries of Kant's ethical theory.

28. A. O. Lovejoy, "On the Discriminants of Romanticism," in his *Essays in the History of Ideas*, Johns Hopkins University Press, 1948.

29. J. S. Mill, "Coleridge," in the *Collected Works of J. S. Mill*, Vol. 10, ed. by J. M. Robson et al., University of Toronto Press, 1963.

30. A. R. Caponigri, *A History of Western Philosophy*, University of Notre Dame Press, 1963-1971, Vol. 3, p. 479.

31. Kant, indeed, used the concept of the thing-in-itself in a quite inconsistent way. See George Schrader, "The Thing-In-Itself in Kantian Philosophy," in R. Wolff, *op. cit.*, pp. 172-180.

32. Caponigri, *op. cit.*, p. 479.

33. Kant, *Fundamental Principles*, p. 13.

34. Jacobi has been largely neglected by English-speaking historians of ideas, which is a pity, since his ideas were more interesting and a good deal less confused than Herder's. See A. Crawford, *The Philosophy of Jacobi*, Macmillan, 1905; & N. Wilde, *F. H. Jacobi: A Study in the Origins of German Realism*, Columbia College Publication, 1894.

35. Lovejoy, "On the Discriminants ..." *op. cit.*

36. Leon Roth, *Spinoza*, Allen & Unwin, 1954. See also Stuart Hampshire, *Spinoza*, Pelican, 1962, especially Ch. 5.

37. Cited in Lovejoy, "Herder and the Enlightenment Philosophy of History," in his *Essays*. For another examination of the relationship between Herder's thought and both nationalism and romanticism, see Albert Guerard, "Herder's Spiritual Heritage: Nationalism, Romanticism, Democracy, in *Annals of the American Academy of Political and Social Sciences*, Vol. 174, 1934, pp. 1–8; and Peter Viereck, *Metapolitics: The Roots of the Nazi Mind.*

38. See J. L. Talmon, *Romanticism and Revolt*, Thames & Hudson, 1967, p. 135. See Ch. 5 for a lively review of developments up to the middle of the nineteenth century. See also Hans Kohn, *The Idea of Nationalism*, Chs. 7 & 8. Hans Kohn, *Prophets and Peoples;* B. C. Shafer, *Nationalism: Myth or Reality*, Chs. 8–11, Royal Institute of International Affairs, *Nationalism*, pp. 35–56.

39. Howard Becker & Harry E. Barnes, *Social Thought from Lore to Science*, Vol. 2, pp. 490–491.

40. *Ibid.*, p. 492.

41. *Ibid.*, p. 491.

42. William Blake, *Songs of Innocence and Experience.* The irony was perhaps not entirely innocent when it is considered that there was a strong streak of neo-Platonism in Blake, on which see G. M. Harper, *The Neoplatonism of William Blake*, 1961, University of North Carolina Press.

43. Patrick Gardner, *Schopenhauer,* Pelican, 1963, p. 173.

44. For a lively analysis of this development, see Peter Viereck, *Metapolitics: The Roots of the Nazi Mind.* Viereck's work, however, is impaired by his untenable position that Nietzsche is not to be included in the tradition of thought that led up to Nazism. Not as exhaustive but in many ways a better book although written under trying circumstances is Rohan D'O. Butler, *The Roots of National Socialism, 1783-1933,* Howard Fertig, 1968.

45. Nietzsche, "The Antichrist," in W. Kaufman (ed.), *The Portable Nietzsche,* Viking Press, 1954, p. 570.

46. William L. Shirer, *The Rise and Fall of the Third Reich,* Pan Books, 1960, pp. 131-132.

47. Georg Simmel, "Freedom and the Individual," in his *Individuality and Social Forms.* All subsequent quotations in this section are from this essay.

48. *Ibid.*

49. See, in particular, Karl Popper, *The Open Society and Its Enemies,* Vol. 2, Chs. 11 & 12. Popper's attempt to place some of the blame for this development on Marxism is utterly unpersuasive. For a sound structural analysis of the role of material demands from the masses in the development of Nazism, see Franz Neumann, *Behomoth: The Structure and Practice of National Socialism,* Oxford University Press, 1964, a solid, dense work which, unfortunately, is not easy reading.

50. Eugen Weber, "Fascism as the Conjunction of Right and Left," in Gilbert Allardyce (ed.), *The Place of Fascism in European History,* Prentice-Hall, 1971, p. 108.

51. E. Weber, *op. cit.,* p. 109.

Chapter 10

Ethnicity, The Modern Crisis and the Possibility of a Secular Reengagement

1. E. R. Dodds, *The Ancient Concept of Progress,* Oxford University Press, 1973, p. 24.

2. Ernest Gellner, *Thought and Change,* Weidenfeld, 1965, p. 218.

3. Racists such as Treitschke have turned the concept of Jewish chosenness against the Jews with disastrous consequences. However, many liberal thinkers have also been greatly offended by it, among them Max Weber, George Bernard Shaw, and H. G. Wells. And many Jews, too, have rejected the idea as dangerous and offensive, for example, Mordecai Kaplan and Moses Mendelssohn. For an excellent treatment of the subject from the viewpoint of a concerned Jewish scholar, see Alfred Jospe, "The Jewish Image of the Jew: On the Meaning of Jewish Distinctiveness," in his *Tradition and Contemporary Experience,* Schocken, 1970, pp. 126–150. On the origins of the Chosen Race doctrine among the Jews, see J. M. Allegro, *The Chosen People,* Hodder and Stoughton, 1971, Chapter 3.

4. Benjamin M. Kahn, "Freedom and Identity: The Challenge of Modernity," in A. Jospe (ed.), *op. cit.,* p. 7.

5. Simone Weil, *The Need for Roots,* G. P. Putnam's Sons, 1953. While Weil's diagnosis of the problem is often brilliant, her prognosis is questionable. Her faith in the past is naive, to say the least, and, partly as a result, her social and political judgments are frequently conservative and out of character.

6. See, in particular, his masterpiece, *The Ritual Process: Structure and Anti-Structure,* Aldine, 1969.

7. Gustave Weigel, *The Modern God: Faith in a Secular Culture,* Macmillan, 1959, pp. 15–16.

8. E. W. F. Tomlin, *Simone Weil,* Bowes and Bowes, 1954, p. 8.

9. Gabriel Vahanian, *The Death of God: The Culture of our Post-Christian Era,* Braziller, 1961, Chapter 3.

10. Karl Barth, "The Epistle to the Romans," in Thomas J. J. Altizer (ed.), *Toward a New Christianity: Readings in the Death of God Theology,* Harcourt, Brace and World, 1967, p. 140.

11. Paul Tillich, "Justification by Doubt and the Protestant Principle," in Thomas J. J. Altizer (ed.), *op. cit.,* p. 162.

12. Vahanian, *op. cit.,* p. 199.

13. R. A. Nisbet, *The Quest for Community,* Oxford University Press, 1969, p. viii.

14. William Barrett, *Irrational Man,* Doubleday Anchor, 1962.

15. Richard Hofstadter in his *Anti-Intellectualism in American Life,* while not recognizing the convergence of which we speak, is at least in no doubt concerning the romantic dangers inherent in traditional American anti-intellectualism.

16. Barrett, *op. cit.,* p. 270.

17. Immanuel Kant, *Fundamental Principles of the Metaphysics of Ethics,* Longmans, 1959, p. 25.

18. Julius Ebbinghaus, "Interpretation and Misinterpretation of the Categorical Imperative," in R. P. Wolff (ed.), *Kant: A Collection of Essays,* University of Notre Dame Press, 1968, pp. 211–227.

19. For a thorough discussion of this issue, especially the distinction between seventeenth century rationalism and eighteenth century empiricism and the use of the concept of reason, see E. Cassirer, *The Philosophy of the Enlightenment,* Princeton University Press, 1968.

20. For a searching assessment of the Enlightenment view of progress from a liberal perspective, see C. Frankel, *The Faith of Reason,* King's Crown Press, 1948, especially pp. 153–158.

21. Sympathetic though penetrating treatments of Enlightenment politics are found in the following: Peter Gay, *The Party of Humanity,* Weidenfeld and Nicolson, 1964; also his *Voltaire's Politics,* Princeton University Press, 1954. On Enlightenment republicanism, see F. Venturi, *Utopia and Reform in the Enlightenment,* Cambridge University Press, 1971. For a summary of the Marxist critique, see L. Goldmann, *The Philosophy of the Enlightenment,* The MIT Press, 1973, pp. 86–89.

22. Hubert Cole, *Christophe: King of Haiti,* Eyre and Spottiswoode, 1967, p. 276.

23. L. Goldmann, *op. cit.,* pp. 14–15.

24. Ernest Gellner, *op. cit.,* pp. 184–185.

Index

Acton, Lord, 72-73, 108
Adams, Robert M., 46
Adaptive ethnic groups, 54-57, 108
Africa, 147
Afro-American Studies programs, 155
Afro-Caribbean societies:
  sociocultural and economic development of, 117-21
  state building in, 87, 88
  See also Guyana; Jamaica
Afro-West Indian segmentary creolization, 120, 121
Agriculture, pristine states and, 46-47
Alexander the Great, 213-17
Algeria, French colonial ethnic elite in, 62, 63, 110
Alienation, 71
  Hebraic crisis as crisis of, 272-76
    personal alienation, 275
    Zionic paradox, 274-76
  of youth in the United States, 160-62

See also Exile
Allegiances, principles of, 115-17
Americanization, 148-49
Ancestor worship, 70
Ancestral spirits, emergence of ruling aristocracy and, 40-42
Anthropology, relativistic, 170
AntiChrist, The (Nietzsche), 258
Antioch, 61
Anti-Semitism:
  black American, 164
  Nazism and, 257
Antiwar movement, 161
Apartheid, relativism and, 171
Arab states:
  not nation-states, 80-81
  See also Islam
Arendt, Hannah, 93
Aristippus, 24
Aristocracy's emergence as ruling class, 38-42, 45
  See also Ruling class
Aristotle, 50-51, 66, 233
Armstrong, A. Hilary, 237
Arnold, Matthew, 206